Heinlein's Juvenile Novels

CRITICAL EXPLORATIONS IN SCIENCE FICTION AND FANTASY
(a series edited by Donald E. Palumbo and C.W. Sullivan III)

1 *Worlds Apart? Dualism and Transgression in Contemporary Female Dystopias* (Dunja M. Mohr, 2005)

2 *Tolkien and Shakespeare: Essays on Shared Themes and Language* (ed. Janet Brennan Croft, 2007)

3 *Culture, Identities and Technology in the* Star Wars *Films: Essays on the Two Trilogies* (ed. Carl Silvio, Tony M. Vinci, 2007)

4 *The Influence of* Star Trek *on Television, Film and Culture* (ed. Lincoln Geraghty, 2008)

5 *Hugo Gernsback and the Century of Science Fiction* (Gary Westfahl, 2007)

6 *One Earth, One People: The Mythopoeic Fantasy Series of Ursula K. Le Guin, Lloyd Alexander, Madeleine L'Engle and Orson Scott Card* (Marek Oziewicz, 2008)

7 *The Evolution of Tolkien's Mythology: A Study of the History of Middle-earth* (Elizabeth A. Whittingham, 2008)

8 *H. Beam Piper: A Biography* (John F. Carr, 2008)

9 *Dreams and Nightmares: Science and Technology in Myth and Fiction* (Mordecai Roshwald, 2008)

10 Lilith *in a New Light: Essays on the George MacDonald Fantasy Novel* (ed. Lucas H. Harriman, 2008)

11 *Feminist Narrative and the Supernatural: The Function of Fantastic Devices in Seven Recent Novels* (Katherine J. Weese, 2008)

12 *The Science of Fiction and the Fiction of Science: Collected Essays on SF Storytelling and the Gnostic Imagination* (Frank McConnell, ed. Gary Westfahl, 2009)

13 *Kim Stanley Robinson Maps the Unimaginable: Critical Essays* (ed. William J. Burling, 2009)

14 *The Inter-Galactic Playground: A Critical Study of Children's and Teens' Science Fiction* (Farah Mendlesohn, 2009)

15 *Science Fiction from Québec: A Postcolonial Study* (Amy J. Ransom, 2009)

16 *Science Fiction and the Two Cultures: Essays on Bridging the Gap Between the Sciences and the Humanities* (ed. Gary Westfahl, George Slusser, 2009)

17 *Stephen R. Donaldson and the Modern Epic Vision: A Critical Study of the "Chronicles of Thomas Covenant" Novels* (Christine Barkley, 2009)

18 *Ursula K. Le Guin's Journey to Post-Feminism* (Amy M. Clarke, 2010)

19 *Portals of Power: Magical Agency and Transformation in Literary Fantasy* (Lori M. Campbell, 2010)

20 *The Animal Fable in Science Fiction and Fantasy* (Bruce Shaw, 2010)

21 *Illuminating* Torchwood: *Essays on Narrative, Character and Sexuality in the BBC Series* (ed. Andrew Ireland, 2010)

22 *Comics as a Nexus of Cultures: Essays on the Interplay of Media, Disciplines and International Perspectives* (ed. Mark Berninger, Jochen Ecke, Gideon Haberkorn, 2010)

23 *The Anatomy of Utopia: Narration, Estrangement and Ambiguity in More, Wells, Huxley and Clarke* (Károly Pintér, 2010)

24 *The Anticipation Novelists of 1950s French Science Fiction* (Bradford Lyau, 2010)

25 *The* Twilight *Mystique: Critical Essays on the Novels and Films* (ed. Amy M. Clarke, Marijane Osborn, 2010)

26 *The Mythic Fantasy of Robert Holdstock: Critical Essays on the Fiction* (ed. Donald E. Morse, Kálmán Matolcsy, 2011)

27 *Science Fiction and the Prediction of the Future: Essays on Foresight and Fallacy* (ed. Gary Westfahl, Wong Kin Yuen, Amy Kit-sze Chan, 2011)

28 *Apocalypse in Australian Fiction and Film: A Critical Study* (Roslyn Weaver, 2011)

29 *British Science Fiction Film and Television: Critical Essays.* (ed. Tobias Hochscherf, James Leggott, 2011)

30 *Cult Telefantasy Series: A Critical Analysis of* The Prisoner, Twin Peaks, The X-Files, Buffy the Vampire Slayer, Lost, Heroes, Doctor Who *and* Star Trek (Sue Short, 2011)

31 *The Postnational Fantasy: Essays on Postcolonialism, Cosmopolitics and Science Fiction* (ed. Masood Ashraf Raja, Jason W. Ellis and Swaralipi Nandi, 2011)

32 *Heinlein's Juvenile Novels: A Cultural Dictionary* (C.W. Sullivan III, 2011)

33 *Welsh Mythology and Folklore in Popular Culture: Essays on Adaptations in Literature, Film, Television and Digital Media* (ed. Audrey Becker and Kristin Noone, 2011)

Heinlein's Juvenile Novels
A Cultural Dictionary

C.W. SULLIVAN III

CRITICAL EXPLORATION IN SCIENCE FICTION AND FANTASY, 32
Donald E. Palumbo *and* C.W. Sullivan III, *series editors*

McFarland & Company, Inc., Publishers
Jefferson, North Carolina, and London

LIBRARY OF CONGRESS CATALOGUING-IN-PUBLICATION DATA

Sullivan, Charles Wm. (Charles William), 1944–
Heinlein's juvenile novels : a cultural dictionary / C.W. Sullivan III.
    p.   cm. — (Critical explorations in science fiction and
       fantasy ; 32)
[Donald E. Palumbo and C.W. Sullivan III, series editors]
Includes bibliographical references.

ISBN 978-0-7864-4463-2
softcover : 50# alkaline paper ∞

1. Heinlein, Robert A. (Robert Anson), 1907–1988 —
Dictionaries. I. Title.
PS3515.E288Z459   2011
813'.54 — dc23   2011020107

BRITISH LIBRARY CATALOGUING DATA ARE AVAILABLE

© 2011 C.W. Sullivan III. All rights reserved

No part of this book may be reproduced or transmitted in any form or by any means, electronic or mechanical, including photocopying or recording, or by any information storage and retrieval system, without permission in writing from the publisher.

Cover illustration by Ed Emshwiller for the 1958 edition of *Have Space Suit–Will Travel* (Carol Emshwiller)

Manufactured in the United States of America

McFarland & Company, Inc., Publishers
   Box 611, Jefferson, North Carolina 28640
      www.mcfarlandpub.com

To my granddaughter, Elle,
in the hope that she, too,
might become a fan of
"Heinlein's Juveniles."

Table of Contents

Heinlein's Juvenile Novels   1

Preface   3

Introduction   7

THE DICTIONARY   13

Appendix I: Plots of Heinlein's Juvenile Novels   169

Appendix II: Some Speculations About Terms and Names Not Found   174

Works Cited   181

Heinlein's Juvenile Novels

<u>Published by Scribner's</u>
1947: *Rocket Ship Galileo (RSG)*
1948: *Space Cadet (SC)*
1949: *Red Planet (RP)*
1950: *Farmer in the Sky (FS)*
1951: *Between Planets (BP)*
1952: *The Rolling Stones (RS)*
1953: *Starman Jones (SJ)*
1954: *The Star Beast (SB)*
1955: *Tunnel in the Sky (TiS)*
1956: *Time for the Stars (TfS)*
1957: *Citizen of the Galaxy (CG)*
1958: *Have Space Suit—Will Travel (HSS)*

<u>Not Published by Scribner's</u>
1959: *Starship Troopers (ST)*
1963: *Podkayne of Mars (PM)*

Preface

I initially set out to compile what I thought of as a "concordance" to Robert A. Heinlein's twelve juvenile novels plus two (see page 1 and below for a list of the novels, their dates of publication, the abbreviation used for each throughout this book, and why there are two extra novels), but after I looked at other concordances, including an online concordance to all of Heinlein's fiction, I realized that I really wanted to do something different. I wanted to identify and then explain the relevance of the various historical and cultural terms in Heinlein's juveniles. In other words, in addition to identifying names and explaining terms, I would also try to discuss why Heinlein used so much material from past and present cultures and terms and names not just from science but also from art, music, philosophy, and more. I began to see that I would be creating a cultural dictionary, not a concordance. That led to the current title, *Heinlein's Juvenile Novels: A Cultural Dictionary*.

The entries in the main part of this book all come from the juveniles themselves and identify the source or sources of the entry, explain what the entry means, and then discuss Heinlein's reason for using that name or term if there is one (as there is in most cases). A sample entry looks like this:

> **Botany Bay** (*RS*, 7; *TiS*, 15): near present-day Sydney Harbour, the site of Captain Cook's first landfall in Australia and later an Australian penal colony. In *RS*, Grandma Hazel asks her son, Roger, if they are headed for Botany Bay after seeing the work schedule he has posted, suggesting that the *Rolling Stone* is a ship like the ones that transported British criminals to Australia in the nineteenth century. In *TiS*, it is an example of a community that has disappeared but is still remembered for its historical importance; Rod Walker is told by Deacon Matson that the town he and the other students founded and developed will have the same historical importance as Plymouth Rock and Botany Bay. See: **Plymouth Rock Colony.**

Preface

The entry in **boldface** appears exactly as it appears in the first novel in which Heinlein uses it. If it is in quotation marks or is italicized in Heinlein's fiction, it appears that way in this text. Albert Einstein will be found as **Einstein** because that is the way Heinlein first, and usually, references Albert Einstein; however, Isaac Newton is listed as **Sir Isaac Newton** (and alphabetized under S) for the same reason. To aid the reader, an entry entitled **Albert Einstein** directs the reader to the full entry, and the same is true with other entries. The entry is followed by parentheses in which the novel or novels and chapter numbers appear; the novel titles are abbreviated (see below), and I refer to chapters rather than specific pages, as different editions have different pagination. The next element explains the entry, followed by an explanation of the relevance to Heinlein's novel or novels. At the end, if necessary, there is a cross-reference in boldface to a related entry or entries so that the same material does not have to be covered twice (in this case, the reference to the **Plymouth Rock Colony** saves the space it would require to explain, again, what the Plymouth Rock Colony was).

Almost all of this material, probably 99 percent of it, can be considered general knowledge, and I consulted various encyclopedias both online and in print to ascertain this information. Where the material was site specific, as in the case of *Shakysides*, I provided the source for the material. All definitions of specific words are from the *Merriam-Webster Online Dictionary*, and all biblical references are to the King James Bible. I provided birth and death dates where I thought it advisable to do so, although a few could not be found, and in cases where there was disagreement (more often than you might think) I used the dates from www.britannica.com. For reasons of length, I chose not to explain astronomical names — Jupiter or Ganymede, for example — unless I felt that those names had thematic significance. In spite of all my work, it is possible that I have missed or misidentified a term or two given the sheer number of terms Heinlein includes in the novels. If so, I hope the omissions are minor and do not seriously detract from what has been as much a labor of love as a scholarly pursuit.

For those who want or need a quick recap, I provide an appendix with a very short plot summary for each novel; I hope that is sufficient for both those who read the novels a long time ago and want to refresh their memories and those who have not read them yet and need to know a bit

Preface

about the works. In addition, placing summaries in an appendix means that I did not have to produce them piecemeal as part of the explanation of each term. I also provide a second appendix containing some terms and names that I could not find, along with some speculation about those items.

I would like to thank those students and colleagues of mine who have encouraged me to "do more work on Heinlein's juveniles," especially Marietta Frank, once a student of mine at Hollins University and now a librarian at the University of Pittsburgh at Bradford and an excellent Heinlein scholar. I would also like to thank Kimberly Thompson, my spring 2010 graduate assistant at East Carolina University, who helped with some of the dreary research (cross-checking birth and death dates) and who attempted with some success to find information on terms that had eluded me (see especially Appendix II). Finally, let me thank the English Department of East Carolina University for a semester of reassigned time for research in the spring of 2009 to get this project started, and my colleague and coeditor for the McFarland series, Don Palumbo, for recommending my proposal to the publisher.

And I want to say a special "Thank You" to my wife, Sheree Scarborough, in whose living room in Austin, Texas, a good bit of reading for this book was done and who has been supportive of the project throughout a rather tumultuous couple of years.

Introduction: Heinlein and Cultural Intertextuality

I have known Robert A. Heinlein since the 1950s. I never met him in person, sadly, but it was his fiction — his science fiction — that was a mainstay of my reading in the late 1950s and early 1960s. I was especially fond of the juvenile novels and had even seen one or two abridged and serialized in *Boy's Life*, but I also read his short stories. "— And He Built a Crooked House —" (1940) and "All You Zombies —" (1960) especially captured my imagination. His adult novels also appealed to me, *The Puppet Masters* (1951), *Double Star* (1956), and *The Door into Summer* (1957) in particular. I continued to read Heinlein, from *The Moon Is a Harsh Mistress* (1966) to *To Sail Beyond the Sunset* (1987), his last novel, but the juveniles remained my favorites — or at least stuck most firmly in my mind.

As I have continued to read and reread Heinlein's juveniles (publications that would be called "young adult" if they were appearing for the first time today), which some of us agree are among his very best writing, and as I began to think about those novels, I came to appreciate them in ways that I could not have, at least not fully, as a juvenile reader. I eventually began to think about them in scholarly and pedagogical ways and began to include one occasionally when and where it seemed to fit in with some course I was teaching. And I began to research and write about the juveniles. I discovered that initial reviewers had given them high marks, for the most part, as did the academic critics who began to weigh in during the 1960s ("Heinlein Criticism"). By comparing Heinlein's books to earlier books, like the Tom Swift series, I realized that Heinlein had almost completely reinvented series fiction, with the different main characters, different settings, and different times allowing him to make use of science fiction's full potential ("Reinventing Series SF"). And I outlined Heinlein's con-

Introduction

tinuing contrast of accurate science and technology to the cartoon or comic strip science and technology that appear in so many other writers' works — much to the detriment of cartoon and comic strip science fiction ("Space Opera"). But one of the aspects of the juveniles that has always interested me, from the time I was a young reader right up to the present, is the way Heinlein inserts references to literature, art, music, philosophy and history (ancient and modern) into what many people, especially the establishment literati, consider mere pulp fiction — good escapism at best, but little else.

But to what end did Heinlein insert these materials? In 1991, Fred Erisman argued that Heinlein "anticipates and illustrates, in short, the principles of cultural literacy" (51), somewhat taking me to task for having suggested that Heinlein's cultural references were something like a trivia game ("Still Contemporary"). Erisman was right, but I do not think he followed through on his initial observation. In addition to cultural literacy, I believe that Heinlein was using the cultural references to make a connection with some of his readers. It is certainly possible to read all of the juveniles and not worry about any of the cultural references in them, as ignorance of those terms does not hinder the reading of Heinlein's novels any more than not knowing that the names of the dwarves in *The Hobbit* come from *The Prose Edda* and *The Poetic Edda* hinders a reading of that book. Heinlein and Tolkien are such superb storytellers that it is not necessary to the story, "as story" (C.S. Lewis), for the reader to know the source of the cultural referents or the dwarf names. Rather, Heinlein was, I think, trying to connect with the "good" readers, the readers who would know some or many of those cultural referents, readers who would, as I did, feel a kind of glow, a frisson, when they ran across a referent they knew — and who probably did not stop to look up the ones they did not know. Heinlein was not only talking about education and the importance of education (see especially the first chapter of *Have Space Suit—Will Travel* for a Heinlein critique of 1950s high school curricula), he was also educating. I believe that he wanted some of us — perhaps the potential engineers among us (or just the "geeks" for whom school, especially junior high and high school, was a somewhat difficult place) — to understand the importance of education in particular and preparedness in general. In Heinlein's novels, it is always the well prepared who survive and, usually, triumph.

Introduction

In doing that, Heinlein created a kind of cultural intertextuality in the series. For Julia Kristeva and her followers, intertextuality seems to mean the various relationships that a particular text might have with other texts (*Desire and Language*). In regard to Heinlein's juveniles, I am extending the concept of intertextuality in several ways. First, there is a general cultural intertextuality. Throughout the series, the terms and names Heinlein includes reach outward from the book to a broad and deep Euro-American culture and history. Heinlein does include some African, Asian, and South American terms and names, but the majority are Euro-American and some date back to ancient Greece and Rome. For example, Abraham Lincoln is mentioned in five novels, Napoleon in four, Geronimo in three, Simon Bolivar in three, Allah in three, Cain in three, Bifrost Bridge in two, Socrates in two, Occam's Razor in two, "Suspenders and Belt Man" in two, Wagner's *Tannhäuser* in two, and so forth.

Second, by including these names and terms, Heinlein makes his fictional future history and culture intertextual with actual history and culture, suggesting, at least, that on one hand the future is a product of the past and on the other that we should learn from the past — not only, as George Santayana suggested, so that we do not make the same mistakes over again, but also so that we see the patterns of the past replicating themselves as we move through the present and into the future. Throughout the juvenile series we are reminded time and again that the exploration of the solar system (and beyond) could parallel the settlement of the North American continent; and we are warned — by the example of the destroyed Moon (*Rocket Ship Galileo*, 11) and the Asteroid Belt remnants of what was once a planet (*Space Cadet*, 12) — that entire planets can be destroyed by their inhabitants through the reckless use of something like atomic power.

The references to actual cultural elements also allow Heinlein to create comparable elements in his future societies without confusing the reader. For example, when Rod Walker says that he does not want to give up Cowpertown, the town he and the other students established while stranded on a distant planet, he is told by his former teacher that Cowpertown is "safe in history, along with Plymouth Rock, Botany Bay, and Dakin's Colony" (20). Heinlein's mention of the Plymouth Rock Colony of seventeenth-century North America and the Botany Bay of eighteenth-

Introduction

and nineteenth-century Australia provides historical referents against which to place his invented colony — Dakin's Colony — so that the reader "knows" what Dakin's Colony was. In *Farmer in the Sky*, Bill Lermer plays *Turkey in the Straw*, Morgenstern's *Dawn of the 22nd Century*, and *The Green Hills of Earth* to convince the cultural and scientific board that his accordion is a cultural asset and that he should be allowed to take it along in spite of its exceeding his personal weight limit (2). "Turkey in the Straw" is an actual tune, of course, and allows Heinlein then to mention other songs without having to explain what they are.

Science fiction, like fantasy, requires objective correlatives within the story so that the reader can understand what is happening. Fantasy relies in large part on the world of medieval history in general and Arthurian legend in particular, and science fiction relies on the extrapolation of the present into a plausible future. In science fiction, the extrapolation of manned rocket ships to Mars and beyond comes from the centuries-old firework rockets, from the German V-2 rockets of World War II and American manned rocket ships to the moon and unmanned rocket ships beyond the moon. Science fiction's extrapolation began with technology, but Heinlein expands that practice in his fiction. Within his extrapolations, Heinlein takes the idea of objective correlatives to the cultural level, pairing actual historical events with invented future ones, actual music and musicians with future ones, actual philosophers and artists with future ones, and so forth. In this way, he makes his future perhaps more real than the futures created by most other science fiction writers ("Realizing the Unreal").

There is also an interesting intertextuality within the series and between the series and the rest of Heinlein's fiction. Within the series, the same character or reference may appear in several novels, and it is important to note, again, that all of the novels in the series have different settings and main characters. For example, the fictional Galactic Overlord appears in both *The Rolling Stones* and *Have Space Suit—Will Travel*, and in both cases references to the Galactic Overlord are part of Heinlein's criticism of cartoon or comic book science fiction. Some repetitions are the names of real people. Einstein's name and theories appear in ten of the books; this is not surprising given that Heinlein's books deal with space travel and with Einstein's theories about the speed of light and about the nature

Introduction

of space itself. Christopher Columbus' name appears in seven of the novels and is relevant as Heinlein compares the exploration of space and its new worlds to the discovery and settlement of the New World. In addition, some of the characters and topics in the series connect with Heinlein's "adult" novels and short stories. The Martians in *Red Planet* have many of the same characteristics and attributes as the Martians in his 1961 novel, *Stranger in a Strange Land* (on which he may have done substantial work in the late 1940s and early 1950s). Hazel Meade Stone, a grandmother in *The Rolling Stones*, appears as a teenager in the 1966 novel *The Moon Is a Harsh Mistress*, and the comments about the Lunar Revolution in *The Rolling Stones* refer to the entire plot of the latter novel. Ezra Dahlquist's sacrifice, briefly mentioned in *Space Cadet* (1), is the subject of the 1948 short story "The Long Watch." And the blind singer Rhysling, the main character in the 1951 short story "The Green Hills of Earth," is mentioned in *Farmer in the Sky* (20).

Finally, it is also worth noting that there are a number of themes that are consistent from novel to novel in the series (and some extend to other Heinlein fiction as well). I have identified some of them: growing up in the atomic age; the importance of education, formal and informal; contemporaries, positive and negative influences; adult advisors/mentors or impediments; powerful aliens, friends or foes; and the elevation of ideals worth dying for ("Growing Up" 26). In addition, some of Heinlein's themes depend, to some extent, on the reader's knowing popular themes (or stereotypes) in science fiction in general, themes that Heinlein occasionally exploits in ironic ways. For example, at a time when most aliens in science fiction were attacking Earth, most of Heinlein's aliens were not. In *Red Planet*, Heinlein creates Willis, a cute little Martian who might well have been the prototype for E.T.; and in most of his other juvenile novels, the only aliens who harm Earth people are those onto whose planets we have stumbled. At the end of the series proper, though, in *Have Space Suit—Will Travel*, the Wormfaces do want to take over Earth, but Heinlein makes that plot something of a red herring, luring the reader into a story that seems to be about a typical science fiction alien menace but is actually about the danger humans pose to themselves rather than any danger posed by the Wormfaces. It is a plot reminiscent of the 1951 film *The Day the Earth Stood Still* and resonates with the main theme of H.G. Wells' 1898

Introduction

novel, *The War of the Worlds*. These elements that reappear throughout the series create a more subtle but no less identifiable intertextuality than do the names and terms from culture and history, a complex intertextuality that made Heinlein's juveniles unique for their time and make them still among the very best young adult science fiction today.

The Dictionary

Aasvogel (*PM*, 4): South African vulture. In *PM*, it is the name of a lodge, like the Elks Lodge on Earth, to which a customs official belongs. Heinlein gives hints that a number of people on Mars are of South African descent, perhaps transported there as convicts. See: **Maori** and **Uncle Tom.**

Abacus (*SB*, 11): Asian device with a wooden frame, wires, and beads used as a calculating instrument. In *SB*, John Thomas Stuart compares an abacus to a slipstick and says that his aunt, who believes in astrology, could not count above ten without the help of one. This is another example of Heinlein criticizing people and beliefs he considers ignorant. See: **Slipstick.**

Abe Lincoln (*FS*, 14; *RS*, 5; *SJ*, 11; *CG*, 20; *PM*, 13): Abraham Lincoln (b. 12 February 1809, d. 15 April 1865), 16th president of the United States. Lincoln was born in a one-room cabin in Kentucky to uneducated farming parents. In *FS*, Bill is describing the house his father has designed on Ganymede and, commenting on its sparseness, says, "Abe Lincoln started with less." See: **Andrew Johnson.** In *RS*, Pollux invokes Lincoln's selling of whiskey in an attempt to justify transporting whiskey-making equipment and ingredients to Mars. In *SJ*, Dr. Hendrix says that Lincoln was "a vulgarian and nervously unstable," an example of the complex nature of human beings. See: **Admiral Lord Nelson.** In *CG*, Thorby, a former slave himself, sheds tears at the replica of the Lincoln Memorial because Lincoln freed the slaves. That the memorial is a replica is one of those "facts" that Heinlein drops into stories without explaining them — in this case leading the reader to assume that the actual Lincoln Memorial was destroyed in some war that occurred before the action of the novel. See: **Bedloe Crater,** *Santa Fé Trail,* and **Statue of Liberty.** In *PM*, Podkayne confuses Lincoln and Gettysburg with Napoleon and Waterloo and comments that Lincoln was sad about the loss of life at Waterloo. See: **Napoleon.**

Acey-Deucey (*ST*, 11): simple, traditional card game with rules that vary. In *ST*, playing acey-deucy is one of the things that the troopers do to pass the time while the ship takes them from one place to another.

Achilles (*TiS*, 15, chapter title; *ST*, 13): Greek hero depicted in *The Iliad* (8th century B.C.) who sailed with Agamemnon's army to Troy, killed the Trojan champion, Hector, and was slain himself when a spear struck his heel, the only unprotected spot on his body. In *TiS*, the chapter title "In Achilles' Tent" refers to the segment of *The Iliad* in which Achilles sulks in his tent and refuses to fight for the Greeks because one of his captives has been taken away from him; he returns to the war only after his best friend, Patroclus, takes his place and is killed. After contact has been reestablished with Earth in *TiS*, all of the formerly stranded students go home, leaving Rod there alone and "sulking" in his hut because he thought all of them would stay. See: **"Here We Rest."** In *ST*, Johnnie is told that he might put on the "best show since Achilles slew Hector" and still not graduate from O.C.S. See: **Hector.**

Achilles and the Tortoise (*HSS*, 6): main characters in Zeno's most famous paradox which says that the faster runner, Achilles, can never overtake the slower runner, the Tortoise, if the slower runner has a head start, because the faster runner will always reach the slower runner's next starting point after the slower runner has left it. This is a variation on the paradox that if you move something halfway to its destination, then halfway again, and so forth, you will never get the thing to that destination but will always be moving it half the remaining distance. In *HSS*, Kip is giving half of the remaining air in one bottle to Peewee every time she runs out and compares that effort to the story of Achilles and the Tortoise.

Achtung! (*RSG*, 16): German for "Attention!" See: ***Aufstieg!***

Acta Mathematica (*HSS*, 7): journal that publishes the latest research in all fields of mathematics. See: ***The Anatomy of Melancholy.***

Adagio Dancers (*SC*, 7): male and female dance pair, most often, who combine a gymnast's strength and agility with a classical dancer's artistic sense and smooth style. In *SC*, the sergeant in charge of the cadets' spacesuit training makes an analogy between the dance move in which the male dancer lifts his female partner over his head and supports her with one hand in the small of her back and the feeling of the cadet's suit jet as it pushes against his back.

Adiabatic [Expansion] (*HSS*, 3): heating or cooling of a gas caused by change in pressure. In *HSS*, Kip reports that the space suit manual says that his air is cooled by "semi-adiabatic expansion."

Admiral Lord Nelson (*SJ*, 11): Sir Horatio Nelson (b. 29 September 1758, d. 21 October 1805), most famous for winning the naval battle at Trafalgar, during which he was killed. In *SJ*, Dr. Hendrix says that Nelson was "a liar, a libertine, and outstandingly undisciplined," an example of the complex nature of human beings. See: **Abe Lincoln**.

Adonis (*BP*, 10): lover of Venus in classical Greek mythology. Adonis disregards Venus' warning about hunting dangerous animals and is killed by a boar; Venus sprinkles his blood on the Anemone, or Wind Flower, as a delicate but lasting memorial. In *BP*, the *Adonis* is a rocket ship of the Venus Republic that is destroyed as ships from Earth approach Venus to invade and retake the planet for the Federation.

AEC (*RS*, 1): Atomic Energy Commission, established after World War II to oversee and regulate the development of atomic energy. In *RS*, "Dealer Dan, the Spaceship Man," modeled on a used car dealer, has a license from the AEC to sell, fuel, and service rocket ships. Later in that same chapter, Grandma Hazel says that she left the AEC because men with less ability were being promoted and she was not. She is an example of Heinlein's strong women and women who have to accept a status subordinate to that of men. See: **Idiot's Mate** and **"Lean and Hungry Look."**

Aes Triplex (*SC*, 11): Latin for "triple bronze," sometimes translated "triple brass," indicating strength; also the title of a Robert Louis Stevenson article on death, first published in 1878. The ship to which Matt, Tex, and Oscar are assigned for their first training cruise as cadets in *SC* is named the *Aes Triplex*, and as the ship was headed out in search of the lost ship, *Pathfinder*, Heinlein might have intended that the name carry both connotations simultaneously. See: **Stevenson**.

Aguinaldo (*FS*, 7; *ST*, 13): Emilio Aguinaldo y Famy (b. 22 March 1869, d. 6 February 1964), a leader of the Philippine independence movement and an ally of the United States government. In *FS*, one of the Boy Scout troops takes the name "Aguinaldo." In *ST*, it is the name of one of the warships of the Federation named for specific foot soldiers.

"Ain'ta Gonna Study War No More" (*ST*, 12) *see* **"Don't Wanta Study War No More."**

Air Academy at Colorado Springs (*HSS*, 1): See: **Colorado Springs**.

Airedale (*SC*, 7): breed of terrier that originated in Yorkshire, England. Airedales have commonly been bred for herding or hunting, and they are also known for their strength and loyalty. The sergeant in charge of training the cadets in the use of space suits in *SC* tells them not to "throw themselves at the far wall like an Airedale heading into a fight."

Ajax Projectors (*RS*, 17): Ajax film projectors for movie theaters and for 8mm home use, many now available as vintage equipment. In *RS*, the Asteroid Belt has a station, Radio City, that uses Ajax three-way projectors to broadcast sight and sound in stereo.

"Alamein Dead" (*ST*, 6): song honoring the almost 5,000 soldiers who died at El Alamein in World War II. See: **El Alamein** and **"*Le Regiment de Sambre et Meuse.*"**

Alamo (*HSS*, 5; *ST*, 13): former Christian mission turned into a military post and famous as the site of a major battle in the Texas War for Independence from Mexico. All of the defenders under Colonel Travis, including Davy Crockett and Jim Bowie, chose to stay and fight, knowing that they would most likely die there but also knowing that their sacrifice would give Sam Houston the time he needed to organize a major force to fight the Mexican army. Their sacrifice gave rise to the cry "Remember the Alamo." In *HSS*, Kip says that being a prisoner of Wormface was as hopeless a situation as being in the Alamo. See: **Colonel Bowie.** In *ST*, it is the name of one of the warships of the Federation fleet.

Alamogordo, NM (*RSG*, 2; *FS*, 6): site of the first atomic bomb test in history on 16 July 1945 at Trinity Site, now occasionally open to tourists. Holloman Air Force Base and the White Sands Missile Range are located nearby. Alamogordo's continuing connection with the development of space exploration, including Space Shuttle *Columbia*'s landing there in 1982, makes that general area a logical place for Heinlein's characters in *RSG* to assemble their rocket ship. In *FS*, the ship's engineer mentions Alamogordo in a discussion of Einstein's equations about mass and energy.

Alate (*PM*, Postlude): Latin for "winged." In *PM*, Clark describes the fairy guarding him and Podkayne as "alate." Although Heinlein shows Clark to be very bright by his actions and Podkayne describes him as very bright, this is one of the few instances where his vocabulary also indicates his intelligence. See: **Ariel** and **Titania.**

Albert Einstein *see* **Einstein**

Albert Memorial (*SJ*, 11): memorial in Hyde Park, London, commissioned by Queen Victoria in memory of her husband and consort, Albert. In *SJ*, it is the name of a star formation that tells the astrogators they have arrived at their plotted destination.

Alexander the Great (*TfS*, 1): Alexander III of Macedon (356–323 B.C.), conqueror of the "known world" and creator of one of the ancient world's largest empires. In *TfS*, Alexander the Great is cited as an example of a great man who seemed destined from the beginning to be great. See: **Einstein** and **Napoleon.**

Alice (*RS*, 3): main character in Lewis Carroll's (Charles Dodgson) 1865 novel, *Alice's Adventures in Wonderland,* and his 1872 novel, *Through the Looking-Glass and What Alice Found There.* See: **Lewis Carroll** and **White Knight.**

"All for One ..." (*SB*, 14; *TiS*, 6): "All for one, and one for all" the motto of the musketeers in the Alexandre Dumas (père) 1844 novel, *The Three Musketeers*. In *SB*, Greenberg uses half of the phrase to try to convince Mrs. Stuart that her son will not be given up to the Hroshii and that the entire Federation will stand against such an act. In *TiS*, Rod, Jimmy, and Jackie agree to be partners and they shake on it while saying this phrase.

Allah (*SC*, 3; *SJ*, 4; *SB*, 3): standard Arabic word for God. A Muslim considers Allah to be supreme, almighty, and solitary. In *SC*, one of the cadets murmurs "Allah the Merciful" when a training ship crashes. In *SJ*, Max sees such strange creatures at Earthport that he assumes only Allah could know whence they came. In *SB*, Judge O'Farrell quotes an ancient fisherman's motto: "Allah does not subtract from man's allotted time those hours spent in fishing."

Alpinist (*HSS*, 4): mountain climber specializing in difficult climbs, originally climbs in the European Alps. In *HSS*, Kip describes the way he and Peewee brace for the skew-flip turnover — with their backs against opposite walls and each one's feet pushing on the other's — as being similar to the way alpinists climb rock chimneys. See: **Skew-Flip Turn-Over.**

Alvin York (*ST*, 13): best known as Sergeant York (b. 13 December 1887, d. 2 September 1964), World War I hero awarded the Congressional Medal of Honor for heroic action during the Battle of Argonne. In *ST*, it is the name of one of the warships of the Federation fleet named for specific foot soldiers. See: **Argonne.**

Amateur Space Lawyer (*SC*, 5) *see* **Bedroll Lawyer.**

Amazons (*TiS*, 2): nation of women warriors that was located, according to Greek mythology and history, in or near Asia Minor. In *TiS*, Rod Walker's older sister, Helen, is an assault captain in the Amazons, who in Heinlein's future world are an established branch of the military in which women serve.

América de Sud (*CG*, 22): Spanish for "South America." In *CG*, it is where Thorby hides out from his Uncle Jack as he prepares to try to take over the company.

Amicus Curiae (*SB*, 3; *CG*, 20): Latin for "friend of the court." In *SB*, Dr. T. Omar Esklund, from the Keep Earth Human League, appears as a "friend of the court" in the Lummox case. Heinlein is being somewhat ironic as Esklund is a friend neither of the court nor of Lummox. In *CG*, James Garsch, Thorby's lawyer, tells him to go ahead with his legal claims and that his "Uncle Jack," who does not want Thorby to have any power within the company, may not even qualify as an *amicus curiae*.

Amphigory (*SB*, 6): nonsense with an apparent meaning that, upon ex-

Anatomy

amination, will prove meaningless. In *SB*, Heinlein characterizes political introductions and compliments as "amphigory" as part of his critical picture of political appointees. See: **Take Me Out to the Ball Game.**

The Anatomy of Melancholy (*HSS*, 7): ostensibly a medical book published in 1621 by Robert Burton but also a philosophical tract encompassing most if not all of the topics that interested the English Renaissance mind. In *HSS*, Kip mentions it as something his father has read, along with *Acta Mathematica* and *Paris-Match*, an indication of his father's breadth of learning and his curiosity.

Andes (*HSS*, 3): mountains that stretch along the western side of the South American continent and one of the longest and highest ranges in the world. In *HSS*, Kip discusses oxygen pressure in a space suit, comparing how much is necessary with how much is available at the heights of the Andes and of Mount Everest. See: **Mount Everest.**

Andrew Johnson (*FS*, 20): Andrew Johnson (b. 29 December 1808, d. 31 July 1875), 17th president of the United States, who, without formal education, taught himself to read and write and was later tutored by his wife. In *FS*, Bill implies that Andrew Johnson had a worse start that the settlers on Ganymede and made something of himself and that, given a chance, the Ganymede settlers can do just as well. See: **Abe Lincoln.**

Annie Doesn't Live Here Anymore (*HSS*, 7): popular 1933 song by Joe Young, Johnny Burke, and Harold Spina about a woman who waits for a man to show up and after waiting for a long time moves away just before he arrives. In *HSS*, one of the humans who has worked for the Wormfaces uses the phrase to make it clear that the Wormfaces no longer have any use for him and his partner.

Ape Escaped a Fifth Way (*TiS*, 2): no specific source found. Probably Heinlein's way of suggesting that however carefully a human prepares there are possibilities he or she might not even consider. Heinlein might be suggesting here that the ape could not discover any of the escape routes the psychologists created and "suicided" as an escape. The "fifth way" might also be a reference to Aquinas' Fifth Way of proving the existence of God, the Egyptian mythological theory that humans consist of five "bodies," and the theory in physics enumerating five dimensions. In *TiS*, Heinlein uses the ape's escape to suggest that humans can find solutions even if there appear to be none.

Aphrodite (*PM*, 9): goddess of beauty, love, and sexuality in Greek mythology. In *PM*, Podkayne puts on makeup copied from an illustration in the most recent issue of *Aphrodite* magazine.

Apollo Belvedere (*PM*, 13): marble sculpture from Classical Greece considered a model of aesthetic male beauty. In *PM*, Podkayne says that "Pinhead" was so horrible on drugs that his non-drugged self was Apollo Belvedere by comparison. See: **Pinhead.**

Apologia (*HSS*, 11): formal defense of or justification for something in which one strongly believes, not an apology in the common sense. *The Apology of Socrates*, Plato's rendition of the speech Socrates gave to the Athenian council that accused him of corrupting the young. See: **Socrates.**

Arabian Nights (*HSS*, 10): title for a collection of folk tales more formally known as *One Thousand and One Nights* in which Scheherazade entertains the king of Persia with a story every night until, instead of killing her as he has others, he accepts her as his wife. In *HSS,* Kip remarks that Peewee's bedroom at the Court of the Three Galaxies, like her bedroom on Vega, looks like something out of the Arabian Nights. See: **Moors.**

Arc de Triomphe (*HSS*, 9): monument in Paris, France, dedicated to those who fought for France, especially during the Napoleonic Wars. In *HSS,* Peewee remarks that the Vegans' city reminds her of Paris as seen from the Arc de Triomphe.

Archangel (*SC*, 9): one of the highest ranks of angels, of which Michael is one of the few named, often used to carry messages from God to man. In *SC*, Bill Arensa drops out of the academy, saying that he "does not want to be an archangel" and cannot imagine atom bombing a city. The Patrol, as Heinlein presents it, would have to bomb any city in any country that started a war, and Heinlein suggests that there are some otherwise fine cadets who could not do that. See: **Flaming Sword.**

Archimedes (*PM*, 9): Greek mathematician, scientist, inventor, and engineer (b. 287 B.C., d. 212 B.C.), most famous for discussing the principles of the lever as well as for several other machines. In *PM*, Podkayne calls her brother a "Young Archimedes" when she warns him not to touch the piano in the hotel suite. See: **Steinway.**

Argonne (*ST*, 13): probably the Battle of the Argonne Forrest (France) in World War I, a major battle in the final Allied push against the Germans in that war, but possibly a reference to a U.S. Navy auxiliary ship commissioned in 1921. In *ST,* it is the name of the transport ship in whose sick bay Johnnie returns to O.C.S.

Ariel (*SB*, 5; *CG*, 16; *PM*, 13): Hebrew for "Lion of God," the name of the spirit that Prospero forces to help him in Shakespeare's *The Tempest* and many others. In *SB*, it is the name of a ship coming from Venus to Earth, but there is no way to tell for which of the many Ariels Heinlein might have named her. In *CG*, the name of the fast mail ship that transports Thorby to Earth from the galaxy's rim. In *PM*, it is the name Podkayne gives to the baby Venerian "fairy" that belongs to her "fairy" guard; Podkayne's naming the baby fairy "Ariel" is an indication of her affection for the creature, an affection that may or may not have gotten her killed at the end of the book. See: **"Samson in the Temple"** and **Titania.**

"Arigato" (*ST*, 3): Japanese word for "thank you" or "thank you very much." See: **"Banzai."**

Aristotle (*RSG*, 10): Greek philosopher (b. 384, d. 322 B.C.) and student of Plato. Considered one of the founding fathers of western philosophy, his writings on logic, among the earliest known, were incorporated into modern formal logic in the late nineteenth century. In a discussion of the nature of the dark, or far, side of the moon in *RSG*, Cargraves calls Ross "Aristotle" and asks him to prove that there is, in fact, a far side to the moon. This challenge to Ross is an example of the way in which Heinlein challenges the reader as well. See: **Scientific Method.**

Arkansas Traveler (*TiS*, 14): traditional fiddle tune dating to the early 1800s and now the state song of Arkansas. In *TiS*, the Saturday night dance is opened with a rendition of "Arkansas Traveler" played as a square dance tune. Heinlein's use of both the traditional tune and the square dance is part of his continuing parallel of the juvenile series to American history, and the specific inclusion in *TiS* illustrates the type of entertainment a frontier community could provide for itself. See: **Square Dance** and ***Texas Star.***

Armageddon (*HSS*, 12; *PM*, 6): scene of the world-destroying battle foretold in Revelations 16: 14–16; more generally, the site of a final and decisive confrontation. In *HSS*, Peewee's father says that they have to call people in the middle of the night because "Armageddon won't wait for office hours." In *PM*, Podkayne says that her brother would not pay attention to anything, even Armageddon, unless he could make a profit from it.

Army Mule (*HSS*, 9) *see* **West Point.**

Arthur Currie (*ST*, 3): World War I Canadian General (b. 5 December 1875, d. 30 November 1933) considered one of the most able military leaders on the Western Front. In *ST*, the first training camp Johnnie attends is named for Arthur Currie.

"As Cold as ..." (*SB*, 6): beginning of several American proverbial comparisons, most notably "as cold as a well-digger's ass" and "as cold as a witch's tit." In *SB*, the Rargyllian negotiator is discussing American idioms and mentions that the person who taught him "two peas in a pod" also taught him some idioms that began "as cold as ..." but are not acceptable in polite company. See: **Two Peas in a Pod.**

"As the Crow Flies" (*SJ*, 11): shortest and fastest way to get somewhere, flying in a straight line that eliminates twists and turns that make a trip longer. In *SJ*, Heinlein suggests that "as the crow flies" is meaningless in space travel as the starships travel from one fold in space to another across the gap in between. See: **Einstein Wall.**

Asgard (*SJ*, 3): Home of the gods in Scandinavian mythology. In *SJ*, the starship *Asgard* is one on which Max's uncle served and on which he, too, will serve; it is an appropriately named ship, as it gets Max what he wants most in life — a career in space. See: **Einstein** and ***The Prince of Wales.***

"Ashes to Ashes, Dust to Dust" (*SJ*, 13): "In the sweat of thy face shalt thou eat thy bread, till thou return unto the ground; for out of it wast thou taken: for dust thou art and unto dust shalt thou return" (Genesis 3:19), traditionally recited at funerals and burials. In *SJ*, these words are recited when astrogator Dr. Hendrix's dead body is launched into space.

Ask Me No Questions and I'll Sell You No Pigs in a Poke (*SJ*, 5; *SB*, 6): "Ask me no questions, and I'll tell you no lies," popular saying attributed to Irish playwright Oliver Goldsmith. Buying a pig in a poke (i.e., a bag) is buying something that you have never seen. In *SJ*, this is one of Sam's fractured sayings. Others include "It's not too late to kill the goose before your bridges are burned" (2), "We'll strike while the iron's in the fire and let the bridges fall where they may" (5), "Let sleeping dogs bury their own dead" (6), "It's an ill wind that has no turning" (6), "When in Rome you shoot Roman candles" (7), "It's an ill wind that gathers no moss" (8), "The best soup usually has a fly in it" (10), "No use cryin' over spilt milk when the horse was already stolen" (18). In *SB*, Greenberg quotes the "when in Rome shoot off Roman candles" fractured proverb.

Assegai (*SJ*, 2): Arabic word for spear or javelin. In *SJ*, it is the name of one of the super-fast trains, all of which have some sort of throwing-weapon name — *Javelin*, *Cleaver*, and *Tomahawk*. See: ***Tomahawk.***

Astarte (*SC*, 16): eastern and southern Mediterranean mythological goddess, cognate with Ishtar, responsible for fertility. Her consort is Tammuz. One of Astarte's symbols was the horse and another was a star within a circle. The horse was a major fertility figure among many European and Middle Eastern peoples, and the planet Venus has long been associated with love and fertility. In *SC*, the cadets discover the one-hundred-year-old wreck of the *Astarte*, the first manned ship sent to Venus. Not only has Heinlein given the ship a name appropriate for the first manned flight to Venus, but also the association with the fertility principle and the fact that she has a consort and not a husband underscores the matrilineal culture of the Little People of Venus, who save the cadets' lives and help them restore the *Astarte* so that they can fly to one of the colonies on the planet.

Athens (*RS*, 1): Greek city that may have been named for Athena, the goddess of wisdom, and considered to be one of the foundations of civilization and one of the oldest cities in Europe. In *RS*, Roger Stone said, when he retired as mayor, that Luna City was "the Athens of the future and the hope of the new age," a comment his fifteen-year-old sons, Castor and Pollux, throw back at him when he suggests that they should go to an Earth university for further education — something they do not want to do.

Atomic Energy Commission (*RSG*, 1) *see* **AEC**.

The Attainability of Celestial Bodies (*SC*, 13) *see* **Hohmann**.

Aubrey Cousens (*ST*, 13): Canadian World War II hero and recipient of the Victoria Cross. Aubrey Cosens was killed (26 February 1945) after successfully capturing the small town of Mooshof, a location considered essential to further operations. In *ST*, it is the name of one of the warships of the Federation fleet named for specific foot soldiers.

Audie Murphy (*ST*, 13): World War II hero (b. 20 June 1924, d. 28 May 1971) and, later, movie actor, one of the most highly decorated U.S. soldiers of World War II. In *ST*, it is the name of one of the warships of the Federation fleet named for specific foot soldiers.

Aufstieg! (*RSG*, 16): German for "rise." In *RSG*, it is used with *Achtung!* as Cargraves orders Morrie to pilot the German "jeep" and attack the German base; it can probably be translated here as "blast-off!" See: *Achtung!*

Augean Stables (*PM*, 3): stables belonging to the Greek king Augeas, owner of more livestock than anyone else in the country. One of Hercules' twelve labors was to clean the Augean Stables, which he did in one day by diverting rivers to run through them and wash away the muck. In *PM*, Podkayne compares changing the diapers of her newborn triplet siblings to cleaning the Augean Stables. See: **What's in a Name?**

Augustus Caesar (*CG*, 14): Roman Emperor (b. 22 September 63 B.C., d. 19 August 14 A.D.) who ushered in the two-hundred year Pax Romana (Latin: Peace of Rome) that allowed the Roman Empire to build a system of roads and cities throughout the Mediterranean and western Europe to promote commerce and military control. In *CG*, it is the name of one of the ships of the Free Traders. See: **Free Traders** and *Hansea*.

Auslander (*FS*, 14): German for "foreigner" or "outsider." In *FS*, Bill joins a scout troop on Ganymede called the "Auslanders."

Auto-de-Fé (*FS*, 12): Spanish for "Act of Faith," an act of public penance dating at least to the Spanish Inquisition. In *FS*, Hank suggests that Bill transfer to a local Scout troop on Ganymede as an act of public penance for suggesting to a local troop that the troop formed on the rocket ship was the equal of the local troops on Ganymede.

Avant-Garde (*TfS*, 3): French for "advance guard," more commonly those who develop new or experimental concepts, especially in the arts. In *TfS*, it is the name of the first long-range spaceship sent to look for inhabitable planets.

Aztec (*CG*, 21): indigenous population of Mexico before the Europeans arrived and conquered the country. In *CG*, Thorby and Leda finally get some privacy when exploring the Aztec exhibit at the Fifth of May Museum, a museum named for the Spanish phrase for the fifth of May, or Cinco de Mayo, a day that commemorates a Spanish-Mexican victory over a much larger French army. The Spanish-Mexican victory may prefigure Thorby's victory over his "Uncle Jack" and the rest of the power structure of the company.

Bach (*PM*, 9): Johann Sebastian Bach (b. 21 March 1685, d. 28 July 1750), German baroque composer, perhaps most famous for works for the organ and for the four *Brandenburg Concertos*. In *PM*, Podkayne thinks that Cantonese sounds like someone vocalizing Bach very badly.

Bad Juju (*SJ*, 12): action that may damage one's aura/soul/karma; an action that may bring the same fate on oneself. In *SJ*, the natives of Halcyon would not kill humans for meat during the day because it is "bad juju" and "the spirit stays around to haunt."

Baden-Powell (*FS*, 7): Lord Baden-Powell (b. 22 February 1857, d. 8 January 1941), founder of scouting in England and indirect founder of the Boy Scouts of America. In *FS*, the boys decide to name their troop Baden-Powell after a skirmish between an English boy who wants to name the troop for Saint George and an Irish boy who wants to name the troop for Saint Patrick. See: **Saint George** and **Saint Patrick.**

Balboa (*TfS*, 12): Vasco Nunez de Balboa (b. 1475, d. 15 January 1519), Spanish explorer best known for being the first European to lead an expedition across the Isthmus of Panama and see the Pacific Ocean. In *TfS*, Tom Bartlett wants to set foot on a new planet and compares that with Balboa's expedition and discovery.

Baldwin Locomotives (*RSG*, 8): American maker of steam locomotives for the railroad. Matthias Baldwin began experimenting with steam engines in the late 1820s and built his first railroad locomotive, Old Ironsides, in 1925. Although the company was very successful as a maker of steam locomotives, it went out of business in the 1950s as the railroads switched to diesel power. In *RSG*, Cargraves suggests going to Baldwin Locomotives for dynamometers, and, given that Cargraves' drive works like a steam engine, Baldwin Locomotives would be a logical place to go for a dynamometer. See: **Heron's Turbine.**

"Banzai" (*ST*, 3): Japanese war cry or cheer, also an expression of enthusiasm or triumph. In *ST*, Sergeant Zim says this when he and an enlistee named Shujumi are about to have a one-on-one contest; Shujumi responds with "arigato." See: **"Arigato."**

Barn Dances (*SJ*, 1): Saturday night dances held in someone's barn. In rural communities, these events gave people from town and the surrounding farms a place to gather and socialize. In *SJ*, Heinlein is creating an exaggerated rural background for his main character, Max, and barn dances are still part of the community's life. See: **Huskings, Side Meat, Squirrel Gun,** and **"Wagon Room."**

Barnard's Satellite (*FS*, 9): fifth moon of Jupiter, discovered by Edward Emerson Barnard (b. 16 December 1857, d. 6 February 1923), an American astronomer with many discoveries to his credit. In *FS*, Bill Lermer suggests that the moon is so small that it would have very low gravity and someone might be able to jump off it and not be pulled back.

Barratry (*CG*, 10): purchase or sale of church or state offices; also, a breach of duty that causes damage to a ship's owner or cargo. In *CG*, one of the trading rituals in which Thorby engages requires that ritual insults be exchanged, and the *Sisu*'s captain accuses the local trader of "everything from barratry to mopery and dopery in the space ways." "Mopery and dopery" is a slang combination meaning foolish or ignorant action.

Barsoom (*HSS*, 5): name for Mars in Edgar Rice Burroughs' (b. 1 September 1875, d. 19 March 1950) Mars series. In the series, Earth man John Carter is mysteriously transported to Mars, where he finds a world derived in large part from medieval romance. See: **Dead Sea Bottoms of Barsoom** and **King Arthur's Court.**

Bastinado (*RS*, 8): particularly painful torture involving beating the bottoms of the feet with a cane or rod or whip. In *RS*, Roger Stone threatens his sons with the rack (a bed-like device on which a person's arms are gradually pulled in one direction and legs are pulled in the opposite direction), thumb screws (a ring that fits over the thumb with a screw through it that tightens down on the thumb), and bastinado strokes if they do not obey his orders about working outside the ship.

Bayreuth [Concord] (*TfS*, 1): city in Germany primarily known now as Richard Wagner's home and the home of the Bayreuth Festival of Wagnerian music and opera. But during World War II it was a center for Nazi ideology and the location of a concentration camp. It is ironic that in *TfS*, the Bayreuth Concord is a treaty that put an end to government investment in space travel for military purposes.

"Be It Ever So Humble ..." (*SJ*, 19): "Be it ever so humble, there's no place like home," from the 1823 song, "Home, Sweet Home," by John Payne and Edward Bishop. In *SJ*, Ellie uses the phrase ironically to refer to the place in which she and Max are held captive by the "centaurs." See: **Centaur**.

"The Bear Went Over the Mountain," (*RS*, 19) *see* **Why Did the Bear Go Round the Mountain?**

"Beauty & the Beast" (*SB*, 5): traditional tale in which a young woman discovers that the beast to whom she has been sent as a wife is actually a handsome nobleman suffering under an enchantment. In *SB*, Mr. Kiku's file on Dr. Ftaeml, the Rargyllian with a Medusa-like head of tendrils, is labeled "Beauty & the Beast" because Mr. Kiku has a severe negative reaction to Dr. Ftaeml's appearance although he respects him as a negotiator.

Beavers (*TiS*, 1): slang term for beards. In *TiS*, Rod Walker sees beards on the emigrants he is watching and assumes from that they have been training for this emigration for months.

Bedloe Crater (*TiS*, 1): reference to Bedloe's Island, later Liberty Island and home of the Statue of Liberty. In *TiS*, it is now Bedloe Crater, having been — one must assume, as Heinlein does not explain — destroyed in a war carried on before the opening of the book. See: **Abe Lincoln**, *Santa Fé Trail*, and **Statue of Liberty**.

Bedroll Lawyer (*SC*, 5; *BP*, 13; *TiS*, 10; *ST*, 5): average person, in *SC* and *ST* a military enlistee who, without fully understanding them, wrongly thinks that he can use the rules to his own advantage. In *SC*, Tex tries to use the rules to avoid a superior's instructions and is told that "amateur space lawyers frequently talked themselves out of the Patrol." In *BP*, when Don wants to be considered as being on detached duty instead of on leave, his lieutenant calls him a "mess hall lawyer." In *TiS*, the community has trouble agreeing on a constitution because so many of them are "Bush Lawyers." In *ST*, an enlistee's insistence on his rights gets him into deeper trouble than he otherwise would have been.

Beethoven's Fifth (*SC*, 2): Symphony No. 5 in C minor, 1804–1808, composed by Ludwig van Beethoven (b. 16 December 1770, d. 26 March 1827) and famous for its dramatic opening bars. These twice-repeated phrases of four notes each are used to introduce the story of Ezra Dahlquist in *SC*, the dramatic music suitable to the story of a Patrol Officer who gave his life to prevent the Revolt of the Colonels in Heinlein's 1948 short story "The Long Watch." See: **Götterdämmerung.**

Dr. Bell (*HSS*, 9): probably Eric Temple Bell (b. 7 February 1883, d. 21 December 1960), mathematician and science fiction writer who published his science fiction under the name John Taine and many of whose nonfiction works on mathematics were written for a popular audience. In *HSS*, when asked about his knowledge of geometry, Kip admits that he has read only the popular mathematical works of Dr. Bell.

Benjamin Franklin (*TfS*, 1): American inventor and printer (b. 17 January 1706, d. 17 April 1790) who became a politician and statesman of the American Revolution and the American republic. In *TiS*, a novel partially about an over-crowded Earth in which families are taxed for having any children beyond the allotted three, he is cited as an example of a youngest child in a large family who became an important person.

Beowulf (*HSS*, 5): main character in the heroic epic poem *Beowulf*, the events of which take place in the 5th century A.D. and feature, as the primary plotline, the slaying of two monsters and a dragon. At the end of the poem, after having helped slay the dragon, Beowulf dies for his people. See: **King Arthur's Court.**

Berlin Sender (*RSG*, 13): could refer to *Reichssender Berlin*, part of the Nazi broadcasting system during World War II and shut down afterwards. A *Sender Freies Berlin* radio station operated in West Berlin from 1954 to 2003. Perhaps in *RSG* Heinlein "foresaw" the reopening of German-controlled radio stations after World War II and assumed that Berlin Sender would be the title (or, perhaps, the American translation of the title). See: **NAA** and **Radio Paris.**

Bernadotte (*ST*, 12): Jean-Baptiste Jules Bernadotte (b. 26 January 1763, d. 8 March 1844), marshall of France selected by the Swedish government to be heir to the throne. His reign was one of peace and prosperity. In *ST*, one of Johnnie's teachers says that wise monarchs like Bernadotte are scarce.

"The Best Things in Life Are Free," (*ST*, 6): 1956 song by Ray Henderson from the movie of the same name and very popular in the 1950s. In *ST*, Mr. Dubois argues that nothing of value is free unless one accepts that the best things in life are bought with things like personal sacrifice, things other than money. See: **Marxist Theory.**

Bethlehem-Antares (*CG*, 16): combination of Bethlehem Steel, which produced big guns and armor plate, ships, aircraft parts, and ordinance for the navy during World War II and a fictional future company, Antares. In *CG*, the name of the company that produced the weapons systems used by the Free Traders to defend themselves from pirates and slavers. See: **Free Traders.**

"Beulah Land" (*FS,* 13): "Thou shalt no more be termed Forsaken; neither shall the land any more be termed Desolate; but thou shalt be called *Hepzibah* and thy land *Beulah*; for the LORD delighteth in thee, and thy land shall be married" (Iasiah 62:4). From that verse, Edgar Page Stiles wrote the gospel hymn "Beulah Land" in 1875 or 1876, which concludes with a chorus describing someone looking across the sea to where mansions are prepared for him. In *FS*, one of the characters who has come to settle on and "terraform" Jupiter's moon, Ganymede, whistles the tune.

Bifrost [Lounge] (*SJ,* 8; *FS,* 3): Rainbow Bridge in Scandinavian mythology linking Asgard, the home of the gods, and Midgard (Middle-earth), the home of the human race. In *SJ*, the Bifrost Lounge is where the officers and guests of the *Asgard* eat and socialize; in other words, it is the place that bridges the gap between the passengers and the officers of the ship. In *FS*, the *Bifrost* is one of four appropriately named ships taking colonists from Earth up to the *Mayflower*, which will carry them to Ganymede. See: ***Daedalus, Icarus,*** and ***Mayflower.***

Big Rock Candy Mountain (*FS,* 13; *PM,* 10): song popular during the Great Depression (1930s) and depicting a paradise especially appealing to the poor for its free food, cigarette trees, lemonade springs, lack of work, and so forth. In *FS*, a range of mountains on Ganymede has been named the Big Rock Candy Mountains, indicating the settlers' hope for the future on the currently almost inhospitable moon of Jupiter. In *PM*, it is the name of an ice cream flavor in an expensive sweet shop on Venus.

Bill Cody [Beard] (*TiS,* 16): William F. Cody (b. 26 February 1846, d. 10 January 1917), also known as Buffalo Bill, famous as a hunter for the railroad and later as a showman with Buffalo Bill's Wild West Show. At the end of *TiS*, Rod Walker is described as being dressed in fringed buckskin and having a "Bill Cody beard and rather long hair," all characteristics of the historical Buffalo Bill Cody. This characterization is part of Heinlein's continuing parallel of the juvenile series to American history and shows the movement of emigrants on horseback and in covered wagons from Earth to faraway planets as being strikingly similar to the American westward movement. See: **Conestoga Wagon.**

Black as the Ace of Spades (*SC,* 14): traditional description of African Americans of particularly dark complexion. In *SC*, Tex mentions that one of the officers is "black as the ace of spades" in an attempt to prove that Matt has no racial prejudice.

Blackboard

Blackboard Jungle (*HSS*, 1): reference to the 1955 movie *Blackboard Jungle*, in which juvenile delinquents disrupt an urban high school. In *HSS*, Kip's father, while criticizing the local high school, mentions that it is at least not a "blackboard jungle." See: **Juvenile Delinquent** and **M.I.T.**

Blackguards (*ST*, 13): traditional term for a person with no principles, an abusive person. In *ST*, Johnnie serves his O.C.S. training mission with Blackie's Blackguards, a unit, like his previous one, the Roughnecks, that prides itself on being "tough" and "nasty."

Blacksheep (*RS*, 16): odd or unusual sheep; in modern slang, anyone who steps out of line or causes trouble. In *RS*, blacksheep refers to the asteroids that do not stay within the boundaries of the Asteroid Belt proper.

"Blessings on Him Who Invented Sleep, the Mantle That Covers All Human Thoughts" (*HSS*, 5): "Now blessings on him that first invented this same sleep: it covers a man all over, thoughts and all, like a cloak" (*Don Quixote*, part 2, chapter 68), Miguel de Cervantes (b. 29 September 1547, d. 23 April 1616). See: **"Sleep That Knits Up the Ravell'd Sleave of Care"** and **"Tired Nature's Sweet Restorer, Balmy Sleep."**

Blind Tom (*SJ*, 9): Tom Wiggins, 19th century African American musical savant and piano prodigy who astonished his audiences, including Mark Twain, with his virtuosity. In *SJ*, Dr. Hendrix compares Max's eidetic memory to Blind Tom's ability.

Blitzed (*RSG*, 15; *BP*, 1; *RS*, 6): suddenly and overwhelmingly attacked. This verb comes from the German noun *blitzkrieg*, the primary definition of which is an intense military air campaign and usually refers to the German air attack on England in general and London in particular, but it can also be used to describe the German military tactics in general. When the *Galileo* is destroyed by Nazis in *RSG*, Cargraves says without knowing who did it but, ironically, correctly, "They blitzed us." See: **Nazis**. In *BP*, Don's roommate at school feels that Don is "blitzing" him by leaving so suddenly. Later in the novel, the earth forces' attack on Venerian ships is called a blitz (10). In *RS*, a friend facetiously describes Castor and Pollux's announcement that they are going to become traders a "blitz" on the other traders.

Blue Bird (*BP*, 15): probably a reference to the 1928 popular song "Back in Your Own Backyard" (Al Jolson, Billy Rose, Dave Dryer), also a reference to the perhaps mythological Blue Bird of Happiness. In *BP*, when Major Phipps realizes that Isobel Costello has had the ring everyone has been searching for, he exclaims, "Talk about the Blue Bird in your own back yard." He follows that with "Talk about Grandma's spectacles," probably referring to the Mother Goose rhyme about grandma's spectacles being in her lap.

Blue Moon (*FS*, 8) *see* **Once in a Blue Moon.**

Bluebeard (*TiS*, 6): title and title character of Charles Perrault's (b. 12 January 1628, d. 16 May 1703) literary fairy tale about a man who murders his wives and the wife who, with the help of her brothers, manages to avoid the fate of her predecessors. In *TiS*, it is the name of Jack Daudet's knife, as Jack eventually turns out to be Jacqueline, "Bluebeard" may be both a serious and an ironic name for the knife she uses to survive. See: **Colonel Bowie, Lady Macbeth,** and **Occam's Razor.**

Bode's Law (*RS*, 15; *TfS*, 12): astronomical formula that roughly predicts the distances between the planets in our solar system. In *RS*, Heinlein invokes Bode's Law to prove that the asteroids between Jupiter and Mars are the fragments of what once was a planet. In *TfS*, the discovery of other solar systems with suns larger or smaller than Earth's sun whose planets also conform to Bode's Law proves that law; scientist Harry Gates says that the discovery will earn him burial beside Galileo. See: **Giuseppe Piazzi, Kepler,** and **Lucifer.**

Bolivar (*SB*, 2) *see* **Simón Bolivar.**

Bolivian Indians (*RP*, 2): possibly the Aymara Indians of Bolivia, who live at high altitudes in the Andes Mountains. See: **Tibetans.**

Bon Marché (*CG*, 14): French for "good market" or, more idiomatically, "good deal"; most popularly, a Seattle, Washington, based chain of retail department stores. In *CG*, it is the name of one of the ships of the Free Traders. See: **Free Traders** and ***Hansea.***

Bonaparte (*SJ*, 12) *see* **Napoleon.**

Bonestelled (*HSS*, 7): Chesley Bonestell (b. 1 January 1888, d. 11 June 1986), painter and illustrator famous for his astronomical and science fictional creations for everything from the pulp science fiction magazines to *Life* magazine and NASA. Bonestell worked on *Destination Moon*, a 1950 film loosely based on Heinlein's juvenile *Rocket Ship Galileo* and on the novella "The Man Who Sold the Moon" and on which Heinlein served as a scriptwriter and technical consultant. Heinlein was an admirer of Bonestell (*Grumbles,* 60). In *HSS*, Kip comments that he has seen pictures of Pluto "bonestelled" to look like photographs, a technique for which Bonestell was famous.

Boojum (*RP*, 3): snark in Lewis Carroll's "The Hunting of the Snark." At the end of the poem, the snark, about to be captured perhaps, "had softly and suddenly vanished away—/ For the snark 'was' a Boojum, you see." In *RP*, MacRae tells the story of a medical lieutenant who tries to "unroll" a Martian and disappears. MacRae draws an analogy between the lieutenant's disappearance and the snark's and, when

Jim does not get the reference, is critical of modern education, one of many such critical comments Heinlein or his characters make throughout the juvenile series. See: **Lewis Carroll.**

Borneo (*HSS*, 5): large island in the South China Sea popularly known as the home of the "Wild Man of Borneo," the epitome of the uncivilized savage. In *HSS*, Kip realizes that he understands the workings of the Wormface's spaceship about as well as a Borneo native would understand the workings of a modern automobile. See: **Brookhaven Atomic Laboratories.**

Botany Bay (*RS*, 7; *TiS*, 15): near present-day Sydney Harbor, the site of Captain Cook's first landfall in Australia and, in the late eighteenth century and well into the nineteenth century, an Australian penal colony. In *RS*, Grandma Hazel asks her son, Roger, if they are headed for Botany Bay after seeing the work schedule he has posted, suggesting that the *Rolling Stone* is a ship like the ones that transported British criminals to Australia. In *TiS*, it is an example of a community that has disappeared but is still remembered for its historical importance; Rod Walker is told by Deacon Matson that the town he and the other students founded and developed will have the same historical importance as Plymouth Rock and Botany Bay. See: **Plymouth Rock Colony.**

Boulder Dam (*RSG*, 3): originally known as Hoover Dam, changed to Boulder Dam as Hoover's reputation fell during the 1930s depression. It was the world's largest concrete structure and energy generating facility as Heinlein wrote *RSG*. Cargraves notes in the future setting of the book that atomic power plants have been built that exceed Boulder Dam's production. In 1947, the year *RSG* was published, Boulder Dam was renamed Hoover Dam.

Bow Bells (*BP*, 5): famous bells of St Mary le Bow Church, Cheapside, London. In *BP*, Don Harvey surmises that, because of the Venerian "Sir Isaac Newton's" Cockney accent, whoever taught him to speak English must have lived very near that church in the heart of London. See **Cockney.**

Bowie (*HSS*, 5) *see* **Colonel Bowie.**

Brainwashed Prisoners (*ST*, 12): U.S. Army prisoners of war in Korea who defected to the enemy in record numbers. Although there is still some debate about the efficacy of brainwashing, brainwashing was a technique developed by the Chinese to break down the psychological stability of the prisoner and induce them to accept a new value structure. Some American prisoners actually became communists and made anti–American statements and such; others pretended to be converted so that they would receive better treatment. In *ST*, an O.C.S. instructor suggests that the brainwashed prisoners were the result of conscript armies and a deterioration of social and moral values in the 1950s. See: **Korean War**.

Brass Hatted [Stupidity] (*SC*, 15): referring to top-ranked officials, especially in the military. "Brass hats" can also refer to decision makers and policy makers who make bad decisions or policy according to those in the ranks below them. In *SC*, Burke feels that the senior Patrol officers who sent the cadets in answer to his distress call had made an unwise decision.

Bread Cast Upon the Waters Does Come Back Seven Hundred Fold (*TfS*, 1): "Cast thy bread upon the waters" (Ecclesiastes 11.1), generally assumed to mean that charity will be returned many times over. In *TfS*, Tom explains that the Long Range Foundation financed scientific research that neither the government nor private industry would undertake and reaped great rewards, especially financial. Here, as he does in *Rocket Ship Galileo*, Heinlein is suggesting, as he also does in the 1949 short story "The Man Who Sold the Moon," that major advances will be made by private individuals or corporations and not the government.

Brennschluss (*RS*, 6): point in a rocket's trajectory when the fuel burns out or is cut off and the rocket continues on under its own momentum. In *RS*, it marks the moment when the *Rolling Stone* goes into free orbit after blastoff.

Brevet (*SB*, 6): temporary authorization, usually military, for someone to hold a rank higher than his or her appointed one. In *SB*, Greenberg is surprised when Mr. Kiku refers to him in a conference as an "associate" rather than as his real title of "assistant" without having informed him of a promotion.

Brickbat (*SB*, 7): piece of some hard material, such as a brick, often used as a missile. In *SB*, Johnnie "pets" Lummox with a brickbat, one of many situations in which Heinlein illustrates the toughness of Lummox's hide.

Brookhaven Atomic Laboratories (*HSS*, 9): now Brookhaven National Laboratory, Upton, New York, originally designed as a nuclear research laboratory. In *HSS*, Kip explains his lack of ability to explain the things he sees on the Mother Thing's planet by saying that a jungle savage, no matter how bright, would be able to understand almost nothing at the Brookhaven Atomic Laboratories, partly because he lacks the centuries of background information and partly because he does not know what questions to ask. See: **Borneo**.

Brownian Movement (*ST*, 4): random movement of particles as a result of the impact of other particles in the same medium. In *ST*, Johnnie describes the movement of individuals in three squads sleeping by herding together on a cold night as a kind of Brownian movement.

Brownie (*RSG*, 10): inexpensive and

simple camera developed by Kodak in 1900. The Brownie, named for the popular cartoon characters created by Palmer Cox, made photography available to everyone, as no special skills were needed to take photographs with the camera. When Cargraves asks Art if he has finished snapping his Brownie in *RSG*, he is making a humorously derogatory remark, as Art is an accomplished photographer.

Buenas Noches (*RP*, 4): Brazilian for "Good Night." In *RP*, it is the end of the song Willis sings. See: *"¿Quién Es La Señorita?"*

"Build That Better Mousetrap and Make the World Beat a Path to Our Door" (*RS*, 17): "Build a better mousetrap and the world will beat a path to your door" (proverb). A proverbial way of saying that if you produce a better product than your competitor people will rush to buy yours instead of the competitor's. In *RS*, Castor uses this saying to suggest that he and Pollux need a gimmick to sell the flat cats.

Bull Pen (*SJ*, 4): previously slang term for prison yard; now a common baseball term for the place where the pitchers warm up. In *SJ*, Sam is leery of cops who might want to throw him and Max into the "bull pen."

Bush Lawyers (*TiS*, 10) *see* **Bedroll Lawyers.**

C-rations and K-rations (*RSG*, 6): food rations used extensively by the military in World War II and Korea. The C-ration continued through the Vietnam conflict. The packages contained canned or dried food, chocolate bars, mixes for fruit drinks and instant coffee as well as basic eating utensils, toilet paper, and cigarettes. Each ration provided a little more than 3,000 calories in the three meals it contained. In *RSG*, Cargraves buys a supply of each for the trip to the moon.

CAB (*RSG*, 6): Civil Aeronautics Board, established by President Roosevelt in 1940 and responsible for safety rules for and accident investigation of the airlines. The CAB's functions were later absorbed by the Federal Aviation Agency (Later Administration, FAA) in 1958, but the CAB would have been, at the time Heinlein wrote *RSG*, the agency that might well have had the authority to inspect such projects.

Caesar (*SB*, 14; *HSS*, 10; *ST*, 2; *PM*, 6): Gaius Julius Caesar (b. 13 July 100 or 102 B.C., d. 15 March 44 B.C.), whose conquest of Gaul, northern and western Europe, extended the Roman Empire almost to the Atlantic; later dictator of the empire. In *SB*, Mr. Kiku remarks that the Hroshii had been planning Lummox's mating since "Caesar fought the Gauls." See: **Gauls.** In *HSS*, the legionary tells Kip that he approves of Caesar. See: **Ovid.** In *ST*, Caesar is an example of a commander who could use "cannon fodder" (food for the enemy's cannons), i.e., platoons of men, usually infantry, who could be sent into battle and be

CalTech

killed without depriving the army of any of its specialists; this is in opposition to the army in *ST*, where everyone, even the men of the infantry, are specialists. Heinlein also suggests (*ST*, 7) that Caesar's sergeants probably began their remarks to their men with "You apes." In *PM*, Podkayne suggests that women should keep their intellects hidden so as not to make men "suspicious and uneasy," as Caesar was of Cassius. See: **"Lean and Hungry Look."**

Cain (*RSG*, 9; *SC*, 15; *FS*, 2): elder son of Adam and Eve, who committed the first murder when he killed his brother, Abel. The popular term "raising Cain" describes an act of violence or, in less serious situations, a mischievous or disruptive act. In *RSG*, Cargraves explains that a rocket could leave the Earth much more slowly but would have to burn much more fuel to do so, raising Cain with the mass-ratio. In *SC*, Burke threatens that his father, a wealthy man with connections, will "raise plenty of Cain" when he discovers that his son was not rescued immediately. In *FS*, George waits to tell Bill about remarrying because he knew Bill would "raise Cain" about it.

"Caissons" (*ST*, 4): "The Caisson Song," a revised version of which, "The Army Goes Rolling Along," is considered the official song of the U.S. Army. See: **"Le Regiment de Sambre et Meuse."**

Calabozo (*SJ*, 6): Spanish for jail or prison. In *SJ*, Sam tells Max that he will go to jail if he returns to Earth after going into space with false identification papers and guild membership. Heinlein, sometimes through Max, is very critical of the guild system, as it opposes individual ability and enterprise.

California Gold Rush (*RS*, 14): 1848–1855 "rush" of approximately 300,000 people to California after gold was discovered at Sutter's Mill in the northern part of the state. News of the discovery spread quickly, and so many people came by land and sea in 1849 that Californians have been known as "Forty-Niners" ever since. In *RS*, Grandma Hazel uses the California gold rush as an example to help Castor and Pollux decide what goods to bring along to sell to the miners in the Asteroid Belt. This is another very obvious element in Heinlein's paralleling of the exploration and settlement of the solar system to the exploration and settlement of the North American continent. Like the California gold rush, the rush to the Asteroid Belt in *RS* made very few people rich, but also, in the same way that the California gold rush had a major impact on California and much of the rest of the American West, the rush to the Asteroid Belt would have a major effect on the development of the solar system.

CalTech (*HSS*, 1): California Institute of Technology, one of the best engineering schools in the USA. In *HSS*, it is one of the schools that rejects Kip. See: **M.I.T.** and **Rensselaer.**

Cambridge

Cambridge (*PM*, 9): Cambridge University, with Oxford University, one of England's best universities. In *PM*, Podkayne's friend Dexter will study paramagnetics and Davis mechanics at Cambridge to be ready for the time the first starships are created. See: **Davis Mechanics** and **Paramagnetics**.

Canaan (*TiS*, 1) *see* **New Canaan**.

Canali (*BP*, 18): Italian word meaning "channels" that astronomer Giovanni Schiaperelli (b. 14 March 1835, d. July 1910) used to describe the long and straight "channels" he thought that he observed on Mars. His "canali" was later mistranslated as "canals," a mistake which was used to support the late 19th and early 20th century belief that there was life on Mars. On the last page of *BP*, the main character observes the "*canali*" as his rocket ship approaches Mars.

Canard (*TiS*, 1; *HSS*, 7): lie, untruth. In *TiS*, as Rod is watching the Asians being herded through a transportation gate to another planet, he feels that the old canard "if you marched the Chinese into the ocean four abreast, they would reproduce so quickly that the line would never end" is true even though he has proved mathematically that it is not. In *HSS*, Kip has a pencil from Jay's Drive-In that advertises the thickest milkshakes in town. He regards that as a canard, saying that he makes the thickest milkshakes in town. See: **Soda Jerk**.

Cannon Fodder (*ST*, 2) *see* **Caesar**.

Captain Bligh (*RS*, 7; *TfS*, 16): William Bligh (b. 9 September 1754, d. 7 September 1817), best known as the captain of the HMS *Bounty*. It is popularly believed that the *Bounty* was seized because Bligh was a tyrannical master. The mutineers put Bligh and his supporters to sea in a small and overloaded boat, and he commanded a remarkable voyage of nearly two months to safety. Unfortunately, Bligh's name has become synonymous with harsh and demanding leadership. In *RS*, Grandma Hazel calls her son, Roger, "Captain Bligh" as a joke. See: **Botany Bay**. In *TfS*, Tom Bartlett refers to his ship's captain, who is ordering him to stay in telepathic contact with his partner for an extraordinarily long time, as Captain Bligh.

Captain Jenks of the Space Patrol (*SC*, 4): futurized novel title based on the late nineteenth-century British music hall song "Captain Jinks of the Horse Marines," which humorously portrays the captain of the title as a dandy and something of a coward "not cut out for the army." It is likely that Heinlein knew the song, if not the stage play, as the song was sufficiently popular in the early and mid twentieth century that it was included in elementary school songbooks. In *SC*, Matt reflects on the novel as an unrealistically heroic portrait of a space patrol officer, a sharp contrast to the rigorous and un-heroic life of a Patrol Academy cadet. By contrasting the song with Matt's training, Heinlein creates a complex pun about both military service and realistic versus "popular" science fiction.

Caravansary (*BP*, 2) *see* **Hilton Caravansary.**

Carboniferous Period (*TiS*, 2): 354 to 290 million years ago, named for the rich deposits of coal that date from at time. In *TiS*, Ramsbotham, mistakenly thinking he is in the Carboniferous Period when he is actually in Rio de Janeiro's botanical garden, is illustrative of the brilliant but impractical or imperceptive scientist.

Carcassonne (*RS*, 18): French fortress captured in 1209 by Simon de Montfort, who imprisoned its viscount, Raymond-Roger de Trencavel, allowed him to die there, and made himself the new viscount. In *RS*, Grandma Hazel, facing death, supposes that everyone has his Carcassonne.

Carnegie (*HSS*, 3): Carnegie Mellon University, one of the best engineering schools in the U.S. Andrew Carnegie, a Scots-American businessman and philanthropist in the late nineteenth and early twentieth centuries, founded the school. In *HSS*, it is one of the schools to which Kip has applied.

Carthage (*ST*, 2): North African city destroyed by the Romans in 146 B.C. after the Third Punic War. According to legend, the Romans covered the ground with salt after destroying the city so that nothing could ever grow there again. In *ST*, Mr. Dubois uses Carthage as an example to counter the concept that violence never solves anything. Dubois then suggests having Napoleon Bonaparte and the Duke of Wellington debate the issue with Hitler as the referee and the Dodo, the Great Auk, and the Passenger Pigeon (all extinct species by the twentieth century) as the jury. DuBois' basic philosophy in *ST* is that force is necessary to defend freedom and that a civilization must always be ready to defend itself from outside aggression. See: **Hitler, Napoleon,** and **Wellington.**

Cassius (*PM*, 6) *see* **"Lean and Hungry Look."**

Castor (*RS*, 1): twin brother of Pollux in Roman mythology. They were the inseparable twin sons of Leda but by different fathers. Castor's father was a mortal, Tyndareus, and the two brightest stars in Gemini are named for them. In *RS*, Castor and Pollux are sons in the Stone family, the main characters in the novel, and are known as the "unheavenly twins" for their propensity to get into trouble. See: **Pollux.**

Catherine the Great (*PM*, 10): Empress of Russia (b. 21 April 1729, d. 28 June 1796), who modernized Russia after western European models and made her country a major power. In *PM*, Podkayne thinks of Catherine the Great as a role model of what a woman can accomplish in a man's world after taking over from her husband. See: **Theodora.**

Caveat Vendor (*RS*, 13): Latin for "let the seller beware." In *RS*, Heinlein uses it as the title for chapter 13, the chapter in which Castor and Pollux are jailed for failing to pay import duties on the bicycles they brought to sell on Mars.

Centaur (*SJ*, 17): creature from Greek mythology with a horse's body and a human torso, arms, and head. In *SJ*, the creatures on the planet look like miniature centaurs about the size of Shetland ponies, but they turn out to be quite dangerous. They capture Max and Ellie and work with other indigenous creatures to try to kill all the humans. See: **Hobgoblins.**

Cessna (*HSS*, 4): small airplane, most popularly the single engine, propeller model that seats two to four people. In *HSS*, eleven-year-old Peewee explains to Kip that her landing of the spaceship was pretty good considering that she had flown only a Cessna before.

Chamberlain (*BP*, 1) *see* **Theory of Colonial Expansion.**

Charles Darwin (*BP*, 5): English naturalist (b. 12 February 1809, d. 19 April 1882) whose 1859 work, *On the Origin of Species*, presented the theory of evolution. In *BP*, Professor Charles Darwin is the name of a Venerian dragon scientist.

Charles' Wain (*SC*, 11): seven bright stars more commonly known as Ursa Major or the Big Dipper. "Wain" is a Middle English word for "wagon," and "Charles" could have come from "Charlemagne" or from the Old English or Old Norse words for "churl." In *SC*, it is the ship to which Pierre is assigned for his first training cruise as a cadet.

Cherenkov [Drive] (*ST*, 10): Pavel Cherenkov (b. 15 July 1904, d. 6 January 1990), 1958 Nobel Prize-winning physicist who observed what has come to be called the "Cherenkov effect," which involves charged atomic particles moving faster than the speed of light. In *ST*, the Cherenkov drive powers the Federation spaceships that travel faster than the speed of light (by jumping from one fold of space to another).

Cherub, Roma, Terra (*RS*, 3): full name of a rocket ship that provides the individual name of the ship, its home city, and its home planet, much as current private sailing ships are now named. In *RS*, the Stone family purchases the ship and renames it the *Rolling Stone*. See: **The Rolling Stones.**

Other names suggested and considered for the ship were *Dauntless* (fearless), *Jabberwock* (the menacing character from Lewis Carroll's poem "Jabberwocky'), *HMS Pinafore* (the name of the ship in the Gilbert and Sullivan operetta of the same name), *The Clunker* (a barely operable old machine, especially a car), *Star Wagon* (derived from the phrase "hitch your wagon to a star"), *Go-Devil* (name for any fast machine, but knowing Heinlein, he might have been referring to the engines in World War II jeeps that were called "Go-Devils"), *Onward* (self-explanatory), *Icarus* (the son of Deadalus; Icarus flew too near the sun, melted the wax holding his wings together, and fell to his death), *Susan B. Anthony* (one of the founders of the women's suffrage movement in the late nineteenth-century United States), *Iron Duke* (nickname of the first Duke of Wellington), *Morning Star* (usually Venus), *Tumbleweed* (a plant that breaks free of its roots and rolls with the wind), *Oom Paul* (a full-bent, large-bowled pipe for smoking tobacco), and *Viking* (Scandinavians who raided, traded with, and settled much of western Europe between 700 and 1000 A.D.). Three other names, *Deadlock*, *Hair Shirt* (a rough cloth made of goat's hair and worn to do penance for one's sins), and *Madhouse*, were suggested as people argued over the other names. All of the names, with the possible exception of *Icarus*, would be suitable for the ship that became the *Rolling Stone*.

Chester Arthur [Jones] (*SJ*, 4): Chester A. Arthur (b. 5 October 1829, d. 18 November 1886), 21st president of the United States and a product of the post–Civil War Republican machine, at least until he took office. In *SJ*, it is the name of Max's uncle, an astrogator who disappeared on a voyage before he could nominate Max to the Astrogators' Guild, an economic machine comparable, perhaps, to Chester A. Arthur's political machine.

Chesterfieldian (*SB*, 5): Chesterfield, a single- or double-breasted topcoat, usually with a fly front and a velvet collar. In *SB*, Mr. Kiku thinks of the Rargyllian negotiator as "Chesterfieldian" because of the alien's choice to appear in the formal wear of the host country or planet.

Chico (*SJ*, 4): Spanish for "little," "small," or "young." In *SJ*, a policeman in Earthport refers to Max as "chico," suggesting not only his youth but also his inexperience.

Chinchilla (*HSS*, 5): small rodent about the size of a chipmunk that is hunted or raised for its soft and dense fur. In *HSS*, Kip describes the Mother Thing's fur as like that of a chinchilla.

Chinese Obligation (*SB*, 17; *PM*, 120): supposed Chinese belief that having helped once one must keep on helping. In *SB*, Mr. Kiku thinks of his job of dealing with extraterrestrials as a Chinese obligation; having successfully dealt with one, he must move on to the next. In *PM*, Podkayne is distressed over her younger brother's disappearance and calls him her "Chinese obligation."

Cholo (*TiS*, 8): derogatory term usually directed at young men of Hispanic or Native American ethnicity.

Chopsticks

Its origin may have come from a word to identify a mixed breed dog or dog of disreputable origin; in general, it is an insult to one's parentage and heredity. In *TiS*, one of the troublemakers from Teller University calls Rod Walker "cholo." See: **Teller [University]**.

Chopsticks (*PM*, 9): piano tune simple enough that children often learn it from each other instead of a teacher; probably got its name because it is played with one finger of each hand. In *PM*, Podkayne plays "Chopsticks" on the piano in the hotel suite. See: **Steinway**.

Christoforo Colombo (*TfS*, 11) see **Columbus**. In *TfS*, it is the name of one of the torch ships. See: **Lebensraum [Project]** and ***Lewis and Clark***.

Churchill [Road] (*ST*, 11) see **Winston Churchill**.

Clambake (*RS*, 4): traditional New England way of steaming a variety of seafood along with corn, sausage, and other additions in a pit lined and covered with seaweed; in American slang, a party or other event. In *RS*, Roger Stone says that he is going to run this "clambake," that is, the family's trip out to the other planets in the solar system.

Cleopatra (*TfS*, 10; *ST*, 13): Egyptian queen (69 B.C.–30 B.C.) renowned for her beauty and for having sons with both Julius Caesar and Mark Anthony. In *TfS*, Tom Bartlett is thinking of her beauty when he suggests that he looks "more like Cleopatra" than Dr. Devereaux "looks like the pretty Dr. Arnault." In *ST*, Johnnie mentions Simon Bolivar marrying Cleopatra as a humorous comment on how each country views its own heroes.

"The Cloud-Capped Towers," (*HSS*, 11): "The cloud-capped towers, the gorgeous palaces / The solemn temples, the great globe itself," William Shakespeare's 1611 comedy, *The Tempest* (IV, I, 152–153). In *HSS*, Kip thinks of these lines as he contemplates the possibility that the Earth will be frozen and the human race extinguished. See: **"These Our Actors ... ."**

Cobber (*CG*, 13): Australian slang for "pal" or "buddy" or "good guy." In *CG*, slang for someone who could make it on the planet Woolamurra. See: **Outback** and **Woolamurra**.

Cock Robin (*ST*, 13): traditional English nursery rhyme and folk song often used metaphorically by its title, "Who Killed Cock Robin?," to refer to a puzzle or mystery. In *ST*, Johnnie's captain uses the expression when Johnnie figures out the weak spot in his platoon.

Cockney (*BP*, 2): refers to working class Londoners and especially the accent with which they speak. In *BP*, the Venerian dragon, "Sir Isaac Newton," speaks English with a Cockney accent. See: **Bow Bells**.

Coelostat (*FS*, 4; *RS*, 7): astronomical instrument that rotates to produce a fixed image of the sun or other astronomical body or section of the sky for navigational purposes. In *FS*, Bill sees a coelostat when he is allowed to enter the control room of the *Bifrost*. In *RS*, it is used to make sure that the ship is properly lined up for her course before the engines are started.

Cofferdam (*ST*, 13; *PM*, 7): wall or barrier built to protect one area from work being done in another; technically, a barrier to keep water out of an area in which people are constructing something. In *ST*, Johnnie talks about cofferdamming an area to protect it from a blast. In *PM*, the outer holds for cargo and water are a spaceship's cofferdam against solar radiation.

Colonel Bowie (*TiS*, 2; *HSS*, 5; *ST*, 13): Jim Bowie (b. 10 April 1796, d. 6 March 1836), American pioneer and adventurer best known for designing the Bowie knife and dying at the Alamo in an effort to liberate Texas from Mexican rule. In *TiS*, it is the name of Rod Walker's favorite knife, an appropriately named weapon/tool for someone going out on a survival test or having to help establish a new society. See: **Bluebeard, Lady Macbeth,** and **Occam's Razor.** In *HSS*, Kip stops feeling "like Bowie at the Alamo" when Peewee tells him that if they can find their space suits they can escape the Wormface's spaceship and walk to Tombaugh Station, some miles across the moon's surface. Kip's image of himself as Jim Bowie is part of his somewhat romantic belief that he will save Peewee or die trying. See: **Alamo, King Arthur's Court,** and **Tombaugh [Station]**. In *ST*, *Colonel Bowie* is the name of one of the warships of the Federation fleet named for specific foot soldiers.

Colorado Springs (*HSS*, 1; *ST*, 12): location in Colorado of the United States Air Force Academy, established in 1954. In *HSS*, Kip thinks that he might get into space if he can be accepted at the air academy in Colorado Springs. For *ST*, see **Saint Cyr.**

Columbus (*RSG*, 3, chapter title; *SC*, 17; *FS*, 4; *SB*, 3; *TiS*, 2; *TfS*, 12; *PM*, 8): Christopher Columbus (b. fall 1451, d. 20 May 1506), Genoese sailor whose trips across the Atlantic turned Europe's attention to the "New World." By entitling the third chapter of *RSG* "Cut-Rate Columbus," Heinlein is referring to both the limited budget for building the rocket ship in the novel and the difficulty Columbus had in financing his voyages. He may also be saying that Columbus' and Cargraves' successes are all that much more admirable in light of the difficulties under which they labored. In *SC*, Tex compares the one-hundred-year-old *Astarte* to Columbus' ships and the Viking ships, suggesting that all are equally primitive. See: **Santa Maria** and **Viking ships.** In *FS*, Bill sees the Earth become rounder and rounder as the rocket ship draws away from it and remarks that Columbus

Comedy

was right, the world is round; here, Heinlein is creating another parallel between American history and Bill's journey to Ganymede, both journeys into the unknown. Later, Bill says that the land on Ganymede is as dead "as Christopher Columbus" (12). And after the discovery of the alien artifacts, Hank says that he and Bill will be famous and that Columbus will look like "a piker" beside them (19). In *SB*, Greenberg suggests that the first "interspatial transition flights" were "as reckless as the voyage Columbus attempted." In *TiS*, it is a name Rod Walker knows from books but does not think about. See: **Otis**. In *TfS*, Tom Bartlett compares stepping onto a new planet with Columbus' setting foot in the New World. Later, he wonders if the new captain, who wants to continue the mission of the *Lewis and Clark* with a skeleton crew, thinks he's Columbus or *The Flying Dutchman* (15). See: **Vanderdecken**. In *PM*, Podkayne's brother asks her if she really wants to pilot an exploratory ship and whether or not she has, not counting Isabella, what Columbus had.

The Comedy of Errors (*RS*, 2): 1552/1554 comedy by William Shakespeare. See: **Hamlet**.

Comic Strip (*HSS*, 2): three- or four-panel illustrated strip, usually humorous, appearing in newspapers. In *HSS*, Kip remarks that Ace Quiggle, his local nemesis, laughs like a comic strip character: "Yuk yuk yukkity yuk!" Throughout the juvenile series, Heinlein contrasts serious science (and science fiction) to the comic strip depictions that are not scientifically grounded—as his fiction is. The comic-strip high school dropout, Ace Quiggle, is a perfect contrast to the well-grounded and well-educated Kip.

Commandant Arkwright (*SC*, 4): possibly British commander Augustus Arkwright (b. 2 March 1821, d. 6 October 1887), a naval officer and conservative politician. In *SC*, Arkwright is the name of the sightless commandant of the academy.

Commander Comet (*HSS*, 8) see ***The Scourge of the Spaceways.***

Comte de Monte Cristo (*TfS*, 16; *HSS*, 5): main character, actually named Edmond Dantés in the 1844 novel *The Count of Monte Cristo*, by Alexandre Dumas (père). Falsely imprisoned, Dantés spends years tunneling out of the prison. In *TfS*, Tom chews up a note smuggled in to him in his food, comparing his unjustified arrest to that of the Count of Monte Cristo or the Man in the Iron Mask. In *HSS*, Kip suggests that a similar escape from the spaceship is impossible, as he and Peewee do not have the same kind of time.

Concentration Camps (*RSG*, 4): most notorious as internment facilities to which Jewish people and others (especially those considered to be of inferior race) were sent for extermination. In *RSG*, Cargraves reminds his sister that her husband was held in a concentration camp as a part of his argument that her son, his nephew, should be a part of the expedition to the moon that Cargraves is planning. In part, this is a setup for the confrontation with the Nazis on the moon at the end of the novel. See: **Nazis**.

Conestoga Wagon (*RSG*, 4; *TiS*, 1): freight wagon that could haul 7 metric tons, first built in the mid–1700s in Pennsylvania, and favorite wagon of both freight haulers and settlers from the southward migration along the Appalachian Mountain chain to the great westward movement of the nineteenth century. In *RSG*, Ross's mother mentions her great-grandparents' trip west in a Conestoga wagon as a comparison to and justification for allowing Ross to accompany Cargraves and the other boys to the moon; here Heinlein is beginning his comparison of the settlement of the American west to the exploration and settlement of "outer space." In *TiS*, a party passing through Emigrants' Gap equipped with Conestoga and steel-bodied Studebaker wagons to haul themselves and their goods is considered well-financed and well-equipped for emigration to their planet as opposed to the impoverished Asiatics that preceded them to a very different planet. See: **Mongol, New Canaan**, and **Studebaker**.

Congressional Library (*HSS*, 9): United States Library of Congress, the largest library in the world, initially established as a research library for Congress in 1800 and expanded ever since.

In *HSS*, Kip tours what he calls the "Congressional Library" of the Mother Thing's planet and recalls that his father believes that library science is the foundation of all sciences.

Coolie (*TiS*, 1): English-language word used to label an Asiatic, primarily Chinese, laborer, especially those who came to America to work on the railroads in the nineteenth century. In *TiS*, Rod Walker sees an "old coolie" being driven through the gate at Emigrants' Gap. See: **Heavenly Mountains** and **Mongol**.

La Coq d'Or (*HSS*, 9): French translation of the 1907 Russian opera title *The Golden Cockerel*, by Nikolai Rimsky-Korsakov, that features a magical bird. In *HSS*, Kip compares Peewee's singing of the name of the Mother Thing's planet to the cockcrow theme from the opera, more evidence of materials with which he has supplemented his high school's meager curriculum. See: **Blackboard Jungle**.

Cordon Bleu (*TfS*, 7): famous cooking school established in France in the late nineteenth century that now has facilities all over the world. The name means "blue ribbon," as the blue ribbon is the award for first place. In *TfS*, Mrs. O'Toole is a cordon bleu chef who conducts cooking classes, one of many classes available to combat the boredom of a long space voyage.

Corset (*RS*, 15): tight garment ... often reinforced — that slims the waist and can also accent the hips and breasts —

worn by women to make them "shapely"; more recently, a slang term for something that restricts freedom. In *RS*, Grandma Hazel feels that artificial colonies have too many restrictions and suggests that the "whole [solar] system has taken to wearing corsets."

Cosmic Great-Circle (*HSS*, 12): route that would take one around the cosmos; also an indirect reference to a great circle route for air travel on Earth in which an arcing route, like that flown by airplanes across the Atlantic Ocean, is a faster way to fly long distances than a straight route would be. In *HSS*, Kip's father suggests that Kip has traveled such a route.

Count of Monte Cristo (*TfS*, 16) *see* **Comte de Monte Cristo.**

Country Cousin (*SC*, 4): innocent or naïve person; one from the country as opposed to a sophisticate from the city. In *SC*, a cynical Girard Burke calls the idealistic Matt a "country cousin" for believing everything he is told or shown as the new cadet candidates are introduced at the Interplanetary Patrol's Terra Base. As it turns out, Burke is the one who is wrong, and he eventually drops out of training.

Coup d'état (*SC*, 2): sudden overthrow of a country's government by a rebel group. In *SC*, Matt and his friends are looking at a placque honoring Ezra Dahlquist for preventing, at the cost of his own life, a coup d'état by the military.

Coventry (*CG*, 7; *HSS*, 10): place to which one is sent for punishment or exile. The origin of the phrase "sent to Coventry" is unknown, but there are some associations with Coventry, England. In *CG*, Thorby feels that his isolation on the *Sisu* is lonelier than Coventry. In *HSS*, Kip at first believes that when the Wormfaces' planet is rotated they are just "being placed in Coventry" until it is explained that their sun does not go with them and that the whole planet will, therefore, slowly freeze solid.

Covered Wagon (*FS*, 14): wagon with an arched canvas top primarily associated with the westward movement in nineteenth-century America. In *FS*, it is the name of a rocket ship that will soon be bringing colonists to Ganymede as the original covered wagons hauled people and freight west in nineteenth-century America. See: **Conestoga Wagon.**

Cow College (*SC*, 6): college or university specializing in agricultural research and degrees, or any rural and unsophisticated college. In *SC*, one of the instructors disparages the cadets by suggesting that they should have gone to cow colleges.

Cracker Jack (*HSS*, 2): popular American snack since the 1890s that consists of popcorn, peanuts, and molasses. Cracker Jack advertised "a prize in every box." In *HSS*, Kip says that his luck is so bad that his Cracker Jack box would be the one without a prize.

Cro-Magnon Man (*SB*, 14): one of the early modern humans, named for a cave in France where the first bones were found, whose remains date back between 17,000 and 30,000 years. In *SB*, the Hroshii have been genetically shaping their race for 38,000 years, a point at which Earth history envisions Cro-Magnon man battling with the Neanderthals for the planet — one of Heinlein's many attempts to show that humans may not be the oldest race in the galaxy or in the universe. See: **Caesar** and **Neanderthal**.

"Cross Your Heart" (*SB*, 1): "cross my heart and hope to die," a traditional oath to indicate that one is telling the truth or means what he or she says. In *SB*, this is an oath that the Lummox has never broken.

Crusades (*ST*, 12): series of military expeditions, 1096–1261, undertaken in fulfillment of a religious vow made by European Christians to deliver eastern holy places, such as Jerusalem, from Mohammedan control and restore them to Christian control. In *ST*, Johnnie argues that the Crusades were different from other wars. He is assigned the task of proving it and discovers that all wars result from population pressure. Hence, the current war between the Humans and the Bugs is about who will get to expand into whose territory.

Cry "Wolf!" (*PM*, 8): from a fable about a shepherd boy who cried "wolf!" several times to get attention; then when a real wolf appeared and he cried "Wolf!" no one came to help him. In *PM*, Podkayne explains that the captain cannot too often demand that people go to the radiation shelters when there is no reason or they will not go when eventually there is a reason because they think he is "crying wolf."

CuiCui Province (*BP*, 9): Cui Cui Island is an island in the Lake District of southern Chile. In *BP*, it is the name of a province and a town on Venus, perhaps suggesting the origin on Earth of some of the settlers of the planet.

Cumshaw (*FS*, 16; *BP*, 2; *PM*, 3): from a Chinese word that can be translated as "grateful thanks" or, more popularly, "gratuity" or "present." In *FS*, Bill's father, George, says the glass for their house is "cumshaw" as a result of his designing the new "glass works." In *BP*, it is a gratuity that Doctor Jefferson pays a desk sergeant who keeps coins for him to use when he forgets to carry money to pay the automated taxis. In *PM*, Podkayne's uncle tells her brother, Clark, that he's getting no "cumshaw" for asking for expenses for the trip.

Cybernetics (*HSS*, 9): from the Greek word for "pilot," the science of communication and control theory particularly focusing on automatic control systems and on the brain or mechanical control systems. In *HSS*, Kip's tour of the Vegans' national library brings up the topic of cybernetics. See: **Congressional Library**.

Dachau (*HSS*, 11): Nazi concentration camp for the internment and execution of "enemies of the state," especially Jews. In *HSS*, Kip wonders how many bad things from Earth history, like the Holocaust, he told his interviewers on Vega, information that will be used when the Court of the Three Galaxies judges the human race. See: **Nazis**.

Daedalus (*FS*, 3): craftsman in Greek mythology who built the Labyrinth for King Minos and then, to escape Crete, made wings for himself and his son, Icarus. In *FS*, the *Daedalus* is one of the four ships taking colonists who want to escape an overcrowded Earth to the *Mayflower*, which will carry them to Ganymede. See: **Bifrost, Icarus,** and **Mayflower**.

Dalai Lama (*TiS*, 6): title given to the leader of the Tibetan Buddhists, in modern times an advocate for peace. In *TiS*, Rod Walker suggests several reasons why they have not been picked up, including the possibility that the Dalai Lama has bombed the rest of the world and destroyed the transportation gates; his real point is that he does not and cannot know what happened, however likely or unlikely, and that they may well be stuck there for the rest of their lives.

Damon and Pythias (*TfS*, 1): friends in Greek mythology whose story symbolizes friendship and trust. Pythias was sentenced to death, asked Damon to be a temporary hostage in his place, and returned just in time to save Damon's life. Dionysus, their captor, was so impressed that he spared both of them. In *TfS*, Tom says that he and his twin brother, Pat, did not have the Damon-and-Pythias relationship that fiction writers believe all twins have.

Danegeld (*SB*, 5): money raised by taxation in England to buy off the Danish invaders in the late tenth century. In *SB*, Mr. Kiku refuses to grant the special interest groups the "Danegeld" they demand, by which he means the attention they want from the government as well a the measures they want the government to undertake.

Dangling Participle (*HSS*, 1): basic error in grammar in which the participle does not modify (refer to) the subject or main clause. Example: Upon entering the room, the picture caught my eye. Explanation: The picture is not entering the room. In *HSS*, Kip's failure to be able to explain a dangling participle to his father is part of Heinlein's critique of American secondary education. See: **M.I.T.**

Daniel Boone (*FS*, 7): American frontiersman, pioneer, and settler (b. 2 November 1734, d. 26 September 1820), led Americans across the Appalachian Mountains and into Kentucky through the Cumberland Gap. In *FS*, one of the Boy Scout troops takes the name "Daniel Boone" in another parallel that Heinlein makes between the move into space and the westward movement in American history. See:

Johnny Appleseed, *Mayflower*, and Plymouth Rock Colony.

"Danny Deever" (*ST*, 5): 1890 poem by Rudyard Kipling, first of the *Barrack-Room Ballads*, depicting the hanging of a soldier who has murdered another soldier and the effect the hanging has on the soldiers forced to watch it. In *ST*, Johnnie thinks that one of the enlistees is going to be hanged and says "they were going to do the 'Danny Deever' to Ted Hendrick," but instead Hendrick is flogged. Heinlein, like Kipling, focuses on the effect of the punishment on the men forced to watch it. See: **Kipling.**

Danse Macabre (*RSG*, 12): art song for voice and piano by Camille Saint-Saëns first performed in 1872 and later reworked as a tone poem for orchestra. The late medieval allegory about the universality of death on which the music is based shows the figure of death leading a row of skeletal dancing figures from all walks of life. In *RSG*, Ross whistles this tune after learning that it was Morrie, not Cargraves, who made the landing on the moon, implying that Ross was leading them toward their death.

Dante (*HSS*, 8) *see* **Dantesque.**

Dantesque (*RS*, 1; *SJ*, 18; *HSS*, 8): probably a reference to *The Inferno* (1847) by Dante Alighieri (b. May or June 1265, d. 13 or 14 September 1321), which relates Dante's journey through the various levels of Hell guided by the Italian poet Virgil. In *RS*, Castor and Pollux cut through the grounds of the General Synthetics Corporation on their way home, and Heinlein describes "the jungle of unlikely shapes" as Dantesque. In *SJ*, Max characterizes the line of humanlike creature caught by the centaurs as "something right out of Dante's Inferno." In *HSS*, Kip refers to the dining room in which all of the Wormfaces died as a "scene out of Dante."

Das Kapital (*ST*, 6) *see under* K.

Davis Drive (*PM*, 10) *see* **Davis Mechanics.**

Davis Mechanics (*PM*, 9): extension of Newton's Second Law of Motion that considers, among other things, long-range projectile factors. See: **Cambridge** and **Paramagnetics.**

Davy Crockett (*HSS*, 6): Tennessee frontiersman and politician (b. 17 August 1786, d. 6 March 1836) most famous for his death at the Alamo. In *HSS*, Kip, impressed with Peewee's map-reading skills, asks her if she was once an Indian scout or Davy Crockett. Surprisingly, the Davy Crockett reference is not about Kip's willingness to die in order to save Peewee. See: **King Arthur's Court.**

De Bello Gallico (*HSS*, 10; *ST*, 13): *Commentarii de Bello Gallico*, Julius Caesar's account of his campaigns in Gaul. At one time, this work was the standard text in a high school second year course in Latin. In *HSS*, Kip mentions that the legionary's vocabulary was not that of *De Bello Gallico* but a mix of many languages into his original Latin. See: **Gaul** and **Legionary**. In *ST*, it is one of the commentaries Johnnie has to read as part of a research project on combat versus non-combat military personnel.

De Facto (*BP*, 9; *TiS*, 8): Latin for "what actually exists," whether by law (de jure) or, especially, without legal authority. In *BP*, the war has placed a de facto embargo on interplanetary shipping, preventing Don Harvey from getting to Mars. In *TiS*, as the group of stranded students gets larger, Rod, who has been the leader, is told that he has no real authority as his leadership is de facto rather than elected, and from this point on, the novel spends a lot of time discussing what sort of government such students might create.

Dead Sea Bottoms of Barsoom (*HSS*, 5): specific area of the planet Mars as envisioned by Edgar Rice Burroughs (b. 1 September 1875, d. 19 March 1950) in his Mars novels, beginning with *A Princess of Mars* (1912) and featuring the heroic adventures of American John Carter and his Martian lover and wife, Dejah Thoris. At the end of the first novel, Carter "dies" back to Earth after saving the population of Mars. See: **Barsoom** and **King Arthur's Court**.

"The Death of the Bon Homme Richard" (*ST*, 5): depicts a Revolutionary War naval battle between the British ship *Serapis* and the American ship *Bon Homme Richard*, commanded by John Paul Jones (b. 6 July 1747, d. 18 July 1792). Jones is supposed to have said, as his ship was sinking and the British captain asked for his surrender, "I have not yet begun to fight." See: **"Horatius at the Bridge."**

Death on a Pale Horse (*ST*, 5): "And I looked, and behold a pale horse: and his name that sat upon him was Death, and Hell followed him" (Revelations 6:8), one of the Four Horsemen of the Apocalypse. In *ST*, Johnnie describes Sergeant Zim this way to emphasize the severity of the situation.

"Death Wish" (*TfS*, 5): psychological condition in which a person does dangerous things that could cause his or her death because of an unconscious desire to die. In *TfS*, Tom accuses the girl he and Pat have been dating of getting ready to tell him he has a "death wish" after she tells him that he has a "will to fail." See: **"Will to Fail."**

de-Camp Joints (*RSG*, 6): joints in a space suit that allow the suit to flex as a body would. Heinlein probably calls them de-Camp joints in *RSG* because he, L. Sprague de Camp (b. 27 November 1907, d. 6 November 2000), and Isaac Asimov (b. 2 January 1920, d. 6 April 1992) worked together at the Philadelphia Naval Yard during World War II. Although de-Camp's time travel stories and some others qualify him as a science fiction writer, his real interest was fantasy, especially sword and sorcery fantasy and heroic fantasy.

"Deef as a Post" (*SJ*, 2): slangier or more "country" version of "deaf as a post," a reference to someone who might actually be deaf or someone who might not listen or pay attention. In *SJ*, Max thinks he has been rendered "deef as a post" by the sonic concussion from the passing high-speed train.

"Deep in the Heart of Texas" (*SC*, 8): song popularized in the 1940s praising various attractive features of the state. In *SC*, after drinking too many mint juleps, an inebriated Tex Jarman tries to get his companions to join him in this song. See: **"Ioway"** and **Mint Julep.**

de Forrest (*RSG*, 14): probably Dr. Lee de Forest (b. 26 August 1873, d. 30 June 1961), often called the father of radio. His "Audion," patented in 1907, is considered the beginning of the modern electronics industry. When Ross questions Art about what he is hearing on the radio in *RSG*, Art suggests that he try using the radio and calls him "Mr. de Forrest."

der Tag (*RSG*, 16) *see under T.*

Designer (*SJ*, 14; *TfS*, 14): "the Designer might have created an infinity of universes." In *SJ*, Heinlein uses "Designer" where others might use "God" when speaking of the creation, but as these are Max's thoughts and as Max is an engineer, "Designer" might be more appropriate to his character than "God." In *TfS*, Tom Bartlett says that he does not believe that "all this complicated universe got here by accident," implying a design and a designer.

Devereux (*ST*, 13): probably Robert Devereux (b. 10 November 1567, d. 25 February 1601), Earl of Essex, military hero, and favorite of Queen Elizabeth I, later tried and executed for treason. In *ST*, it is the name of one of the warships of the Federation fleet named for specific foot soldiers.

DEW Line (*HSS*, 10): Distant Early Warning Line, a radar line near the Arctic Circle in Canada built to detect an air strike of bombers from the Soviet Union during the Cold War of the 1950s and 1960s. In *HSS*, Kip imagines a ship undetectable by the DEW Line waiting for the order to rotate the Earth away from its sun and thereby killing all living things on it if the Court of the Three Galaxies decides that Earth is a future menace to their civilizations.

Dexter (*PM*, 9): referring to the right, as in right-handed or the right side of something. In *PM*, the young man of Venus Podkayne meets is named Dexter, and he makes a pun about his name being wrong as he is left-handed and perhaps could have been named "Sinister" (referring to the left, as in left-handed or the left side of something) but for the

Dextrocardia

negative connotations of that word. See: **Sinister.**

Dextrocardia (*TfS*, 2): medical condition in which the heart is on the opposite side of the chest from where it would normally be. In *TfS*, the Bartlett twins are mirror images of each other, one right-handed and the other left handed, one with his heart on the right side and one with his heart on the left.

Digitalis and Curare (*HSS*, 9): examples of how both a medicine and a poison can come from the same plant as well as the way modern medicine can learn from traditional herbal healers. In *HSS*, Kip says the Vegans' interest in human medicine and science could be compared to modern science's interest in traditional herbal healers.

Dillinger (*ST*, 8): John Dillinger (b. 28 June 1902, d. 22 July 1934), American bank robber during the 1930s who killed a number of law officers but was idealized as a modern-day Robin Hood. In *ST*, Dillinger is the name of a recruit who deserts and, later, kills a baby girl. See: **"To Understand All Is to Forgive All."**

Diogenes (*CG*, 23): third or fourth century Greek famous for supposedly walking through the streets with a lantern and claiming to be looking for an honest man. In *CG*, Thorby asks his lawyer, James Garsch, where he can find ten honest men and is told that Diogenes would have settled for one.

Dip Water with a Knife (*CG*, 5): "You can't dip water with a knife," traditional phrase referring to doiong the impossioble. In *CG*, Thorby regards the possibility of his rescuing Baslim from the police as dipping water with a knife.

Doctor Slop (*FS*, 18): rather grotesque physician in Thomas Sterne's novel series *Tristram Shandy*, the first of which appeared in 1759. In *FS*, it is a nickname given to Bill for his "omnibus stew."

Dodo (*ST*, 2): flightless bird native to the island of Mauritius, hunted to extinction in the seventeenth century. See: **Carthage.**

Dom Pedro (*TfS*, 17; *PM*, 9): Dom Pedro I or Dom Pedro II, the seventeenth- and eighteenth-century emperors of Brazil. In *TfS*, Emperor Dom Perdo III presents medals to the returning crew members of the *Lewis and Clark*. See: **Lewis and Clark.** In *PM*, Podkayne spends some evenings at the Dom Perdo Casino, where there is a figure dressed like an emperor who walks around in the casino.

Don Juan (*SJ*, 17): fictional lover whose name has become synonymous with legendary romantic and sexual escapades. In *SJ*, Ellie calls Max a "reluctant Don Juan." She is being very ironic in this case, as Max, like many of Heinlein's young male characters, has absolutely no clue about how to deal with women, let alone romance them, even though Ellie has given him more than enough hints.

Donner Party (*TiS*, 1): group of Americans headed for California who became snowbound in the Sierra Nevada Mountains in the winter of 1846–1847 and resorted to cannibalizing members of the party who had died of exposure and starvation. In *TiS*, Deacon Matson refers to the Donner Party, but without mentioning the cannibalism; from there, he goes on to mention the First Venus Expedition, implying that the same thing happened to them. This is both part of Heinlein's continuing parallel of the juvenile series to American history and an example of how dangerous humans can be to each other in extreme situations. See: **King of the Beasts.**

"Don't Make My Boy a Soldier, the Weeping Mother Cried" (*ST*, 12): "I Didn't Raise My Boy to be a Soldier," 1915 World War I antiwar song. See: **"Don't Wanta Study War No More."**

Don't Teach Your Grandpop [Grandmother] How to Suck Eggs (*SJ*, 14; *SB*, 11): "Don't try to teach your Grandma to suck eggs" (proverb); i.e., don't give advice to someone more experienced that you are. In *SJ*, Kelly says this to Max when Max starts to tell him to do something he is already doing. In *SB*, Betty says, "Don't teach your grandmother," a shortened form of the proverb, to Johnnie when he warns her to watch out for people looking for them; the shortened form suggests that Heinlein expected his readers to know the whole proverb.

"Don't Wanta Study War No More" (*ST*, 12): "Ain't Gonna Study War No More," traditional antiwar song recorded by, among others, the Weavers. In *ST*, one of the songs the officer candidates sing, all of which, unlike the songs such by the recruits at training camp, are very downbeat. Perhaps Heinlein is suggesting that whereas the recruits needed positive and lively songs during their training to help them become enthusiastic and good followers the officer candidates needed to understand the full spectrum of emotions concerning war so that as leaders they would be more thoughtful about the decisions they were making.

Doodlebugging (*FS*, 18): American folk speech referring to using a dowsing stick or divining rod to find water. In *FS*, Bill says that the mineralogist is "doodlebugging ... for ores."

Doomsday Bomb (*RSG*, 5): bomb theoretically capable of ending all, or nearly all, life on Earth. Though no Doomsday Bombs have yet been developed, they have been a feature of literature, especially science fiction, since the conception of the atomic bomb. In *RSG*, Ross and Art see the crater made by the UN's test of a small doomsday device and then discuss the UN police as ensuring there will be no more war. Also in *RSG*, the trial of the Doomsday Bomb has produced the Doomsday Crater (6). See: **UN.**

Douglas MacArthur [Okajima] (*FS*, 7): World War II general (b. 26 January 1880, d. 5 April 1964) who served in the Pacific, would have overseen the invasion of Japan, accepted the Japanese surrender, and supervised the occupation of Japan in the early 1950s. In *FS*, Heinlein briefly mentions a young man named Douglas MacArthur Okajima, an obvious Japanese-American combination.

"Dragged Through a Knothole" (*SC*, 3): idiomatic expression for someone who looks very tired, worn out, or used up. In *SC*, Matt says that one of his fellow trainees looks as if he had been dragged through a knothole.

Dramatic License (*RS*, 2) *see* **Poetic License.**

Druid (*RS*, 2): member of the priestly, intellectual, and artistic class of the ancient Gauls or Celts. In *RS*, Grandma Hazel incorrectly identifies "Geronimo" as an ancient Druidic phrase. See: **Geronimo.**

Duke University (*HSS*, 5): private research university in Durham, NC, known for its research into such powers of the mind as telepathy and telekinesis. In *HSS*, Kip says that his communication with the Mother Thing is not like that kind of thing.

Duodecahedron (*TfS*, 4): geometric form, any polyhedron with twelve faces. In *TfS*, it is the approximate pattern outward from Earth that the torch ships will take in their explorations. See: **Lebensraum [Project]** and ***Lewis and Clark.***

Dupont (*CG*, 14): chemical company that began in the early 1800s as a maker and supplier of gunpowder, also the name of the family that founded the company. During World War II, the Dupont Company made many things, from tires to nylon, for the war effort. In *CG*, it is the name of one of the ships of the Free Traders. See: **Free Traders** and ***Hansea.***

Durance Vile (*BP*, 9; *PM*, 4): imprisonment. In *BP*, Don Harvey refers to his working for Old Charlie as a dishwasher at the Two Worlds Dining Room as "durance vile." Charlie, of course, is not his warden; Don is imprisoned by circumstances caused by the rebellion of Mars and Venus against Earth. In *PM*, Podkayne's uncle jokingly refers to the delay during which their travel credentials are examined as "durance vile" to make the point to Podkayne that such minor delays are sometimes necessary.

E=MC² (*FS*, 6): equation developed by Albert Einstein in which E equals energy, M equals mass, and C^2 the speed of light squared (multiplied by itself). The equation is the basis for the nuclear reaction and has led to speculation that as a body (such as a rocket ship) approaches the speed of light time slows down. Such speculation has led to many science fiction stories, such as Heinlein's *Time for the Stars*, in which people traveling in a fast rocket ship do not age as quickly as people left behind on Earth. See: **Einstein** and **Einstein Wall**.

Each Cat His Own Rat (*CG*, 13): variation of American proverbs "to a good cat a good rat" and "a bad cat deserves a bad rat." In *CG*, Captain Krausa explains the saying to Thorby by telling him it means each person has his own place.

Eastern Mysticism (*TfS*, 5): general term embracing the mystical traditions of the Near East, India, and the Far East. In *TfS*, Tom Bartlett says that he and his twin brother, Pat, do not have to do any of that "Eastern mysticism nonsense" to speak to each other telepathically. Tom's statement indicates both how easy it is for twins to speak telepathically and how little he knows of the world.

Eboracum (*HSS*, 10): city in Roman Britain, in Yorkshire, on the site of the present city of York. See: **Gaul**.

Echo (*HSS*, 5): mountain nymph in Greek mythology in love with the sound of her own voice. In *HSS*, Heinlein has Kip answer his own question by saying "Echo answers mournfully."

Eddington's *The Nature of the Physical World* (*RSG*, 2): series of lectures by A.S. Eddington (b. 22 December 1882, d. 22 November 1944) at the University of Edinburgh in 1927 and later published in book form. In *RSG*, this is one of the books on the boys' clubhouse shelf. See: **Jules Verne**.

Egg in Your Suds (*HSS*, 12): "What do you want, egg in your beer?" is a phrase that originated during World War II asking if you wanted a bonus. In *HSS*, one of the scientists asks the other, who has told him that they might have discovered a way to stop nuclear reactions and therefore a bomb from a long distance, if there's anything else. The other scientist responds, "What do you want? ... Egg in your suds?"

"Eight-Six" with the Reuben Steuben (*TiS*, 15): to "eighty-six" something is to throw it away, cut it or cancel it, or mean that it is no longer available. It may have originated in the restaurant business (www.phrases.org.uk). In *TiS*, the Rod threatens the film crew he feels has invaded his territory, and one of of the crew says, "It's an 'eight-six' with the Reuben Steuben." Although no definition could be found for "Reuben Steuben," it sounds like a Cockney rhyming term or other slang terminology for "rube," a word denoting an ignorant country person that Rod might appear to be to the members of the film crew.

Einstein (*RSG*, 4; *SC*, 10; *RP*, 4; *FS*, 6; *BP*, 16; *SJ*, 3; *TiS*, 2; *TfS*, 1; *HSS*,

Einstein

9; *PM*, 13): Albert Einstein (b. 14 March 1879, d. 18 April 1955) was born in Germany and remained there until 1933. He produced his most striking work in theoretical physics at a relatively young age. He renounced his German citizenship for political reasons, emigrated to the United States, and taught as a professor of theoretical physics at Princeton University. In *RSG*, Cargraves cites Einstein as an example of someone who did his best work at an early age. See: **Manhattan Project** and **Sir Isaac Newton**. In *SC*, Matt says he'll "never be an Einstein" when questioned about his course work in atomics. In *RP*, the *Albert Einstein* is a rocket ship the travels between Earth and Mars. In *FS*, the ship's engineer comments on Einstein's equations about the speed of light and says that no one knows what would happen to a ship that could exceed the speed of light. Later in *FS*, Bill uses Einstein's $E=MC^2$ to figure out the conversion of ice to air on Ganymede (12). In *BP*, "Doctor Einstein" is the chosen English language name of one of the Venerian dragon scientists. In *SJ*, Einstein is one of the previous names of the starship *Asgard*. See: ***Asgard*** and ***The Prince of Wales***. In *TiS*, it is a name Rod Walker knows from books but does not often think about. See: **Otis**. In *TfS*, Einstein is cited as an example of a great man who seemed destined from the beginning to be great. See: **Alexander the Great** and **Napoleon**. Throughout *TfS*, Einstein is invoked several times because the novel is about telepathic communication being instantaneous no matter how far apart the telepaths are, thereby calling the theories about travel at the speed of light into question and how the person traveling at or near the speed of light does not age as rapidly as a person remaining on Earth. In *HSS*, the ability of the spaceships of the Mother Thing's people to travel almost instantaneously from one place in space to another seems to defy Einstein's theories so completely that Kip thinks that Einstein must be referred to as "Whirligig Albert" by these advanced races. See: **Whirligig**. In *PM*, Podkayne's brother sarcastically refers to "Pinhead" as "Albert Einstein." See: **Pinhead**.

Einstein Barrier (*SB*, 8) *see* $E=MC^2$ and **Einstein Wall**.

Einstein Time Effect (*TfS*, 6) *see* **Einstein**.

Einstein Wall (*SJ*, 7; *SB*, 8): speed of light. In *SJ*, Max is explaining the ship's drive and an astrogator's job to Ellie and says that they that have to go through that wall to jump from the fold of space that they are leaving to the fold of space where their destination is located. See: **"As the Crow Flies"** and $E=MC^2$. In *SB*, John Thomas Stuart does not find ships that can break through the Einstein barrier at all remarkable.

El Alamein (*ST*, 13): city in northern Egypt that was the site of two World

War II battles, the second of which signaled the end of German and Italian power in North Africa. In *ST*, it is the name of one of the warships of the Federation fleet. See: **"Alamein Dead."**

El Nido (*CG*, 11) *see under N.*

Elephant's Child (*RS*, 18): "The Elephant's Child," one of the stories in Rudyard Kipling's 1902 *Just So Stories*. "The Elephant's Child" tells the story of how the elephant got its trunk. In *RS*, when their scooter runs off course in the Asteroid Belt, Grandma Hazel tells Buster this story to keep him quiet while she calls for help. See: **Kipling.**

Eliza (*HSS*, 6): character in Harriet Beecher Stowe's 1852 antislavery novel, *Uncle Tom's Cabin*, whose most famous scene may be Eliza's escape from bloodhounds by running and jumping across breaking ice in the Ohio River. In *HSS,* Kip compares his attempted escape across the surface of the Moon to Eliza's crossing the ice.

Elizabeth Regina (*SJ*, 22): Elizabeth the Queen. In *SJ*, it is the name of the ship to which Max is assigned as assistant astrogator at the end of the novel.

Emigrants' Gap (*TiS*, 1): there are at least two, one in the ridge where the California Trail crosses the Sierra Nevada mountain range so steep that nineteenth-century travelers had to lower their wagons down the slope with ropes, and another on the Oregon Trail west of Casper, Wyoming. In *TiS*, one of the Ramsbotham Gates through which settlers can travel almost instantaneously from one planet to another is called Emigrants' Gap. See: **Otis, Peter the Great,** and **Witwatersrand [Gate].**

"The Emperor's New Clothes" (*HSS*, 9): 1837 short story by Hans Christian Andersen. Two tailors delude a king by selling him nothing but telling him that his new clothes will be visible only to worthy subjects; when the king parades his new clothes in public, no one says anything until a small child tells the truth and says that the emperor has no clothes on. In *HSS*, because the helmet on Peewee's new space suit is invisible, Kip asks her if it's a case of "the Emperor's new clothes" when she tells him she is wearing it. See: **Hans Christian Andersen.**

Empire State Building (*RSG*, 3): completed in 1931 and the world's tallest building for more than four decades. In *RSG*, Cargraves compares the profitability of his proposed moon trip to the riches Europe gained from Columbus' discovery of the Americas by suggesting that the backers of Columbus' voyages never expected him "to come back with the Empire State Building in his pocket."

Emulate the Red Queen (*RP*, 14): actually the White Queen, in Lewis Carroll's *Through the Looking-Glass*, who says that she sometimes believes

En Banc

as many as six impossible things before breakfast (chapter 5). In *RP*, when Jim Marlowe protests that Doctor MacRae is asking him to assimilate too much material at once, MacRae tells him to "Emulate the Red Queen." Perhaps MacRae misremembered; perhaps Heinlein did. See: **Alice** and **Lewis Carroll.**

En Banc (*SB*, 3): French for "the full bench," as in a judge's bench in a court of law. In *SB*, Sergei Greenberg suggests that he and Judge O'Farrell sit en banc on the Lummox case.

En Brosse (*TiS*, 9): French term for hair cut so short that it is stiff and stands up. In *TiS*, Carmen wears her hair this way at her wedding. Moreover, it is a sensible style for this essentially frontier community the students have established on the planet where they have been marooned.

"Eniac" (*RSG*, 9; *TiS*, 2): Electronic Numerical Integrator and Computer. Built for the U.S. Army and first operated in 1946 to calculate artillery-firing tables, Eniac was the first multi-purpose computer. The computer that helps operate the *Galileo* in *RSG* is called "Joe" and its cam was designed by Eniac, which Heinlein correctly locates at that time at the University of Pennsylvania. In *TiS*, Eniac is an ancestor to the Rakitiac computer. See: **Maniac** and **Univac.**

Erska (*RS*, 17): derives from Icelandic and also other Scandinavian languages. In *RS*, the Erska family of the Asteroid Belt speak what may be Icelandic. Their appearance in the novel is brief, and the identification of them as Icelandic indicates Heinlein's attention to detail.

Eskimo (*SC*, 11; *RP*, 4; *FS*, 18): various Native American tribes inhabiting the very cold regions of northern Canada, Russia, and Alaska especially. In *SC*, Captain Yancey, discussing hydroponics, mentions a rust infection that left him with no more shipboard farm "than an Eskimo." Later in the book, Matt praises Oscar for his negotiating skills by suggesting that he could sell "snow to the Eskimos," a variant of the more popular phrase about selling refrigerators to the Eskimos, in both cases something they do not need (15). See: **Hydroponics.** In *RP*, Eskimos are among the settlers on Mars who can best stand the extreme cold. See: **Tibetans.** In *FS*, Bill quotes an Eskimo as saying "food is sleep" when as camp cook he has to produce four meals a day for the exploring party.

Espiritu Santo (*ST*, 11): Spanish for "Holy Spirit." In *ST*, the capital city of the planet Sanctuary, a Federation world well hidden from the enemy.

Esprit de Corps (*BP*, 13; *CG*, 16; *ST*, 11): morale, or the enthusiasm of the members of the group for each other and for the task at hand, usually used in regard to military operations; literally, a French term meaning "the spirit of the corps" or group. In *BP*, Don Harvey comments on the high level of esprit de corps in the guerilla rebel group he joins. In *CG*, Thorby joins the Hegemonic Guard, an outfit with a great deal of esprit de corps. In *ST*, Johnnie says that his outfit had esprit de corps but also says that they did not know that the Federation was losing the war. Later in *ST*, he says that the esprit de corps is the result of free men having chosen to go to war to protect their civilization (13).

Estates General (*BP*, 9): eighteenth-century legislature of France composed of representatives of the clergy, the nobility, and the common people, formed before the French Revolution. It was called and dismissed by the king and had no real power. In *BP*, the Republic of Venus has an "Estates" that, Heinlein suggests, has in just a few weeks grown almost too unwieldy to actually get anything done.

Estivate (*PM*, 8): state of summer sleep like hibernation in winter. In *PM*, Podkayne is bored while being cooped up during the solar flare and comments that a Venerian would just estivate.

Et Tu (*TiS*, 10): Latin for "and you." According to Shakespeare, in the 1599 tragedy, *Julius Caesar*, Caesar's final words upon seeing his best friend, Brutus, among his assassins, were, "Et tu, Brute? Then fall, Caesar!" (III, ii, 76). Today, "et tu, Brute?" signifies any betrayal by a friend. In *TiS*, Jimmy uses the phrase humorously when Jacqueline suggests that he does not fully understand something and is not very bright.

Euclid (*RS*, 8): Euclid of Alexandria, ca. 300 B.C., often called the father of geometry. In *RS*, Pollux's father assigns him extra homework to continue until he masters non–Euclidean geometry both as a learning experience and as a punishment for allowing his twin brother to take and pass the high school course for him.

Evangeline (*ST*, 12): "Evangeline: A Tale of Acadia," 1847 poem published by Henry Wadsworth Longfellow (b. 12 February 1807, d. 24 March 1882). The poem sets Evangeline's search for her lover, Gabriel, against the background of the Acadians' exile from Canada to Louisiana. Although Evangeline does not find him until the end of the poem, when both of them are old and he is dying, they pass close to each other several times without knowing it. In *ST*, Johnnie compares his meeting with his own father, as he is leaving the ship and his father is boarding, to Evangeline's story.

"Every Civilized Man Has Two Planets, His Own and Ganymede" (*SC*, 9): corruption of "every civilized man has to consider that he has two homes, his native home and Syria," a phrase attributed to French archaeologist André Pareau that appears in a lot of advertisements for travel in Syria.

Ex Cathedra

In *SC*, a cadet from Ganymede uses the phrase in a discussion of homesickness, through which Heinlein implies that we all have two homes, the one where we were raised and the one we have adopted. In Matt's case, his second home is the patrol.

Ex Cathedra (*ST*, 10): Latin for "from the chair," usually used to refer to pronouncements from the pope designating that his official pronouncements "from the chair," sent by God, are infallible truths. In *ST*, when Sergeant Jelal wants something corrected, he invokes the lieutenant and, according to Johnnie, is speaking ex cathedra.

Exeunt Omnes (*SB*, 5): Latin for "exit all," generally a stage direction that all characters should leave the stage at this point. In *SB*, Mr. Kiku suggests that Greenberg's decision in the Lummox case should have had everyone exiting and laughing.

Faith, Hope, and Charity (*TfS*, 1): "And now abideth faith, hope, and charity, these three; but the greatest of these is charity" (1 Corinthians 13:13). In *TfS*, they are the names of Tom and Pat Bartlett's three sisters.

Fakir (*RP*, 6; *RS*, 19): Indian Sufi who can perform feats of endurance such as sleeping on nails or walking on fire. In *RP*, Frank mentions fakirs to Jim when they are trying to survive a Martian night by crawling into a giant Martian plant, suggesting that they, too, can exist on less oxygen than seems possible. In *RS*, Grandma Hazel claims to have used a fakir's trick to survive when she ran short of air. See: **Houdini.**

Farmer in the Sky (*FS*, cover): title of Heinlein's fourth juvenile novel. This novel is about "terraforming" Ganymede, one of Jupiter's moons, so that humans can inhabit it without any special breathing apparatus or pressurized cities, as exist on Earth's moon in Heinlein's future. In addition to getting the reader to think about farming and terraforming, the title is a play on the children's game rhyme "The Farmer in the Dell." See: **Terraforming.**

Fate-Worse-Than-Death (*HSS*, 5): phrase referring to anything that could happen to a person that would be worse than dying, traditionally associated with rape and the belief that a dishonored woman was better off dead. In *HSS*, Kip uses the phrase to refer to continued capture and interrogation by the Wormface and actually means it. This is one of the ways in which Heinlein emphasizes how frightening these aliens are.

Fatted Calf (*BP*, 2; *SJ*, 4): "And bring hither the fatted calf, and kill [it]; and let us eat and be merry" (Luke 15:23). This can be a metaphor for welcoming someone or celebrating, a more complete statement usually includes the word "kill" or "killing," as in "we'll kill the fatted calf when you get here." In *BP*, Dr. Jefferson says that he will "pick out a fatted calf and butcher it" to welcome Don Harvey to New Chicago. In *SJ*, Sam asks Max if the Astrogators Guild killed "the fatted calf," i.e., welcomed him as a long-lost member, when he showed up.

Featherbedding (*CG*, 10): requiring an employer to hire more workers than necessary by union rule or safety statute. In *CG*, the Free Traders never allow anyone else inside their ships to load or unload cargo even if they have to pay the locals who would have done the job not to do it.

Fiddlesticks (*TiS*, 2): literally, a violin bow; in modern slang, something of little value. In *TiS*, Rod Walker's sister uses the word to mean "nonsense."

Fifth Amendment (*HSS*, 2): amendment to the Constitution of the United States that guarantees, among other things, that an accused person cannot be forced to make self-incriminating statements. In *HSS*, Kip ends his spiel for Skyway Soap by creating the metaphor that the soap is so pure that it refuses to take the Fifth Amendment.

Fifth Column [Activity] (*RP*, 11; *HSS*, 7): secretly undermining a group by using people within that group. In *RP*, MacRae contacts friends who work for the company to help him and the other settlers and workers who are trying to overthrow the company. In *HSS*, Kip calls the two humans working for the Wormfaces "fifth columnists."

The Fifth Way (*TiS*, 2, chapter title) *see* **Ape Escaped a Fifth Way.**

Finest Hour (*HSS*, 7) *see* **Their Finest Hour.**

"Fire When Ready, Gridley" (*ST*, 3): "You may fire when ready, Gridley," famous command with which Commodore George Dewey (b. 26 December 1837, d. 16 January 1917) began the Battle of Manila Bay in 1898 during the Spanish-American War. The command has become part of popular American speech and can be used to tell someone to begin an activity or process. In *ST*, Sergeant Zim says this to one of the enlistees who has accepted his challenge to personal combat.

"Fish, or Cut Bait" (*TiS*, 8 and chapter title): idiomatic expression instructing someone to make a decision about which course of action he or she will follow. In *TiS*, Rod uses this idiom to tell lazy students from Teller University that they have to work in the community just like everyone else or leave. See: **Teller [University]**.

Flaming Sword (*SC*, 9): probably refers in this case to the flaming sword of the archangel who escorted Adam and Eve out of Eden (Genesis 3:24). In *SC*, Bill Arensa leaves the academy, saying that he does not want to carry a flaming sword, which means he does not want to be the enforcer of the Federation's laws. See: **Archangel.**

Flea in Your Ear (*SJ*, 10): plant an idea in someone's mind; also a criti-

Fleshpots

cism or rebuke. In *SJ*, Simes is criticizing Max for what Simes suspects is a trick Max has played by pretending to have an eidetic memory. See: **Put a Flea in His Ear.**

Fleshpots of Egypt (*TiS*, 14): originally a reference to the pots in which Egyptians cooked meat or the opulent lifestyles of the Egyptians (Exodus 16:3); more recently, places of carnal luxury. In *TiS*, the phrase is meant to refer to luxuries. When one of the women wishes for lipstick, her husband humorously comments that she longs for "the fleshpots of Egypt."

Flicka (*PM*, 3): name of the main character, a horse, from Mary O'Hara's popular 1941 children's novel, *My Friend Flicka*. The novel was the first of a trilogy and the source of several films and television series. In *PM*, Podkayne's uncle calls her "Flicka" after the spirited filly of the novel.

Flit Gun (*RSG*, 18): hand-held, pump-action sprayer for liquid insecticide. Flit was a commercial insecticide used between the 1920s and the 1950s, and the Flit gun was its official dispenser. As a result of a large advertising campaign, the brand name, Flit, became a household word. In *RSG*, Cargraves says that if Morrie and Art are late he will come after them "with a Flit gun"; he is humorously suggesting, perhaps, that the boys are pests.

Flophouse (*ST*, 1): cheap hotel or rooming house, a place where one can "flop" (sit or lie down in a heavy or clumsy manner). In *ST*, Johnnie does not know if he has bombed a church, a flophouse, or a military headquarters; the mission of his platoon is to cause destruction and scare the population of the planet.

Florence Nightingale (*FS*, 7): known as "The Lady with the Lamp" (b. 12 May 1820, d. 13 August 1910) for her work as a nurse during the Crimean War and very influential in the development of the nursing profession. In *FS*, Bill's half sister, Peggy, joins a Girl Scout troop named for Florence Nightingale, causing Bill to wonder why girls copy what boys do.

The Flying Dutchman (*TfS*, 15) *see* **Vanderdecken.**

"Fog-Eater" (*BP*, 1): slang term for someone who lives on Venus, the second planet from the sun, which has a very dense atmosphere. In *BP*, one of Don's schoolmates calls him a "fog-eater," and Heinlein comments that the use of a slang term like "fog-eater" can be either innocent slang or deliberate insult. See: **"Limey," "Skin Head,"** and **"Yank."**

"For This Relief, Much Thanks" (*TiS*, 11): "For this relief much thanks" (1, i, 8) in Shakespeare's 1603 tragedy, *Hamlet*. At this point, Bernadro is relieving Francisco as watchman on the walls of the castle on a very cold night, and Francisco thanks him. In *TiS*, Carol writes the phrase in her notebook when she thinks that Rod and Roy will be back in two days to ease her concern about Rod's being away.

Form a Turtle (*HSS*, 11): Roman military maneuver in which the soldiers hold their shields to the front, rear, and sides as well as overhead to protect themselves from arrows, spears, and other missiles. In *HSS*, the Roman legionary challenges The Court of the Three Galaxies to combat, one at a time or formed up as a turtle.

"Foxes Have Holes and Birds of the Air Have Nests —" Matthew viii:20 (*BP*, 8): "Foxes have holes and birds of the air have Nests, but the Son of Man has no place to lay His head" (Matthew 8:20). Jesus makes this statement in response to someone who said he would follow Jesus wherever he went, but Jesus's response indicated that Jesus was not here to build a kingdom on earth but would return to heaven soon. In *BP*, it is the title of chapter 8, about Don Harvey's first day on Venus and which recounts how, without money, he finds a job and a place to stay. But the statement suggests that while Don is on Venus he is really not of Venus.

Frankensteinian Monster (*ST*, 12): creature built like Dr. Frankenstein's monster in the 1818 novel, *Frankenstein, or the Modern Prometheus*, by Mary Shelley (b. 30 August 1797, d. 1 February 1851), in which a creature of superhuman powers is abandoned by its creator to run amok in nineteenth-century Europe. In *ST*, the commander at O.C.S. always worries that, in spite of the training, he might be turning a Frankensteinian monster, in the person of a newly commissioned officer, loose on an experienced combat team.

"Frankie and Johnny Were Lovers" (*SB*, 12): traditional American popular song about a woman, Frankie, who finds her lover, Johnny, with another woman and shoots him. In *SB*, Mr. Kiku sings this song to himself from time to time, and at the end, he sings the last verse: " ... This story has no moral, this story has no end. This story only goes to show that there ain't no good in men" (17). He is referring to the recent dealings with the Hroshii and the intermediary/translator, a Rargyllian, and may mean that they, like him, were not always truthful in their negotiations.

Free Traders (*CG*, 3): society that lives totally aboard their spaceships, traveling from planet to planet in the Galaxy and making a living by trading with the people on those planets. In *CG*, Heinlein loosely bases the Free Traders on the Romany, or Gypsies, who lived, and in some places still do, without fixed homes and traveled by wagon from place to place and were known as sharp traders. See: **Hansea.**

Galactic Overlord (*RS*, 2; *HSS*, 12): villain of the serial Hazel Stone is writing in *RS*. See: ***The Scourge of the Spaceway***. In *HSS*, the Galactic

Overlords are part of Ace Quiggle's ridicule of Kip and his desire to go into space. In both *RS* and *HSS*, the Galactic Overlords represent comic book science fiction villains and comic book science fiction in general, just the opposite of the kind of science fiction Heinlein was writing and promoting. Ironically, the actual Galactic Overlords in *HSS* are dedicated to keeping the peace.

Galahad (*SC*, 5; *RS*, 2; *TfS*, 10): knight of the Arthurian Round Table who searched for and found the Holy Grail. Galahad was considered the perfect knight and his name has come to symbolize the best of chivalry and courtesy. In *SC*, Burke calls Matt "Galahad" when Matt seems shocked at the idea of sneaking more than the allowed weight of possessions up to the *James Randolph*. In *RS*, Roger Stone calls John Sterling, the hero of *The Scourge of the Spaceways*, a "mealy-mouthed Galahad," meaning that he is devious and cannot or will not state the facts directly. See: ***The Scourge of the Spaceways.*** In *TfS*, one of the crew suggests that even Sir Galahad could get nowhere with Prudence Mathews because her telepathic twin, Patience, back on Earth, would not allow it. See: **"Pease Porridge Hot."**

Galileo (*RSG*, title; *BP*, 16; *TfS*, 12): Galileo Galilei (b. 15 February 1564, d. 8 January 1642), Italian astronomer, mathematician, and physicist now considered the father of modern sciences whose improvements to the telescope led him to support the Copernican theory that the Earth revolved around the sun. Galileo was forced by the Inquisition to recant his support of the Copernican theory. Heinlein's use of Galileo's name for the boys' model rocket club and for the actual rocket to the moon in *RSG* is indicative of the controversy surrounding their flight and their correctness in doing it. In *BP*, Galileo Galilei is the chosen English language name of one of the Venerian dragon scientists. In *TfS*, the proving of Bode's law is considered as important as Galileo's discoveries.

Gallic (*SB*, 6): referring to the Gauls (or Celts) of ancient Europe and to those who claim descent from them, especially the French. In *SB*, the Rargyllian negotiator spread his hands "in a gesture that was purely Gallic," meaning that he used his hands in conversation as a stereotypical Frenchman does.

Gallipoli (*ST*, 13): World War I battle on the Turkish peninsula in which both sides suffered heavy casualties and the British and French alliance failed to capture Istanbul. In *ST*, it is the name of one of the warships of the Federation fleet.

Gamov (*RSG*, 2): George Gamow (b. 4 March 1904, d. 19 August 1968), born Georgiy Antonovich Gamow. A Russian physicist and cosmologist, he moved to the United States in 1934, worked at George Washington University, and published articles with

Edward Teller, among others. Gamov worked on many projects and theories, including the radioactive decay of the atomic nucleus and the big bang theory. In 1956, he was awarded the Kalinga Prize by UNESCO for his work in popularizing science. In *RSG*, the boys have read "Gamov's new book." It is interesting that Heinlein uses the correct Russian form of the name in *RSG* as opposed to the American version by which he is better known. See: **Pollard and Davidson**.

Garand Rifles (*RSG*, 6): more popularly known as the M-1, the primary semiautomatic rifle used by U.S. forces (and the Allies to whom the U.S. provided them) during World War II and the Korean War. In *RSG*, Cargraves buys two Garands when prowlers become a problem and stows the guns aboard the *Galileo* before takeoff. Even though he sees no reason for them on such a voyage, his impulse to be prepared proves beneficial when he and the boys encounter the Nazis on the moon.

Gargantuan (*BP*, 17): adjective form of the name Gargantua, a giant in the sixteenth-century novels of French writer François Rabelais (b. ca. 1494, d. 9 April 1553). In *BP*, Heinlein capitalizes the word when he uses it to describe some of the rooms in the Venerian dragon Sir Isaac Newton's dwelling place. As Gargantuan is not usually capitalized when used as an adjective in English, I suspect that Heinlein was directing the reader's attention to the source of the word.

Gary (*SC*, 13): several U.S. Navy vessels over the years, including the *Gary* (DE-326), that served during World War II. I can find no connection to Girard Burke's ship, *Gary*, in *SC*, but perhaps it was named for manufacturing center Gary, Indiana.

Gat (*RSG*, 18): slang for "gun," popular in the 1930s, probably from Gatling Gun, the precursor of the automatic or machine gun. In *RSG*, Morrie refers to a German's gun as a "gat," suggesting, perhaps, his familiarity with popular literature and film about 1930s gangsters.

Gaul (*HSS*, 10): area of Roman conquest including the modern countries of Belgium, France, Luxembourg, and Germany west of the Rhine River. In *HSS*, the legionary captured by the Court of the Three Galaxies says that he served in Gaul before being stationed at a British garrison in Eboracum, north of Londinium. See: **Eboracum** and **Legionary**.

Gauls (*SB*, 14): generally, the tribes of northwestern Europe conquered by Julius Caesar and now referred to popularly as the Celts. See: **Caesar** and **Gallic**.

Gekko (*RP*, 3): Martian who befriends Jim and Frank. Perhaps Heinlein wanted the reader to think of *gecko* when reading *RP*.

"Gentlemen Rankers" (*ST*, 12): 1892 poem by Rudyard Kipling and a term for soldiers who might be de-

George

moted officers or might be educated sufficiently to be officers but are not. It was later set to music and, still later and somewhat modified, became the "Whiffenpoof Song," a popular song at Yale and Harvard universities. See: **"Don't Wanta Study War No More"** and **Kipling.**

"George" (*ST*, 13): from "Let George do it" and usually referring to the lowest ranking person in the group, who gets all the odds and ends jobs or the "extra" jobs, especially the ones no one else wants. In *ST*, Johnnie, as a cadet on a training mission, gets to be "George."

German War Rockets (*RS*, 11): V-2 rockets used by the Germans during World War II. V-2 rockets were the first ballistic missiles and hit cities in England and on the European continent. In *RS*, the shuttle rockets on Mars are slightly more powerful than "German war rockets." See: **Nazi V-2 Rockets.**

Geronimo (*RSG*, 8; *RS*, 2; *ST*, 13): Chiricahua Apache military leader (b. 16 June 1829, d. 17 February 1909) who fought against both the Mexican army and the United States cavalry in an attempt to keep Euro-American settlers from moving into traditional Apache lands. His name was adopted by paratroopers, in honor of his leap from Medicine Bluff, and was shouted as they jumped from airplanes during World War II; the name has since become a synonym for daring. Morrie yells "Geronimo" in *RSG* when he sees Cargraves take off testing the *Galileo* and its new power train. In *RS*, Grandma Hazel shouts "Geronimo" when she, her son, Roger, and the twins, Castor and Pollux, head out to see about buying a used rocket ship. In *ST*, it is the name of one of the warships of the Federation fleet.

Gettysburg (*ST*, 13): famous battle of the American Civil War that effectively ended the South's northward invasion and turned the war in favor of the North. In *ST*, it is the name of one of the warships of the Federation fleet.

Giuseppe Piazzi (*RS*, 15): Italian astronomer (b. 7 July 1746, d. 22 July 1826). Piazzi discovered and named the asteroid Ceres, the largest asteroid in the Asteroid Belt, thinking it was a planet. See: **Bode's Law, Kepler,** and **Lucifer.**

Gladiator (*HSS*, 11): Latin for "swordsman," armed fighters who entertained Roman audiences by fighting each other or condemned criminals in the centuries just before and after the birth of Christ. In *HSS*, Iunio offers a "gladiatorial challenge" to the Court of the Three Galaxies.

Gladstone (*SB*, 2): probably William Gladstone (b. 29 December 1809, d. 19 May 1898). Gladstone was several times prime minister of Great Britain. He championed self-government for Ireland, and had difficult dealings with Queen Victoria throughout his years in public service. In *SB*, Henry Gladstone Kiku is "Permanent Under Secretary for Spatial Affairs," his job is, essentially, anything to do with interplanetary relations, and he constantly "manages the actual Secretary," a political appointee who needs all the help he can get. See: ***Take Me Out to the Ball Game.***

Glory Road (*BP*, 2): road of one who is on a quest for fame and glory. In *BP*, it is the name of the rocket ship that will take Don Harvey from Earth to the Circum-Terra space station and, more important, will start him down his own Glory Road. Incidentally, the only Heinlein novel that can be called fantasy rather than science fiction is *Glory Road*, published in 1963.

Goddard (*BP*, 5; *SB*, 2): Robert Goddard (b. 5 October 1882, d. 10 August 1945), one of the first scientists to be interested in rocketry and the first to launch a liquid-fueled rocket. In *BP*, a hotel on the space station, Circum-Terra, is named for him. In *SB*, exchange students to Earth are from a school on Procyon VII named after Goddard.

Goddess of Liberty (*TiS*, 1) *see* **Statue of Liberty.**

Gold Rush (*RS*, 14) *see* **California Gold Rush.**

Golgotha (*FS*, 13): Aramaic for "skull," and the name for the hill on which Christ was crucified, the "place of skulls." In *FS*, Bill and his father, George, are looking over their land on Ganymede, and all they see is rocks. One formation looks like a skull, and George, looking at it, calls it "Golgotha," indicating his dismay at the amount of work it will take to make the land ready to cultivate. See: **Milk and Honey** and **Promised Land.**

Golliwog (*SB* 1; *TiS*, 11): children's literature character from Florence Upton's (b. 22 February 1873, d. 16 October 1922) books that looked like a black-face minstrel rag doll; in and after the 1950s, a term of racial insult. In *SB*, Lummox has a "simple-minded golliwog" smile, reminiscent of the exaggerated smiles of the rag dolls and the blackface minstrels after which they were designed. In *TiS*, the animals called "dopey joes" have a golliwog facial expression, leading the students to believe, erroneously, that the animals are harmless.

Gonoph (*RS*, 1): Hebrew for "pickpocket" or "thief." In *RS*, Grandma Hazel calls Dealer Dan, the Spaceship Man a "gonoph" after hearing the price he wanted to charge Castor and Pollux for a used spaceship on his lot.

Good Hope Mountain and Mount Waddington (*ST*, 9): principal mountains in the Coast Range of British Columbia, Canada. In *ST*, it is part of the setting for Camp Sergeant Spooky Smith.

Good Samaritan (*SC*, 11; *SJ*, 2, chapter title): New Testament story about a Samaritan who is the only person to stop and help a Jew who has been beaten and robbed. The story is im-

Götterdämmerung

portant, as Jews and Samaritans did not associate with each other. In *SC*, Operation Samaritan is the search for the lost ship, *Pathfinder*. In *SJ*, Heinlein uses this chapter title in a doubly ironic way. Sam, the "samaritan" of the chapter's title, first helps Max by giving him food and a place to sleep, then he steals valuable books and an ID from Max; later in the novel, he helps Max achieve his desire to go into space and, in the end, dies to save Max's life.

Götterdämmerung (*SC*, 2): German for *The Twilight of the Gods*. First performed in 1876, this is the last of the four operas that make up Wagner's *Der Ring das Nibelungen* (*The Ring of the Nibelungs*) that depicts, through the story of Siegfried and Brünnhilde, the downfall and destruction of the Norse gods. In *SC*, the Valhalla theme from this opera plays at the end of the presentation of Ezra Dahlquist's story, marking his death as sufficiently heroic to merit his entrance into Valhalla, the "heroes' hall" of the Norse gods. See: **Beethoven's Fifth** and **Wagnerian Opera.**

Grand Canyon (*PM*, 11): deep canyon or gorge in Arizona carved by the Colorado River. In *PM*, Podkayne believes that the artificial view for the hotel "window" is of the Grand Canyon of Eldorado or Colorado. The Colorado reference is correct, but El Dorado is one of the legendary Seven Cities of Gold for which Spanish explorers searched the American southwest, including the Grand Canyon area, and parts of northern Mexico.

Grand Opera (*TiS*, 13): opera in which the text is sung and which features a large cast and orchestra. In *TiS*, Jimmy calls the creatures that make loud noises during the night "grand opera."

Grand Rapids (*BP*, 14): city in western Michigan noted for furniture manufacture. In *BP*, Don Harvey is admiring the human furniture in Venerian dragon Sir Isaac Newton's home and discovers that the dining room chairs have "'Grand Rapids' stamped on their undersides."

Grandma's Spectacles (*BP*, 15) *see* **Blue Bird.**

Great Auk (*ST*, 2): flightless bird hunted to extinction by the middle of the nineteenth century. See: **Carthage.**

Great Divide (*SB*, 8): Continental Divide of the United States that separates the waters that drain into the Caribbean and the Atlantic Ocean from the waters that drain into the Pacific Ocean, generally the peaks of the Rocky Mountain chain. In *SB*, Johnnie takes Lummox to hide in the woods on the slopes of the Great Divide, one of the few areas of wilderness left on the continent.

Great Fire of Rome (*TiS*, 7): week-long fire that destroyed much of Rome in A.D. 64. See: **Nero.**

"**Great Globe**" (*BP*, 2) *see* "**These Our Actors ...**"

"**Greater Love Hath No Man**" (*SJ*, 21; *ST*, 8): "Greater love hath no man than this, that a man lay down his life for his friends" (John 15:13). In *SJ*, Max considers this for Sam's epitaph after Sam has died so that Max and Ellie can escape to the ship, thereby saving not only the two of them but the rest of the ship's company as well because Max is the only one left who can navigate the ship back to the known planets. Max rejects this epitaph in favor of one even more fitting. In *ST*, Mr. Dubois intentionally misquotes this saying, without changing its intent, to argue that it illustrates all moral problems.

Green Cheese (*RSG*, 10): young cheese, not fully matured, usually an extremely light color. Saying that the moon is made of green cheese refers not to the color green but to the pale white or yellow color of the moon that resembles the color of young or immature cheese. In *RSG*, Cargraves suggests that, by a certain logic, the argument that the moon is made of green cheese is valid. See: **Scientific Method**.

Greenwich [Time] (*RSG*, 12; *FS*, 7; *BP*, 7; *RS*, 2; *SJ*, 21; *TfS*, 9; *HSS*, 6): Greenwich Mean Time (GMT); local time at the 0° meridian passing through Greenwich, England. Although it is not as accurate as an atomic clock and does not actually apply during daylight savings time months, the Greenwich meridian is still considered the place from which we measure the day, time, time zones, and longitude in the popular imagination. In *RSG*, Tycho will be the Greenwich for the moon. In *FS*, the *Mayflower*'s decks are organized as time zones, with A deck on Greenwich time. In *BP*, the *Nautilis*, which is taking Don Harvey to Venus, operates on Greenwich time. In *RS*, the Stone family lives on Greenwich time even though it does not correspond to the moon's day/night cycle. In *SJ*, when the *Asgard* gets ready to try to get back to known space, the ship returns to Greenwich time. In *TfS*, there are two clocks in the mess room, one showing the ship's time and the other showing Greenwich time; both clocks read the same at the start of the voyage, but as the voyage continues, the difference between the clocks grew and Greenwich time became irrelevant to most of the crew. In *HSS*, Kip says that he should have been able to read Greenwich time from the moon by looking at the Earth but that his inexperience and his and Peewee's travel in the mountains prevent him from doing so.

Groundhog (*RS*, 1): rodent, also known as a woodchuck or whistle-pig, that burrows into the ground. In *RS*, an insulting slang term that dwellers on the moon use to refer to people who live on Earth.

Guggenheim [Grant] (*HSS*, 7; *PM*, 1): grants presented by the John Simon

Guilds

Guggenheim Memorial Foundation for research in the natural sciences, social sciences, creative arts, and humanities. In *HSS*, Kip comments that Professor Tombaugh had a Guggenheim grant to build a telescope to photograph Pluto. See: **Tombaugh [Station]**. In *PM*, Podkayne's father is a university professor on leave with a Guggenheim grant.

Guilds (*SJ*, 2): association of craftsmen of a particular trade. Guilds flourished in the Middle Ages and through the Renaissance in Europe and began to wane in the eighteenth and nineteenth centuries with the advent of the Industrial Revoluion. In the future of Heinlein's *SJ*, almost all forms of employment, from crafts people to professionals, are organized into and overseen by guilds. Max cannot become an astrogator because his father was not one and his uncle, who was, did not nominate him to an apprenticeship in the Astrogators' Guild. Heinlein, as a Libertarian, is critical throughout the novel of the Guilds' control over human freedom and considers it, in part, a result of the high-density population of Earth, calling the planet a "jail" (5) and comparing it unfavorably to the frontier world of Nova Terra, where, among many other positive conditions, there are no guilds (6). At the end of the novel, Max ponders the situation and thinks *the guilds were set up wrong; the rules ought to give everybody a chance* (22).

Guillotine (*HSS*, 7): method of execution developed during the French Revolution (1789–1799). A weighted blade is dropped down a wooden structure onto the neck of a kneeling prisoner to chop off his or her head. The guillotine came to be a symbol of the excesses of the French Revolution but was the official method of execution in France until the latter part of the twentieth century. According to legend, Dr. Guillotin was beheaded by the machine named after him as one of its developers, but he actually died of old age in 1814. In *HSS*, Kip describes one of the gangsters as being "as coldly vicious as a guillotine."

Gulliver's Travels (*TiS*, 2; *CG*, 19): 1726 novel by Jonathan Swift (b. 30 November 1667, d. 19 October 1745) describing the fantastic travels of Lemuel Gulliver to lands that were satiric exaggerations of and comments on Swift's England. In *TiS*, Heinlein mentions *Gulliver's Travels* and then refers indirectly to Swift's "A Modest Proposal," in which Swift satirically proposes the fattening and sale for food of Irish babies as a solution to the overpopulation problem of Ireland, a problem which the Earth of *TiS* is solving by encouraging or forcing people to emigrate to other planets. See: **Malthus**. In *CG*, Thorby feels that his "Uncle Jack" and the others are preventing him from finding out any useful information by making him wade through a lot of meaningless documents. He says that he feels "tied up with a thousand threads" like "the fellow in ... 'Gulliver and His Starship.'"

"Gus" (*CG*, 14) *see* **Augustus Caesar**.

Haber (*HSS*, 2): Fritz Haber (b. 9 December 1868, d. 29 January 1934), prominent German scientist in the field of aviation medicine and space science. See: **Stapp** and **Strughold**.

Hades (*SJ*, 11): brother of Zeus and Poseidon in Greek mythology; also, ruler of the Underworld. Hades is used more now as a place name than to refer to the god himself. In *SJ*, Hendrix says that Max's failure to take a doppler reading to check his calculations might have ended them in Hades, crashed into the River Styx (the boundary river between Earth and the Underworld).

Hadrian's Wall (*HSS*, 10): famous fortification the Romans built in the north of England from the River Tyne to the Solway Firth to define and defend the border of the Roman Empire in Britain. In *HSS*, Kip thinks at first that the legionary is talking about Hadrian's Wall when he talks about being on guard duty where a wall was being built but realizes that the legionary was not talking about that wall but another one, farther north. Heinlein must have been referring to the Antonine Wall on which construction was begun in about A.D. 144. See: **Eboracum**, **Legionary**, and **Victrix**.

Haggard's *When the Earth Trembled* (*RSG*, 2): H. Rider Haggard (b. 22 June 1856, d. 14 May 1925), best known for the novels *King Solomon's Mines* (1885) and *She* (1887), published *When the World Shook* in 1919. The 1918 dedication page has this title, but a retitled version might have been published in the United States. In *RSG*, it is one of the books on the boys' clubhouse shelf. See: **Jules Verne**.

"Hail, Caesar, We Who Are About to Die—" (*TiS*, 1): "Ave, Caesar, morituri te salutant," Latin for "Hail, Caesar, we who are about to die salute you," traditionally considered the phrase gladiators directed to the Roman emperor before they began their combats. More commonly now used, sometimes ironically, before starting some risky task. In *TiS*, Jimmy uses the phrase to describe the survival test he and the rest are about to undergo. See: **Nos Morituri —**

Halcyon (*SJ*, 6): place or time of peace and prosperity, as in halcyon days. In *SJ*, it is the name of a planet that is attractive but cold; it is also the title of chapter 12, the chapter in which Max is quite happy with his position aboard ship.

Half a Loaf (*TfS*, 4 and chapter title): "Half a loaf is better than none" (proverb); i.e., getting half of what you want is better than getting none of it. In *TfS*, Pat Bartlett suggests using this argument with their parents to show them that having one son at home is better than having no sons at home, but his brother, Tom, knows that it won't work. See: **Ninety and Nine.**

"Halls of Montezuma" (*ST*, 4): as "The Marines Hymn," the official song of the U.S. Marine Corps. See: *"Le Regiment de Sambre et Meuse."*

Hamlet (*RS*, 2): 1603 tragedy by William Shakespeare. In *RS*, Roger Stone complains about Grandma Hazel's introduction of the Galactic Overlord into *The Scourge of the Spaceways* serial (which she has taken over writing) as a "preposterous" and "over-used" device, to which Grandma Hazel replies that for the next episode, she will "equip *Hamlet* with atomic propulsion and stir it in with *The Comedy of Errors*." See: **Galactic Overlord** and *The Scourge of the Spaceways.*

The Handbook of Chemistry and Physics (*RSG*, 2): now in its 89th year and also available on CD-Rom. As Heinlein gives only the title, this may not be the book; but it is certainly old enough to be a companion to *Marks' Standard Handbook for Mechanical Engineers*. In *RSG*, it is one of the books on the boys' clubhouse shelf. See: **Jules Verne.**

Handwriting on the Wall (*BP*, 2; *HSS*, 7): general metaphor meaning that something is obvious. The original handwriting on the wall appeared in the Bible (Daniel 5:25). In *BP*, Dr. Jefferson uses this phrase to refer to a government announcement that has just appeared on a large screen declaring that the Venus colonials have rejected the Earth government's most recent offer. In spite of the government's reassurance, Jefferson's comment suggests that war is on the way. In *HSS*, one of the former gangsters says that you have to change allegiances when you see the handwriting. Heinlein is suggesting that the gangster has no principles but only follows the strongest boss. See: **"Mene, Mene, Tekel, Upharsin."**

Hanky-Panky (*SJ*, 10): devious or mischievous activity. In *SJ*, Simes accuses Max of "hanky-panky," suggesting that his eidetic memory is just some sort of trick he has played on the officers.

Hans Christian Andersen (*HSS*, 5): Danish author (b. 2 April 1805, d. 4 August 1875) and popularizer of literary fairy tales based on traditional folk tale formulae. In *HSS*, Kip refers to Andersen's story "The Princess and the Pea," saying that the princess would find no problem sleeping on a hard floor in the moon's low gravity.

Hansea and ***New Hansea*** (*CG*, 14): Hanseatic League, also the Hansa or Hanse, thirteenth- to seventeenth-century trading league of Northern European countries along the North Sea and the Baltic Sea. The Hanseatic League was essentially a cooperative trade monopoly with its own laws and armed forces. In *CG*, it is the name of one of the ships of the Free Traders, who operate much as did the Hanseatic League. Many of the Free Trader ships have names that denote commerce or travel, but there are other ships' names, like *Galactic Banker* and *Country Store*, which have no specific cultural referents, or *Deimos* and *Vega*, which are astronomical and have neither cultural nor commercial referents. Ships like the *Joseph Smith* are named for the founder of Mormonism and have American historical referents, while others, like the *Caesar Augustus*, are named for figures from ancient history. See: **Free Traders.**

Hara-Kiri (*SJ*, 19): ritual Japanese suicide performed by one who believes that he has dishonored himself, his family, or his country. In *SJ*, Sam suggests that the *Asgard* captain's death was not by natural causes but honorable hara-kiri, the result of his having failed at his command.

Harry Weinstein (*RS*, 17): self-taught musician (b. 14 July 1914, d. 27 March 2009) who played throughout the Midwest before World War II, helped build aircraft engines during the war, and became a CPA after the war. In *RS*, Heinlein mentions Harry Weinstein's Sunbeam Six, a musical group.

Harvard (*RS*, 1; *SB*, 3; *ST*, 2): highly respected university and oldest institution of higher learning in the United States. In *RS*, Roger Stone wants to send his sons back to Earth to continue their higher education at Harvard, but instead, the family purchases a rocket ship and heads out into the solar system as part of Heinlein's paralleling the exploration of space to the exploration and settlement of the North American continent. In *SB*, both Judge O'Farrell and Sergei Greenberg discover that the other graduated from Harvard Law School. In *ST*, Johnnie's father is planning to send him to Harvard and the Sorbonne so that he can take over the family business. See: **Sorbonne.**

Harvard-Carnegie Expedition (*RP*, 2): fictional future expedition to Mars sponsored by Harvard University and possibly the Carnegie Institution for Science. Here, as he does many times in his science fiction, both juvenile and adult, Heinlein is suggesting that it will not be the government but private concerns that will invest in this kind of exploration and expect to profit from it. In *RP*, this leads to a sequence of colonial exploitation and revolution based on English and American relations in the late seventeen hundreds.

Hassan the Assassin (*ST*, 12): Hassan-I Sabbah (b. 11th century, d. 12th century), founder of the assassins known as the Hashshashin. In *ST*, a cadet named Hassan is nicknamed "The Assassin."

"Hasta la Vista, Amigo!" (*HSS*, 8): Spanish phrase meaning, "Good-bye, my friend." In *HSS,* Kip says this to his space suit when he believes he will not make it back to the shelter on Pluto before freezing to death.

Hastings (*ST*, 13): 1066 battle in which the Norman French forces of William the Conqueror defeated the forces of Edward the Saxon and turned the British Isles away from its northern European heritage in favor of a Mediterranean one. In *ST*, it is the name of one of the warships in the Federation fleet.

Have Space Suit—Will Travel (*HSS*, title and 12): take off on the title of the popular 1957–1963 western series, *Have Gun—Will Travel*. The television show starred Richard Boone as the title character, known only as Paladin, who was a gunfighter for hire but only on the side of justice. Every week, he left his San Francisco hotel to travel somewhere in the West, dressed in black, the knight chess piece symbol on his holster, rifle stock, and calling cards. Paladin was well educated and cultured, and he often solved problems without violence. The title is both suitable and ironic for *HSS*. On one hand, Kip refers to himself several times as a knight who will protect Peewee and acts accordingly when he can; on the other hand, it turns out in *HSS* that humans are their own worst enemies, facing possible extermination by the Three Galaxies Confederation as a potential danger (a situation very much like that portrayed in the 1951 film *The Day the Earth Stood Still*). At the end of the novel, Ace Quiggle teasingly suggests that Kip go into the hero business with "Have Space Suit—Will Travel" as his advertising slogan (12).

Hawk from a Handsaw (*BP*, 2; *RS*, 1): from Shakespeare's 1603 tragedy, *Hamlet* (II, ii, 361–2). Hamlet says, "I am but mad — north — north — west; when the wind is / southerly, I know a hawk from a handsaw." He is suggesting that he is only mad at times and that at other times he is perfectly sane. In *BP*, Dr. Jefferson uses the phrase "I know a hawk from a handsaw" as we currently do to indicate that we know the truth. See: **These Our Actors ...** In *RS*, Roger Stone calls his sons' plan to buy a rocket ship a "hare-brained scheme" and says that he himself "can tell a hawk from a handsaw," meaning that he can't be fooled. His mother, Grandma Hazel, then creates a pun using "Hawk" and "Hanshaw," the names of two kinds of rocket ships.

Hayden Planetarium (*HSS*, 4): public planetarium located in New York City. In *HSS*, the Hayden Planetarium took reservations for trips to the moon should such ever become a reality. Peewee's trip to the moon was the result of her father's registering for such a trip when he was a boy.

Hayseed (*SC*, 11): derogatory term for someone from a rural area, as opposed to someone from the city, referring to the possibility of hay seeds in one's clothing or hair. In *SC*, Tex calls Matt a hayseed because Matt has been assigned to the ship's hydroponic tanks as ship's "farmer." See: **Hydroponics.**

"He Is a Stranger and Therefore a Barbarian" (*SB*, 6): "Therefore if I know not the meaning of the voice, I shall be unto him that speaketh a barbarian, and he that speaketh [shall be] a barbarian unto me" (1 Corinthians 14:11). In *SB*, the Rargyllian ambassador suggests that this is God's greatest joke, because "it never grows stale." The implication, of course, is that however well one speaks another's language, cultural worldview will still make complete understanding impossible.

Heavenly Mountains (*TiS*, 1): remote mountain range in northwestern China. In *TiS*, the suggestion that the mass of Asiatic emigrants are heading for a planet named Heavenly Mountains is meant to be ironic, as the emigrants appear to be of the lowest and poorest classes of the Australasian Republic. See: **Coolie** and **Mongol.**

Heaviside Layer (*HSS*, 8): layer of ionized gas between about 60 and 100 miles above the Earth that affects radio waves but is also affected by the time of day such that at night radio waves can travel further. In *HSS*, Kip wonders if this is why the Mother Thing wanted the beacon triggered at night.

Hector (*ST*, 13): Trojan hero depicted in *The Iliad* (8th century B.C.), son of the Trojan king Priam, and defeated and killed by the Greek hero Achilles. See: **Achilles.**

Heil dem Fürher (*RSG*, 16): German phrase popularly translated as "Hail to the Leader." In *RSG*, Heinlein's Germans say that instead of the more widely known "Heil Hitler," as Hitler died at the end of World War II.

Hekate (*CG*, 14): Greek goddess (Hecate in Latin) associated with magic, fertility, and the underworld; perhaps best known now as the chief witch in Shakespeare's *Macbeth*. In *CG*, it is the name of the planet on which "authentic Terran *Coca-Cola* is licensed for bottling." Heinlein seems doubtful about the drink's authenticity or, perhaps, its quality.

Helen of Troy (*RS*, 19; *PM*, 5): legendary Greek beauty whose husband led the Greek forces against Troy in the Trojan War when Helen went there with her lover, Paris, King Priam's son. In *PM*, Podkayne suggests that an older and attractive woman on the ship looks more "Helen-of-Troyish" in contrast to Podkayne's youth.

Hemlock (*PM*, 13): plant that was the source of the poison that Socrates drank. In *PM*, Podkayne's uncle says that he would rather drink Hemlock than betray his duty to Mars. See: **Socrates.**

Henry Hudson (*TfS*, 6): English explorer (b. in 1565, d. after 22 June 1611), best known for his discovery of the Hudson River in New York State and Hudson's Bay in Canada in his search for a western route through the rivers of North America to Asia. On his last voyage, his crew mutinied and put Hudson and his followers adrift in a small boat; he was never heard from again. In *TfS*, it is the name of one of the torch ships. See: **Lebensraum [Project]** and ***Lewis and Clark***.

"Here We Rest" (*FS*, 18; *TiS*, 14): Alabama state motto adopted after the Civil War, during Reconstruction, and replaced in 1939 with a new motto, "We Dare Maintain Our Rights" (www.netstate.com/states/mottoes/al_motto.htm). In *FS*, Paul, the "general specialist" in charge of integrating information, chooses to stay on Ganymede, saying "Here I rest," rather than return to Earth, because he fears that there will be global war on Earth in forty to seventy years. In *TiS*, Rod says, "Here we rest!" to himself when he realizes how happy he is on the planet where he and the other students have been stranded.

Hermes (*PM*, 7): Greek messenger god characterized by his winged sandals and who today appears as the symbol for FTD (Florist's Transworld Delivery). In *PM*, Hermes Station will send out a message to warn spaceships of deadly solar flares so that all personnel can get to safe places within the ship.

Heron's Turbine (*RSG*, 8): steam turbine in which water below is heated so that steam comes up through a cylindrical or circular device that spins horizontally. This turbine was first documented by mathematician, physicist, and engineer Heron of Alexandria (A.D. 10–85). In *RSG*, Cargraves uses Heron's turbine to explain how his atomic drive works.

Hespera (*SJ*, 8): one of the Hesperides who tend the Golden Apples of Immortality in Greek mythology. In *SJ*, it is Ellie's home planet.

Hesperus (*ST*, 12): Evening Star, a point of light that the Greeks did not realize was the same celestial object as the Morning Star, Venus. In *ST*, Johnnie thinks his roommate's name, "Angel," is an odd one for a trooper, but perhaps Heinlein was correct in thinking that "angel" might be a good name for someone from Venus.

"Hey, Rube!" (*SJ*, 15): traditional call for assistance by circus people when a fight breaks out. In *SJ*, Sam uses the phrase to describe the start of a brawl about the *Asgard*.

H.G. Wells (*RSG*, 2): English science fiction writer (b. 21 September 1866, d. 13 August 1946). His most famous science fiction novels are *The Time Machine* (1895), *The Island of Doctor Moreau* (1896), *The Invisible Man* (1897), *The War of the Worlds* (1898), and *The First Men in the Moon* (1902). In *RSG*, Wells' *Seven Famous Novels* is one of the books on the boys' clubhouse shelf. See: **Jules Verne**.

High Tea (*SJ*, 20): afternoon or evening meal, now generally available only in high-end hotels and restaurants; primarily a British tradition. A high tea usually includes sandwiches, pastry, jams and butter, fruit, and tea. In *SJ*, Max is served a high tea when he returns to the ship after his captivity among the centaurs.

Hillside Snee (*FS*, 19): possibly an imaginary creature like the "side-hill wampus" which supposedly had legs shorter on one side than the other from walking around the hill the same way all of the time. In *FS*, Bill comments that the alien transport vehicle can adjust its legs over rough terrain "like the fabulous hillside snee."

Hilton (*BP*, 2; *PM*, 9): one of a chain on hotels founded by Conrad Hilton (b. 25 December 1887, d. 3 January 1979) and considered one of the premier hotel chains in the world at the time Heinlein was writing the juvenile novels. See: **Hilton Caravansary** and **Tannhäuser**.

Hilton Caravansary (*BP*, 2): Hilton hotel that takes its name from the Middle Eastern and Asian "caravansaries," inns along major trade routes and built around courtyards that could accommodate large caravans. In *BP*, it is the hotel where Don Harvey stays in New Chicago and therefore qualifies as an inn on a major trade route.

Hilton Tannhäuser (*PM*, 9) *see* **Tannhäuser**.

Hippocratic Oath (*RS*, 8): oath taken by doctors to practice ethically, supposedly written by Hippocrates (b. ca. 460 B.C., d. c. 375 B.C.), the "Father of Medicine." In *RS*, it is the oath that Edith follows when she goes onboard another ship to attempt to diagnose and treat the mysterious and sometimes fatal illness on that ship.

Hiroshima (*RSG*, 8): Japanese city on which the United States dropped an atomic bomb on 6 August 1945. When Cragraves test flies the *Galileo* in *RSG*, he tells the boys that if they see a Hiroshima mushroom cloud that they should go to the nearest town and report it to the authorities.

"His Strength Is as the Strength of Ten Because His Heart Is Pure" (*HSS*, 7) *see* **"My Strength Is as the Strength of Ten Because My Heart Is Pure."**

Hitler (*RSG*, 16; *SC*, 9; *HSS*, 7; *ST*, 2): Adolf Hitler (b. 20 April 1889, d. 30 April 1945), leader of Germany before and during World War II, member and head of the National Socialist German Workers Party, popularly known as the Nazi Party. In *RSG*, the German rocket scientists are from "Hitler's crumbled empire," indicating that these new Nazis are both carrying on the old Reich and starting a new one. In *SC*, Lieutenant Wong explains to Matt that the Patrol can't just bomb a potential Hitler but that the Space Marines might go in and deal with such a threat in its early stages. Heinlein develops this military theory more fully in *Starship Troopers*.

Hobgoblins

See: **Nazis**. In *HSS*, Kip notes that Hitler wrote *Mein Kampf* while in prison. See: **O. Henry** and **Saint Paul**. In *ST*, Mr. Dubois uses Hitler as an example that violence does settle things.

Hobgoblins (*SJ*, 17; *HSS*, 5): small, hairy, human-shaped creatures in British folklore that can be friendly or troublesome. More recently, the goblin, or troublesome and sometimes evil part, has been increasingly emphasized, especially in J.R.R. Tolkien's novels *The Hobbit* (1937) and *The Lord of the Rings* (1954–1955). In *SJ*, Ellie refers to the balloon-like creatures as hobgoblins. See: **Centaur**. In *HSS*, Kip refers to the Wormfaces as hobgoblins.

Hoboken Gate (*TiS*, 1): city in New Jersey, part of the New York metropolitan area and home of the Hoboken Terminal, a major transportation hub. In *TiS*, Rod heads home through the Hoboken Gate. His family home is on the Grand Canyon Plateau, which is an "out county" of Greater New York City, evidence of the overpopulated Earth for which the gates to other planets offer some relief.

Hogshead (*SB*, 10): large cask or barrel used primarily to store liquids and holding about 63 gallons. In *SB*, Lummox quenches her thirst with "a few hogsheads of clear mountain water."

Hohmann Orbit (*RSG*, 8; *SC*, 13): elliptical trajectory named after Walter Hohmann (b. 18 March 1880, d. 11 March 1945) that allows a spaceship to move from place to place with the least amount of expended energy. Interested in interplanetary space flight as early as 1911, Hohmann published *The Attainability of Celestial Bodies* (1925) in which what are now called Hohmann transfer orbits were described. In *SC*, Heinlein briefly explains Hohmann orbits. See: **S-trajectories**.

"Holy Moses!" (*SC*, 16): popular phrase used to express surprise; a mildly irreverent oath. In *SC*, Tex's surprise at discovering the *Astarte*'s log causes him to exclaim, "Holy Moses!" See: ***Astarte***.

Homer (*RS*, 1): blind Greek poet (8th century B.C.) who composed the epic poems *The Iliad* and *The Odyssey*. In *RS*, Roger Stone says that he is using ideas from Homer in his science fiction serial, *The Scourge of the Spaceways*. See: **Stevenson**.

Homestead Claim (*SB*, 3): the post–Civil War Homestead Act promised ownership of a 160-acre parcel of land to a person or family who would cultivate it for the five years following the filing of a claim. In *SB*, Betty talks Johnnie into "homesteading" Lummox as a way of protecting his pet.

Honoris Causa (*SB*, 2): honorary degree. In *SB*, Mr. Kiku has an honorary degree, a Litt. D. (doctor of letters), from Capetown University. It is an indication of his status. See: **O.B.E.** and **Oxon**.

Hoosegow (*TiS*, 12): American slang for "jail." In *TiS*, Grant threatens to throw Rod and Roy in the "hoosegow" for being away much longer than they were supposed to be. See: **Laurel.**

Hoover Medal (*PM*, 1): medal awarded to engineers for civic and humanitarian achievements by a board representing five engineering societies. In *PM*, Podkayne's mother has won a Hoover Medal. Her Christiana Order, Knight Commander, seems to have been made up by Heinlein. This is another instance of Heinlein's pairing something known with something of his own invention.

Horace Mann [Grammar School] (*HSS*, 7): American education reformer (b. 4 May 1796, d. 2 August 1859) who worked for better pay for teachers, compulsory education through age 16, professional training for teachers, better equipped schools, a broader curriculum, and other improvements. In *HSS*, it is the name of the grammar school in which Kip learned not to be a crybaby.

"Horatius at the Bridge" (*ST*, 5): legend in which one man, Horatius, stood on the bridge over the Tiber River and kept the Etruscan army from crossing and invading Rome; as a result, Rome renounced kings and became a republic. In *ST*, Sergeant Zim suggests that one of the enlistees read "Horatius at the Bridge" and "The Death of the Bon Homme Richard" if he does not believe that one man can make a difference in battle. Later in *ST*, *Horatius* is one of the names of the warships in the Federation fleet named for specific foot soldiers (13). See: **"The Death of the Bonne Homme Richard."**

Horst (*SJ*, 7): name associated with jet engine development since World War II in Germany. In *SJ*, Max explains to Ellie that it is the Horst anomaly that lets them move from one point to another in space. See: **Horst-Conrad Drive.**

Horst-Conrad Drive (*BP*, 16; *SJ*, 3): Max Conrad (b. 1903, d. 1979), famous small-plane pilot. In *BP*, the Horst-Milne equations lead to the Horst-Milne-Conrad Drive that becomes, in *SJ*, the Horst-Conrad Drive. Milne may be a Heinlein tribute to Francis Milne, a Royal Australian Air Force pilot officer who died while serving with a U.S. crew in World War II. See: **Horst.**

Hot Potato (*SB*, 3): children's game involving tossing an object quickly so as not to be holding it when the music stops. More recently, a slang term for anything that's difficult to handle. In *SB*, Judge O'Farrell thinks that the lawsuit about Lummox will be a "hot potato."

Houdini (*RS*, 19): Harry Houdini (Erich Weiss: b. 24 March 1874, d. 31 October 1926), professional magician most famous for his ability to escape from almost any containment and for exposing people who claimed they could contact the dead. In *RS*, Grandma Hazel uses a Houdini breathing technique to survive in space when her oxygen runs out. See: **Fakir**.

Housemaid's Knee (*TfS*, 5): inflammation of the soft tissue that lies in front of the kneecap, usually caused by a fall or direct blow to the knee but popularly believed to be caused by spending a lot of time on one's knees as housemaids do when scrubbing floors and such. In *TfS*, when Tom Bartlett says that he has been inoculated for everything from "housemaid's knee to parrot fever" he is exaggerating the thoroughness of the physical he was given before takeoff. See: **Parrot Fever**.

Hroshii (*SB*, 5): interstellar race invented by Heinlein. While this term has no real-world cognates, it may be that Heinlein coined it so that he could have McClure, the secretary for Spatial Affairs, mispronounce it as "Hoorussians" (12). That is a conflation of "Hroshii" and "Russian" and another element in his characterization of the secretary as an inept political appointee. See: **Russian Roulette** and *Take Me Out to the Ball Game*.

Hudson's Manual (*RS*, 4): *The Engineer's Manual*, Ralph Gorton Hudson, 1917. In *RS*, Castor and Pollux tell their father that they have read Hudson's Manual and know it by heart in an effort to impress him with their knowledge. See: **Castor, Pollux,** and **Hyper-Ideal**.

Huskings (*SJ*, 1): gatherings of people in rural communities to remove the husks from corn prior to its being cooked and preserved in cans or jars. In *SJ*, Heinlein is creating an exaggerated rural background for his main character, Max, and huskings are still part of the community's life. See: **Barn Dances, Side Meat, Squirrel Gun,** and **"Wagon Room."**

Hydra (*CG*, 14): in Greek mythology, a snake-like beast with at least nine heads. Hercules killed the Hydra of Lema as one of his twelve labors. In *CG*, the *Hydra* is a fast, heavily armed ship of the Hegemonic Guard, whose mission is to "prowl for outlaws" along the outer rim of the galaxy. Heinlein probably called it the *Hydra* for its multiple weapons systems.

Hydroponics (*RSG*, 6; *FS*, 10; *RS*, 17)): method of farming in which plants are grown in a nutrient solution rather than soil. Hydroponics can take less space and weigh less than soil-based farming; both considerations make hydroponics a logical method for producing both food and oxygen in a rocket ship. In *RSG*, Cargraves installs a hydroponic tank for rhubarb "to make the air self-refreshing" in the structure that he and the boys build on the moon. In *FS*, the hydroponic sheds on Ganymede are named "Oahu," "Imperial Valley," and "Iowa" for three major growing regions in Hawaii, California, and the Midwest. Hydroponics began in the 1930s, but Heinlein may have known about the

U.S. Army's use of hydroponics at overseas bases during World War II. In *RS*, Mrs. Fries, the wife of the mayor of the Asteroid Belt, has a hydroponic garden.

Hyper-Ideal (*RS*, 4): probably a reference to hyperideal circle patterns, part of geometric topography. In *RS*, Roger Stone gives his twin sons a page of mathematics, including "hyperideal" equations, to show them that they do not know as much as they think they do.

"I Should Have Baked a Cake" (*TiS*, 7 and chapter title): "If I knew you were comin' I'd've baked a cake," a popular 1950s song by Eileen Barton that tells what the singer would have done had she known the visitor was coming. In *TiS*, Jimmy says that he should have baked a cake when Bob Baxter and Carmen Garcia arrive unexpectedly; he is being ironic, as he and Rod and Jacqueline are, at the time, surviving on what they can hunt.

"I Wept That I Had No Shoes — Till I Met a Man Who Had No Feet" (*PM*, 10): supposedly a Persian proverb, stating that one should not complain because there is always someone else who is in worse circumstances. In *PM*, Podkayne stops feeling sorry for herself when she realizes her friend Girdie is in much worse financial straits.

IBM (*RS*, 4): International Business Machines, now an information technology and computer company, began making business machines in the late nineteenth century. In *RS*, an IBM company representative installs the ballistic computer in the *Rolling Stone*.

Icarus (*FS*, 3): son of the Greek mythological craftsman Daedalus. Icarus flew on wings his father made so that they could escape from Crete, where they were being held by King Minos, but Icarus flew too close to the sun, the wax in his wings melted, and he fell to his death. In *FS*, the *Icarus* is one of the four ships taking colonists escaping an overcrowded Earth to the *Mayflower*, which will carry them to Ganymede. It seems an ironic name for a rocket ship except for the element of escape in the original story, unless, of course, Heinlein was subtly underlining the danger of space travel — something he always recognized and included in his novels. See: **Bifrost, Daedalus,** and **Mayflower.**

ICS Correspondence Courses (*RS*, 4): International Correspondence School, perhaps the oldest institution in the world providing correspondence courses for home study. In *RS*, Castor and Pollux will study through ICS while traveling with the family from the moon to Mars and beyond.

"Idiot Savant" (*SJ*, 9): complex term referring to people who lack general knowledge and abilities but have unusual expertise in one small area. In *SJ*, Dr. Hendrix is amazed at Max's total recall of everything he has read.

Idiot's

But because Max is a capable person in all other areas, Dr. Hendrix states that Max is not an "*idiot savant.*"

Idiot's Mate (*SJ*, 19): move in 3-D chess, probably similar to the fool's mate in regular chess. In *SJ*, Max that he is teaching Ellie how to play 3-D chess and thinks she is pretty good "for a girl." But late in the novel, she reveals that she is a chess champion and beats him several times, once with the idiot's mate, explaining to him that "the world being what it is ... women sometimes prefer not to appear too bright." Ellie is an example of the strong women in Heinlein's juveniles and women who feel it necessary to seem less intelligent that they actually are. See: **AEC** and "**Lean and Hungry Look.**"

I.G. Farbenindustrie (*PM*, 11): German chemical industry that was, at one time, the fourth largest corporation in the world but was broken up after World War II. In *PM*, Podkayne's uncle says that if Earth, the moon, Mars, and Venus operate under the same rules, they all will lose their freedoms and be as tightly structured and as tightly run as General Motors and I.G. Farbenindustrie.

In Loco Parentis (*RP*, 5; *PM*, 11): Latin for "in the parents' place." Up until the students' rights movement of the 1960s, schools, and especially boarding schools, colleges, and universities, used this philosophy to govern the conduct of their students, even off campus. In some cases, such as curfew hours, colleges and universities were actually stricter than the students' parents would have been. In *RP*, Headmaster Howe uses this phrase to describe his position as a school administrator in charge of students; he also uses it to justify his seizure and imprisonment of Jim Marlowe's pet, Willis. In *PM*, her uncle eases Podkayne's guilt about her brother's disappearance by saying that it is his fault, as he is "in loco parentis" for them both on this trip — and then he makes a joke that her parents were "loco" (crazy) to entrust the children to him.

In Xanadu Did Kubla Khan / A Stately Pleasure Dome Decree — (*PM*, 9): mythical land in Samuel Taylor Coleridge's (b. 21 October 1772, d. 25 July 1834) incomplete 1797 poem, "Kubla Khan," of which Heinlein quotes the first two lines: "In Xanadu did Kubla Khan / A stately pleasure dome decree." In *PM*, Podkayne describes the Dom Pedro Casino as a "stately pleasure dome."

***Inferno*, Dante's** (*SJ*, 18) *see* **Dantesque.**

Infinity (*TfS*, 16): name of one of the new "irrelevant" spaceships. See: **Serendipity.**

Les Invalides (*ST*, 9): group of buildings, plazas, and monuments in Paris that commemorate and otherwise relate to the military history of France. Napoleon's coffin is located there. See: **Napoleon.**

Invasion-from-Mars (*HSS*, 58): radio broadcast, 30 October 1938, of a dramatized version of H.G. Wells' *The War of the Worlds* by Orson Welles, American actor (b. 6 May 1915, d. 10 October 1985). It was believed to have been an actual newscast by many and caused widespread panic. In *HSS*, Kip suggests that after people got to the moon and Venus, they stopped believing in the possibility of finding life anywhere else; the irony of the novel is that the Wormfaces really want to conquer Earth but are not the real threat to humanity. See: ***Have Space Suit—Will Travel.***

"Ioway" (*SC*, 8): "Iowa Corn Song," which begins "Let's sing of grand old Ioway." While not the official state song, it is probably better known and more popular than the official song. In *SC*, an inebriated Tex, who cannot get anyone to join him in singing "Deep in the Heart of Texas," declares that he is broad-minded enough to sing about another state. See: **"Deep in the Heart of Texas"** and **Mint Julep.**

Ipse Dixit (*RP*, 1): Latin for "he himself said it," referring to a statement that has been asserted or accepted but cannot be proved. In *RP*, MacRae suggests that Willis should stay with Jim because Willis wants to for reasons that cannot be proved. MacRae then says that there is a lot about Mars that the settlers from Earth do not yet and may never know.

Iron (*RSG*, 15): slang term for a gun, usually a pistol, found more often in westerns than in science fiction novels. In *RSG*, Heinlein describes one of the Germans attacking the *Galileo* as "still reaching for his iron" when he is shot by one of the boys.

Irrelevant (*TfS*, 16): name of one of the new "irrelevant" spaceships. See: **Serendipity.**

Isabella (*PM*, 8): queen of Spain (b. 22 April 1451, d. 26 November 1504) best known for financing Columbus' first expedition in 1492. See: **Columbus.**

Iskander (*ST*, 1): Iskander Bey, Albanian for Lord Alexander or Leader Alexander and a name/title of Albanian national hero Gjergj Kastrioti Skanderberg (b. 1405, d. 17 January 1468), Iskander being a Turkish version of Skanderberg. He was also called the Dragon of Albania. In *ST*, Sergeant Jelal is a Finno-Turk from, appropriately, the planet Iskander.

I. T. & T. (*BP*, 18): International Telephone and Telegraph, a communications company founded in the 1920s. In *BP*, I. T. & T. operates an interplanetary radio station on Mars.

Ivanhoe (*RS*, 1): 1819 novel by Sir Walter Scott (b. 15 August 1771, d. 21 September 1832). *Ivanhoe* is essentially historical fiction set in twelfth-century England and focuses on the tension between the Anglo-Saxon inhabitants and the Norman French conquerors.

In *RS*, Roger Stone suggests that his sons should read great literature, and they reply that they have already read *Ivanhoe*, a novel that was in fact on suggested and required reading lists in public high schools in the 1950s. Heinlein is also juxtaposing respected literary works with the low-quality space opera Roger Stone is writing. See: **The Mill on the Floss** and **The Scourge of the Spaceways**.

Iwo (*ST*, 13): short for Iwo Jima, island site of a major and fiercely fought battle in the Pacific during World War II. The photo of the raising of the flag on Iwo Jima became an inspiration for Americans late in the war. In *ST*, it is the name of one of the warships in the Federation fleet.

Jack Spratt (*PM*, 1): one of the main characters in the children's rhyme "Jack Spratt could eat no fat / His wife could eat no lean / And so betwixt them both / They licked the platter clean." In *PM*, Podkayne says that her parents are like Jack Spratt and his wife, her father interested in the past and her mother in the future.

Jacques de Barre de Vigny (*HSS*, 7): name that the fat gangster gives Kip, but Kip does not believe it is his real-name. While there seems to be no real world cognate for the name, it is possible that Heinlein was thinking of the "Duke and the Dauphin" episode from Mark Twain's 1884 novel, *The Adventures of Huckleberry Finn*, in which two con men give themselves aristocratic names to impress Huck and Jim as well as to avoid giving their real names. The fact that the other gangster gives his name as Timothy Johnson, however, may negate this possibility. See: **Mark Twain's *Life on the Mississippi*.**

"J'ai soif" (*SC*, 14): French for "I am thirsty." In *SC*, Thurlow speaks French in his delirium. See: *"Maman."*

James B. Quinn (*CG*, 14): engineer in the United States Army Corps of Engineers. There is no way of knowing if this is the person Heinlein had in mind when, in *CG*, he used the name for one of the ships of the Free Traders. See: **Free Traders** and **Hansea**.

James Joyce [Fogarty] (*PM*, 3): Irish author (b. 2 February 1882, d. 13 January 1941) best known for such modernist and stream of consciousness works as *Ulysses* (1922) and *Finnegan's Wake* (1939), much of which were written in Joyce's self-imposed exile from Ireland. In *PM*, James Joyce Fogarty is the name of an express tunnel on Mars, a planet that, as a prison colony, has been the home of exiles.

James Madison [Marlowe] (*RP*, 4): one of the "Founding Fathers" of the American republic (b. 16 March 1751, d. 28 June 1836), primary writer of the Constitution of the United States of America, and later fourth president of the United States. In *RP*, Heinlein begins naming characters after important historical figures, especially American figures who contributed to the founding and building of the nation. James Madison Marlowe is named for James Madison and will be a significant factor in the Martian struggle for independence.

Jato Units (*RS*, 15): originally Jet [fuel] Assisted Take Off Units, used to provide additional thrust. These units were used in both rocketry and jet plane development. In *RS*, they are used to help the *Rolling Stone* maneuver in the Asteroid Belt.

Jerome K. Jerome (*HSS*, 1): British writer (b. 2 May 1859, d. 14 June 1927) most famous for the humorous novel *Three Men in a Boat*. In *HSS*, Kip's father rereads the novel so often that Kip thinks he must know it by heart. See: **Three Men in a Boat.**

Jerry Talk (*RSG*, 16): slang term for the German language. The British slang term for Germans during World War II was "Jerries"; the term was later adopted by Americans as well. In *RSG*, Ross says that he has had Art "translating the Jerry talk" onboard the German ship that they seize after the *Galileo* has been destroyed.

Jitterbug (*FS*, 8): lively dance, as opposed to the slower and more formal waltzes, fox trots, etc., that became popular during the "swing era" of the 1930s and was a part of the "rock and roll" explosion of the 1950s and 1960s. In *FS*, the shuttle that transports people from the interplanetary rocket ship down to the surface of Ganymede is named *Jitterbug* and provides a rough ride down.

Joan of Arc (*HSS*, 7): French heroine and Catholic saint (b. 1412, d. 30 May 1431) who led the French army to several victories during the Hundred Years' War and was burned at the stake for heresy by the English at age 19. In *HSS*, Kip regards Peewee's cooperation with the Wormfaces as less likely than the possibility of Joan of Arc recanting.

John Paul Jones (*ST*, 12) see "The Death of the Bon Homme Richard."

John Sterling (*RS*, 2): hero of Roger Stone's future serial, *The Scourge of the Spaceways*. In *RS*, Roger Stone's and, later, Grandma Hazel's hero has the sort of clichéd hero's name common to comic book heroes. See: **The Scourge of the Spaceways.**

John Thomas [Stuart] (*SB*, throughout): slang reference for a man's penis. Given Heinlein's history of disagreements with Scribner's editor Alice Dalgliesh, as recorded in *Grumbles from the Grave* (ed. Virginia Heinlein, New York: Ballantine, 1989: 41–80), including one about the sexual reproduction of Martians that he wanted to include in *Red Planet*, I like to think it is very possible that he slipped this slang term into *Star Beast* on purpose. In *SB*, the reader discovers in chapter 12 that Lummox, having been the pet of numerous John Thomas Stuarts in succession, believes that she has been raising them, "raising John

Johnny

Thomases" as it were, slang for causing a male human to have an erection.

Johnny Appleseed (*FS*, chapter 13, title and *passim*): John Chapman (b. 26 September 1774, d. 18 March 1845), who became a legendary figure for introducing apple trees throughout much of middle America. In *FS*, Heinlein uses the name as a chapter title and as the local nickname for Johann Schultz, an established farmer who grows apples and gives away some of the seeds. All of the varieties of apples Heinlein mentions are grown on Earth. Some of the locals use the name derisively; Heinlein, however, is presenting Schultz as a positive role model for Bill Lermer. See: **Daniel Boone, *Mayflower*,** and **Plymouth Rock Colony.**

Johnny-Come-Latelies (*FS*, 12): idiomatic reference meaning "newcomer" or "latecomer." In *FS*, the settlers from the *Mayflower* are "Johnny-Come-Latelies," and Bill and his scouting friends, as "Johnny-Come-Latelies," run into difficulties with the local established scouting organization.

Johnson's Hole (*CG*, 17): incorrect reference to Jackson Hole, Wyoming. In *CG*, Thorby's "Uncle Jack" tells him that the family estate, Rudbeck, is located where there was once a small city named "Johnson's Hole, or some such." Heinlein may well have foreseen the development of the Jackson Hole region into a summer and winter playground in the last third of the twentieth century

Jo-Jo the Dogface Boy (*HSS*, 10; *PM*, 13): Fedor Jefticheive (b. 1868, d. 31 January 1904), Russian who became a performer with P.T. Barnum's sideshows and was known as Jo-Jo the Dog-Faced Boy (later Man). Jefticheive suffered from hypertrichosis, a physical condition causing excessive hair growth. In *HSS*, Kip refers to the Neanderthal who has been captured by the Court of the Three Galaxies as Jo-Jo the dogface boy. See: **Neanderthal.** In *PM*, it is the name Podkayne's brother gives Pinhead. See: **Pinhead.**

Jolly Roger (*PM*, 13): flag used by pirates, usually with a black background and a white skull and crossbones. In *PM*, Podkayne refers to *Treasure Island* and says that she should have been able to escape capture, run the Jolly Roger down, and raise the Union Jack, a symbol of good triumphing over evil. See: ***Treasure Island*** and **Union Jack.**

Jonah (*TiS*, 1): swallowed by a whale while trying to avoid doing God's wishes in the Old Testament book of Jonah. In *TiS*, when a student complains that the survival test isn't fair and isn't like real life, Deacon Matson suggests that's what Jonah said when he was swallowed by the whale. Here, Matson is articulating a basic Heinlein belief that the successful person is the one who is the best prepared for all eventualities and able to roll with the punches, as it were, when he or she encounters something unanticipated.

Joseph Smith (*CG*, 14): founder of the Church of Latter Day Saints, more commonly known as Mormonism, who led his followers west to Missouri and Illinois before his assassination (b. 23 December 1805, d. 27 June 1844). In *CG*, it is the name of one of the ships of the Free Traders. See: **Free Traders**, **Hansea**, and **Mormons**.

Josephine (*SJ*, 12): Joséphine de Beauharnais (b. 23 June 1763, d. 29 May 1814), first wife of Napoléon Bonaparte and ancestress of several modern royal lines. In *SJ*, the Josephine Hotel is the only hotel in Bonaparte City, Halcyon, an ironic contrast to the splendor of the French court.

Josephus (*HSS*, 9): Titus Flavius Josephus (A.D. b. 37, d. c. A.D. 101), Jewish-Roman historian who wrote histories of the Jewish people for a Roman audience and who believed in the compatibility of Jewish and Roman thought. He also wrote some of the earliest accounts of Jesus Christ. In *HSS*, Kip refers to the Vegan historian, who is gathering information from him about Earth's history and cultures, as Professor Josephus Egghead.

Jove (*HSS*, 11): Sky god and leader of the gods in Roman mythology. See: **Mars**.

A Joyous Noise Unto the Lord (*HSS*, 5): "Make a joyful noise unto the LORD" (Psalm 98:4). In *HSS*, this is Kip's first description of the music that is the Mother Thing's speech.

"Judge Not According to the Appearance" John vii:24 (*BP*, 15): "Judge not according to the appearance, but judge with righteous judgment" (John 7:24). In *BP*, this is the title of Chapter 15, the chapter in which Don Harvey's ring, which appears to be worthless plastic, is discovered to be the key to winning the rebellion. The ring is worthless to Don, who is not a scientist, but extremely valuable to the scientists who know how to use it (judge with righteous judgment). As the Vererian dragon and scientist Sir Isaac Newton comments, Don has mistaken "simple appearance for simplicity."

Jules Verne (*RSG*, 2): French science fiction author (b. 8 February 1828, d. 24 March 1905) whose most famous works are probably *Journey to the Center of the Earth* (1864) and *Twenty Thousand Leagues Under the Sea* (1869). In *RSG*, his books being on the boys' clubhouse shelves, along with fictional works by Wells and Haggard and scientific works by Ley and Eddington, among others, as well as "dozens of pulp magazines," mirror the kind of reading, though not necessarily the same texts, Heinlein himself did at that age. The mixture of books represents both Heinlein's belief in a serious science education (within a broader education) and his belief that science fiction is good for the imagination, especially as it prepares the reader for the future. See: **H.G. Wells**.

Julius Caesar (*ST*, 2) *see* **Caesar.**

Junebug (*HSS*, 3): kind of beetle. In *HSS*, Kip uses "Junebug" to refer to himself in his imaginary calls to "Peewee."

Junior League (*RS*, 5): nonprofit and charitable organization established in 1901 to help develop women's potential as civic leaders and improve communities. In *RS*, a delegation from the Lunar Junior League comes to bid Meade Stone farewell as the Stone family leaves the moon. See: **The Rolling Stones.**

Junípero Serra (*FS*, 7): Miguel Jose Serra i Ferrer (b. 24 November 1713, d. 28 August 1784), a Franciscan friar who founded missions in California. In *FS*, one of the Boy Scout troops takes the name Junípero Serra.

Juvenile Delinquent (*HSS*, 2): technically, a person under the legal age (usually 18) who has committed a crime; more popularly, especially in the 1950s, the cigarette-smoking and leather-jacket-wearing toughs who, if in school, caused disruptions in the classroom or, if out on the street, defied the authorities, went "joy riding" in cars, and met and fought in "gang wars." In *HSS*, Ace Quiggle is a high school dropout who makes fun of Kip's desire to go into space and about whom Heinlein wonders, in the person of Mr. Charton, how much "civilization is retarded by the laughing jackasses, the empty-minded belittlers?" (3). See: **Blackboard Jungle.**

Kaibab [Gate] (*TiS*, 2): one of six national forests in Arizona named for a tribe of the Paiute Indians. In *TiS*, it is the name of the transportation gate nearest Rod Walker's family's house.

Kaiser Wilhelm [Institute] (*RSG*, 4; *RS*, 16): Kaiser Wilhelm II (b. 27 January 1859, d. 4 June 1941), ruler of Prussia and Germany from 1888 to 1918 and a believer in imperialism and militarism. The Kaiser Wilhelm Institute of Anthropology, Human Heredity, and Eugenics was founded in 1927 and was closely associated with the Nazi theories of eugenics and racial hygiene. In *RSG*, Cargraves invokes the memory of her husband's resistance to those theories to help persuade Art's mother to allow him to make the trip to the moon. See: **Nazis.** In *RS*, one of the major strikes in the Asteroid Belt is named for Kaiser Wilhelm.

"Kallikak Family" (*BP*, 6): Henry H. Goddard's 1912 study in eugenics, *The Kallikak Family: A Study in the Heredity of Feeble-Mindedness*, theorizes that intelligence, morality and criminality, among other traits, can be inherited. Goddard follows a double family tree with the same father, one side descended from a "feebleminded" woman and the other from a normal woman. In *BP*, the television series *Kallikak Family* follows the fortunes of a family in which activities from murder to cheating on ration stamps make up the story and may be

Heinlein's negative comment on the intellectual level of television fare.

Kamehameha (*ST*, 13): first king of Hawaii (b. November 1758, d. 8 May 1819), best known for preserving Hawaii's independence and for passing a law protecting noncombatants in times of war. In *ST*, it is the name of one of the warships of the Federation fleet named for specific foot soldiers.

Kangaroo Court (*HSS*, 10): court with no real legal jurisdiction characterized by irresponsible, unauthorized, or irregular proceedings and often preordained outcomes. The term originated in the United States in the middle of the nineteenth century but is of otherwise unknown origin. In *HSS*, the spokesperson for the Wormfaces claims that the Court of the Three Galaxies is a kangaroo court.

Das Kapital (*ST*, 6): major three-volume work by Karl Marx published in 1867, of which the last two volumes (1885 and 1894) were edited and published after Marx's death by Friedrich Engels (b. 28 November 1820, d. 5 August 1895). See: **Marxist Theory**.

Karl Marx (*ST*, 6) *see* ***Das Kapital*** and **Marxist Theory**.

Kepler (*RS*, 15): Johannes Kepler, German mathematician and astronomer (b. 27 December 1571, d. 15 November 1630). Kepler wrote, "Inter Jovem et Martem Planetam Interposui" ("Between Jupiter and Mars I put a planet"). See: **Bode's Law, Giuseppe Piazzi,** and **Lucifer.**

Kilgore [Equations] (*FS*, 6): possibly a reference or tribute to Senator Harley Kilgore (b. 11 January 1893, d. 28 February 1956). In 1944, Kilgore proposed a bill to establish the National Science Foundation that would have given funding priority to government laboratories and still been able to award research funds to colleges and universities. Although his colleagues convinced him to wait on this bill, which led to an almost six-year delay in the creation of the NSF, Kilgore's intent was one with which Heinlein would have agreed.

Kilkenny Cats (*TiS*, 14; *TfS*, 12): two cats in Kilkenny, Ireland, who thought that there should be only one cat in Kilkenny, fought about it, and destroyed each other. In *TiS*, the improved defenses of the community include traps for the "dopey joes" so that they will fall into deep pits and "chew on each other like Kilkenny cats." In *TfS*, Tom Bartlett thinks that Earth may solve the overpopulation problem the same way as the Kilkenny Cats did before the means to transport people to other planets is found.

Kilroy Was Here (*SC*, 1): graffito with a person peeking over a wall (above the words) scrawled by American GIs wherever they went in World War II and Korea; now a popular expression. There are dozens of legends about the origin of the graffito and about its impact. If nothing else, it

Kine

was a sign to one serviceman that another one had been there and was, therefore, a comfort. In *SC*, it is the name of the first manned rocket to Mars, which crashed upon return to Earth, killing all aboard. When asked, Matt incorrectly identifies Kilroy as Admiral "Bull" Kilroy of the Second Global War, obviously confusing him with Admiral "Bull" Halsey; Matt's new friend, Tex, is impressed with Matt's knowledge. Heinlein is probably criticizing Matt's know-it-all attitude as well as the boys' general lack of historical knowledge.

The Kine That Tread the Grain (*FS*, 16; *ST*, 12): "Thou shalt not muzzle the mouth of the ox that treadeth out the corn" (1 Corinthians 9:9). In *FS*, Bill's father quotes this line when he explains that window glass won't bee too expensive for them because he designed the glassworks. See: **Cumshaw.** In *ST*, Johnnie's father uses that saying, telling Johnnie that he gave the man he appointed to run his business a share of that business and implying that someone who has a share of a business has it in his best interest to take good care of the business.

King Arthur's Court (*HSS*, 5): medieval court of knights and ladies known for its style and for establishing a period of peace. In *HSS*, Kip has a dream that includes King Arthur's Court, Barsoom, *Beowulf*, and Tristan and Iseult. The combination of these figures from epic literature, medieval romance, and heroic fantasy — as well as some elements from Kip's real life — reflects Kip's previous thoughts and his decision to "take care of her [Peewee] ... or die trying." See: **Barsoom, Beowulf,** and **Tristan and Iseult.**

King Log and King Stork (*TiS*, 10): traditional fable in which frogs ask for a king. The first king they are given is a log, but when the log does nothing, they ask for a more powerful king; their second king is a stork that proceeds to eat them. Many feel that this fable is about the political power a monarch or government should have. In *TiS*, on the day after a contentious community meeting, the new mayor, Grant Cowper, who had been throwing his weight around, is described as more like King Log and less like King Stork.

King of the Beasts (*TiS*, 1): phrase generally used to refer to the African lion. In *TiS*, Deacon Matson uses the phrase ironically to voice Heinlein's continuing belief that humans are the most dangerous animals in the known universe. See: **Donner Party.**

King Solomon (*TfS*, 4) *see* **Solomon.**

Kingdom Come (*FS*, 6): appears as "Thy Kingdom Come" in the Christian Lord's Prayer and refers to heaven and, perhaps, the end of the world. In *FS*, Bill looks out of a large viewport on the *Mayflower* and feels that there is nothing between him and Kingdom Come.

King's Kodiak Bears (*ST* 12): Kodiak bears, also known as grizzly bears, found primarily in southwest Alaska, the largest of the brown bears, and equal in size to polar bears. In *ST*, one of the units is named King's Kodiak Bears.

King's X (*HSS*, 8): term from children's folk speech meaning "truce." When someone calls "King's X," for example, the game stops where it is until the problem is resolved. In *HSS*, Peewee says that the Wormfaces grabbed the Mother Thing when in a King's X situation.

Kipling (*FS*, 20): Rudyard Kipling, English writer (b. 30 December 1865, d. 18 January 1936) most famous for poems and short stories set in India. In *FS*, Bill remembers a phrase, "I have lived and worked with men," but cannot remember if the line is from Kipling or Rhysling. Rhysling is "the blind poet of the spaceways" in Heinlein's fiction, most especially in the 1947 short story "The Green Hills of Earth."

Knight-Errant (*HSS*, 6): knight who wanders (errant) in a certain search of adventure in order, especially in medieval romances, to prove himself. In *HSS*, Kip speaks dismissively of himself as a knight-errant when he discovers that he cannot get to the oxygen-helium tank he had planned to use to recharge Peewee's diminishing air supply. Even in self-criticism, Kip continues to think of himself as Peewee's rescuerer and defender. See: **King Arthur's Court** and ***Sans Peur et Sans Reproche.***

Kodiak Bear (*ST*, 12) *see* **King's Kodiak Bears.**

Kong Christian (*RS*, 8): "Kong Christian Stod Ved Hojen Mast" ("King Christian Stood by the Lofty Mast"). The song and music are the Danish royal anthem, one of the oldest anthems in the world and seen as a tribute to sailors. In *RS*, it is the name of a ship that suffered an accident involving welding.

Korean War (*ST*, 12): technically, the 1950–1953 war between North Korean and South Korean that has been suspended since the armistice of 1953. The United States and the United Nations came to the aid of South Korea, and the People's Republic of China came to the aid of North Korea. Skirmishes continue. In *ST*, Johnnie's teacher at O.C.S. brings up the issue of brainwashing during the Korean War to suggest a problem with conscript armies. See: **Brainwashed Prisoners.**

Korpsbruder (*ST*, 3): German, literally "corps brother," a close friend in the military; more idiomatically, a fellow member of a student dueling society. In *ST*, Sergeant Zim asks one German trainee who speaks English if his korpsbruder, who doesn't understand the language, is ready; the two Germans have answered Zim's challenge to the trainees, asking if any of them are willing to fight him.

Kosher (*PM*, 10): from Jewish dietary laws about the correct preparation of food; more generally, the correct or proper way of doing something. In *PM*, Podkayne explains the system of bartered brides on Venus and says that whatever money changes hands and how it changes hands is "all kosher."

Kraal (*TiS*, 8): South African word for a livestock enclosure or corral. In *TiS*, it is the wall protecting the area in which the students live.

Kraken (*CG*, 14): legendary monster supposed to inhabit the North Atlantic waters and capable of pulling a ship to the bottom of the sea, also the focus of an 1830 poem by Alfred, Lord Tennyson (b. 6 August 1809, d. 6 October 1892). In *CG*, it is the name of a ship of the Free Traders. See: **Free Traders** and **Hansea**.

Krishnamurti (*CG*, 15): Jiddu Krishnamurti (b. 11 May 1895, d. 17 February 1986), famous speaker on spiritual and philosophical subjects who stressed concepts of freedom and responsibility. In *CG*, Krishnamurti is a medical officer who places Thorby under hypnosis to interview him about the slave trade information that Baslim the Cripple made Thorby memorize. By the end of the novel, Thorby will have real conflicts with the concepts of freedom (which he wishes he had to spend all his time trying to shut down the slave trade) and responsibility (which forces him to stay on as the head of Rudbeck). See: **Merry Widow**.

La Coq d'Or (*HSS*, 9) *see under C.*

La Savate (*TiS*, 14; *ST*, 5) *see under S.*

Lady Godiva (*PM*, 7): Anglo-Saxon noblewoman who, according to legend, rode naked through the streets of Coventry, England, so that her husband would cancel the oppressive taxes he had placed on the citizenry. In *PM*, Podkayne understands the necessity of getting to a place of safety should there be a solar flare warning but does not intend to be a Lady Godiva in the process.

Lady Macbeth (*TiS*, 2; *PM*, 13): wife of Macbeth in Shakespeare's 1606 tragedy, *Macbeth*, considered by some to be the instigator of and power behind the bloody deeds of the play. In *TiS*, it is the name of Helen Walker's favorite combat knife, an appropriately named weapon for an assault captain in the Amazons. See: **Amazons, Bluebeard, Colonel Bowie**, and **Occam's Razor**. In *PM*, Podkayne's brother refers to their captor, Mrs. Grew, as "Lady Macbeth," perhaps for her cruelty or for her willingness to break the law for her political ends.

Lafayette Law (*SB*, 8): for the Marquis de Lafayette (b. 6 September 1757, d. 20 May 1834), a Frenchman who fought for America in the Revolutionary War. After that war, the state of Maryland made Lafayette an honorary citizen; in 2002, the United States Congress recognized Lafayette as an honorary citizen. In *SB*, Heinlein creates a Lafayette Law that would allow Johnnie, as a citizen of Mars, to claim land there.

Laguna Serenidad (*FS*, 13): Spanish for "lagoon of serenity." In *FS*, it is a lake that borders Bill's property and is a name in sharp contrtast to some of the others that describe the land on Ganymede. See: **Golgotha**.

Lake of the Forest (*HSS*, 3): resort area west of Kansas City, KS. In *HSS*, Kip has been invited to Lake of the Forest for Labor Day weekend. Heinlein, who grew up in Kansas City, MO, would have known about Lake of the Forest.

Laocoön (*SJ*, 17): Trojan who warns the people about the wooden horse the Greeks have left, immediately after which serpents coil around him and his sons and crush them to death. In *SJ*, when Max and Ellie are roped by the centaurs, Heinlein describes them as "being held like Laocoön."

Laurel (*TiS*, 12): leaves that form the traditional crown honoring Olympic athletes or others of significant achievement. In *TiS*, when Rod and Roy return from their search after having been given up for dead, Grant says that he does not know whether to throw them "in the hoosegow" or crown their "brows with laurel." See: **Hoosegow**.

"Lay On, Macduff, and Curs'd Be Him That First Cries, 'Hold, Enough'" (*HSS*, 6): from Shakespeare's 1606 tragedy, *Macbeth*, "Lay on, Macduff, / and damned be he that first cries, 'Hold, enough'" (V, vii, 63–64). In *HSS*, Kip uses this quotation to redirect his and Peewee's search for the path to Tombaugh Station as they attempt to escape from their captors on the Moon. Peewee thinks that, the quotation came from Shakespeare's *King Lear*, but Kip corrects her. Heinlein uses the occasion to suggest that, although Peewee may be a genius, Kip is smart and well educated as well, having independently supplemented the meager offerings of his high school. See: **M.I.T.**

"Le Regiment de Sambre et Meuse" (*ST*, 4) *see under R.*

League of Nations (*HSS*, 10): international governmental organization founded after World War I. The failure of the League of Nations to prevent World War II, as well as the refusal of the United States to join it, caused it to be disbanded. In *HSS*, Kip says that the Court of the Three Galaxies is like the League of Nations or the United Nations. See: **United Nations**.

"Lean and Hungry Look" (*PM*, 6): from Shakespeare's 1599 tragedy, *Julius Caesar*: "Yond Cassius has a lean and hungry look, / He thinks too much; such men are dangerous" (I, ii, 194–195). In *PM*, Podkayne says that, if you are a woman, it is not good to show men that you are smart, as they become as uneasy as Caesar when he notes Cassius' "lean and hungry look." This is another Heinlein comment

Lebensraum

about women having to hide their intelligence or women being assumed to be less intelligent than men. See: **AEC, Caesar,** and **Idiot's Mate.**

Lebensraum [Project] (*TfS*, 3): space required for life or growth or activity. In *TfS*, Project Lebensraum was established to send twelve ships out to find inhabitable planets for Earth's expanding population.

Lefty Gomez (*TfS*, 12): All-Star baseball pitcher and five-time World Series champion with the New York Yankees, 1930–1942, sometimes identified as Mexican-American but more often as Portugese-American and known for his quick wit and self-deprecating sense of humor. In *TfS*, it is the name of a cook eaten by a large carnivorous lizard. Tom, the narrator, remarks that no one would have figured the assistant pastry cook for a hero but that more people would have died had Lefty been "the kind of man who insists on living forever."

"Legion Étrangère" (*ST*, 6): March of the French Foreign Legion. See: **"Le Regiment de Sambre et Meuse."**

Legionary (*HSS*, 10): professional soldier in the army of the Roman Empire, 1st through 3rd centuries A.D. In *HSS*, a Roman legionary is one of the Earth people the Court of the Three Galaxies has captured to examine before deciding whether or not to exterminate all humanity. See: **Neanderthal.**

Leif Ericsson (*TfS*, 9): Scandinavian explorer (b. ca. 970, d. ca. 1020) considered to be the first European to reach the shores of North America based on literary evidence in the Icelandic sagas and archeological evidence at L'Anse aux Meadows in Newfoundland. In *TiS*, it is the name of one of the torch ships. See: **Lebensraum [Project]** and ***Lewis and Clark.***

Lemmings (*TiS*, 13): small arctic rodents commonly and mistakenly believed to commit mass suicide by jumping from cliffs into the water and swimming until they drown. In *TiS*, Rod Walker compares the "dopey Joes," a small but dangerous animal, and their sudden migration to the popular belief about lemmings.

Leonardo da Vinci (*TfS*): Leonardo di sur Piero da Vinci (b. 15 April 1452, d. 2 May 1519), a polymath who was everything from an engineer to a painter, the ideal Renaissance man, most famous for two paintings, *Mona Lisa* and *The Last Supper*. In *TfS*, Tom Bartlett is Thomas Paine Leonardo da Vinci Bartlett, his given names coming from his father's interest in American history and his mother's interest in art. The names reflect Heinlein's belief in a well-rounded education. See: ***Thomas Paine.***

Les Invalides (*ST*, 9) *see under I.*

"Let the Blind Lead the Blind" (*SB*, 5): "And if the blind lead the blind both shall fall into the ditch" (Matthew 15:14). In various forms, "the blind leading the blind" has become a popular expression. In *SB*, Mr. Kiku suggests that he and Greenberg meet the Rargyllians; when Greenberg humorously doubts his ability to help, Mr. Kiku suggests that the blind can lead the blind.

Lewis and Clark (*TfS*, 3): Meriwether Lewis (b. 18 August 1774, d. 11 October 1809) and William Clark (b. 1 August 1870, d. 1 September 1838) led an expedition (1804–1806) to survey the northern sectors of the Louisiana Purchase by way of the Missouri and Columbia rivers, among others. The Lewis and Clark expedition paved the way for much of the westward expansion that followed. In *TfS*, the torch ship to which Tom Bartlett is assigned is named the *Lewis and Clark*, an appropriate name for a ship going out to find new and inhabitable planets (as are the names of the other ships in the project). Heinlein is again paralleling the juvenile series to American history.

Lewis Carroll (*RP*, 3; *RS*, 3): pen name of Charles Lutwidge Dodgson (b. 27 January 1832, d. 14 January 1898), mathematician most famous for writing *Alice's Adventures in Wonderland* (1865) and *Through the Looking-Glass and What Alice Found There* (1872). See: **Alice** and **Boojum**.

Leyport (*RS*, 5): spaceport on the moon, probably named for Willy Ley. There is currently a crater on the moon named for Ley. See: **Ley's *Rockets*** and **Willy Ley**.

Ley's *Rockets* (*RSG*, 2): Willy Ley's *Rockets* (1944), the first in a series of nonfiction books about space travel expanded and revised over the next two decades. In *RSG*, it is one of the books on the boys' clubhouse shelf, and later the source for the estimate of the possibility of being hit by a meteor (10). See: **Jules Verne, Leyport,** and **Willy Ley.**

Leyte (*ST*, 13): Philippine site of the largest naval battle of World War II in which the U.S. Navy dealt a crippling blow to the Japanese navy. In *ST*, it is the name of one of the warships of the Federation fleet.

"The Life and Times of T.P. Bartlett, Gent." (*TfS*, 9): title Dr. Devereaux suggests for Tom's diary. In *TfS*, Devereaux's suggestion is modeled after eighteenth- and nineteenth-century English novels often about young men who start out badly and out of place but end up successful and composed, such as *The Life and Opinions of Tristram Shandy, Gentleman*, Laurence Sterne's series begun in 1759.

"Life, Liberty, and the Pursuit of Happiness" (*ST*, 8): "[humans] are endowed by their Creator with certain unalienable Rights; that among these are life, liberty, and the pursuit of happiness," probably the most famous words from the United States Declaration of Independence (4 July 1776). In *ST*, Mr. Dubois contends that there is no such thing as "unalienable rights" and concludes a long passage

Limbo

by asserting that liberty is never free and must be continually bought with the blood of patriots.

Limbo (*TiS*, 2): according to some Christian beliefs, the place where the impure, but not damned, souls wait to be purified so that they can enter heaven. In *TiS*, Rod Walker's sister, Helen, says, "There is no point being the best dressed ghost in Limbo," telling him not to be over-equipped for the survival test but to rely on his instincts. Heinlein believed in being prepared, but he believed even more in trusting in one's skills.

"Limey" (*FS*, 7; *BP*, 1): insulting slang term for Englishman used primarily by Americans and Canadians, believed to have originated from the British navy's use of lime juice to prevent scurvy. In *FS*, in a debate over what to name the Boy Scout troop, Bud Kelly, who is Irish, calls John Edward Forbes-Smith, who is English, "a limey." See: **"Fog-Eater," "Skin Head,"** and **"Yank."**

Lincoln, Abraham (*SJ*, 11) *see* **Abe Lincoln.**

Lingua Franca (*BP*, 9): mixture of various languages used among mixed peoples as a common or commercial language. In *BP*, it is the language of the small business people and their customers in the side streets of New London on Venus.

Little America (*FS*, 4): scientific research station in Antarctica established and maintained by the United States. In *FS*, Bill spots Little America from the rocket ship. Heinlein may have included Little America as a reminder of how humans have been able to adapt to and control hostile environments as the characters in *FS* will have to do on Ganymede.

Little Buttercup (*BP*, 16): one of the main characters in W.S. Gilbert (b. 18 November 1836, d. 29 May 1911) and Arthur Sullivan's (b. 13 May 1842, d. 22 November 1900) operetta *H.M.S. Pinafore*. Buttercup sells sundries to the sailors aboard the ship but also holds the key to Ralph Rackstraw's future. In *BP*, Little Buttercup is the chosen English language name of one of the Venerian dragon scientists; she will help the others unlock the key to success in the rebellion of Mars and Venus against Earth. Ironically, Major Phipps, who points Little Buttercup out to Don Harvey, says that no one "knows why" the dragon calls herself Little Buttercup, echoing the song from the operetta in which the woman sings, "I'm called Little Buttercup, dear Little Buttercup / Though I could never tell why"— an interesting bit of Heinlein humor.

Little David (*BP*, 18): Biblical character who killed the giant Goliath with a stone from a sling. The story of David and Goliath is an archetypal story about someone smaller and weaker overcoming someone larger and stronger. In *BP*, *Little David* is the ship that makes the trip from Venus to Mars with the new drive and the new "weapons" that will prevent the Federation from destroying the rebels on Mars. In Heinlein's *The Moon Is a Harsh Mistress* (1966), Little David's Sling is the catapult that the rebels on the moon use to bombard Earth with rocks.

The Little Lame Prince (*HSS*, 1): 1875 classic story for children by Dinah Maria Mulock Craik (b. 20 April 1826, d. 12 October 1887). In that story, a lame prince is given a magical traveling cloak by his fairy godmother and, during his travels, develops wisdom and understanding. In *HSS*, Kip is reading *The Little Lame Prince* and thinks a king is coming because his father has a royalty (payment for a publication or a public lecture) coming. Interestingly, Kip's winning a space suit will make it possible for him to go on a great journey and starts him on the road to wisdom and understanding.

Lochiel of Cameron (*ST*, 6): usually written Cameron of Lochiel, a reference to the Scots clan and clan leaders, considered to be particularly fierce fighters. In *ST*, the current Cameron donates a set of bagpipes to Camp Arthur Currie after his son dies in training there.

Lockheed (*HSS*, 9): short for the Lockheed Martin Corporation, a manufacturer that traces its history back to the early days of airplane flight. In *HSS*, Kip refers to a Lockheed ultrasonic courier.

Londinium (*HSS*, 10): Roman name for the present city of London. See: **Gaul.**

Long-Haired [Stuff] (*SC*, 9): American slang for "intellectual" or "sophisticated." In *SC*, a marine sergeant suggests to Matt, who has been struggling with his astrogation homework, that he should give up "that long-haired stuff" and join the space marines. Heinlein creates this choice for Matt, who has to decide whether to take the easy way out and join the space marines or stay in the patrol and continue to exert himself. Later in the novel, the findings onboard the *Pathfinder* will be turned over to the "long-hairs" (13).

Long Johns (*HSS*, 3): slang term for long underwear, long-sleeved and complete-legged underwear worn primarily for warmth. In *HSS*, Kip compares his deflated space suit to "a pair of limp long johns."

Long Pig (*TiS*, 7): slang term for human flesh used as meat for eating. In *TiS*, Jimmy says that they should try to attract others to their campsite, and he humorously suggests that if he and Rod and Jackie don't like the newcomers, there would be "long pig" for dinner.

"Lord Giveth and the Lord Taketh Away. Blessed be the Name of the Lord." (*TiS*, 11): "Then Job arose, and rent his mantle, and shaved his head, and worshipped, And said, Naked came I out of my mother's womb, and naked shall I return thither; the Lord gave, and the Lord hath taken away; blessed be the name of the Lord (Job

Lord

1.21). In *TiS*, Caroline uses this verse as a comment when one of the members of the community is killed on a hunting trip; her use of this verse, from a Bible story about a man who suffers greatly, indicates that she (and, by implication, the others) have been accustomed to the hardships and dangers that surround them.

Lord Haw-Haw (*RSG*, 17): name given to British radio propagandists for the German cause in World War II, most closely linked to William Joyce. In *RSG*, Cargraves calls the German moon-base commander Lord Haw-Haw because of the English accent he used when the Germans destroyed the *Galileo*. William Joyce was captured, tried, and hanged for treason by the British after the war. Cargraves' use of this term for the German commander suggests that the commander will be executed for his crimes as well. See: **Oxford Accent.**

Lord High Executioner (*RP*, 9): character from the 1845 Gilbert and Sullivan operetta, *The Mikado*, who moves from condemned criminal to Lord High Executioner. In *RP*, MacRae refers to one of the company's representatives as "the Lord High Executioner," perhaps because the company is trying to prevent the colonists from moving south for the winter as they have always done.

Lost Sheep [Parable] (*TfS*, 4) *see* **Ninety and Nine.**

Lowell [Academy] (*RP*, 4): school, probably named for the astronomer Percival Lowell. See **Percival Lowell.**

Luau (*TiS*, 12): traditional Hawaiian feast held to celebrate various important events. In *TiS*, the community holds a luau, a special feast, upon the return of Rod and Roy, who had been gone so long searching for caves into which the community could move that everyone assumed they had been killed.

Lucifer (*SC*, 12; *RS*, 13): Latin for "Bringer of Light" and a name interchangeable with Satan. In *SC*, Professor Thorwald theorizes that the Asteroid Belt is the remains of a planet whose inhabitants had destroyed themselves and the planet "by artificial nuclear explosion." By calling the planet Lucifer, Heinlein, through Thorward, is suggesting something of the enormity of such self-destruction. In *RSG*, Morrie suggests that the inhabitants of the moon destroyed themselves by atomic war, but the name Lucifer does not appear in that novel. In both cases, Heinlein is, of course, warning that the same thing could happen to Earth (11). In *RS*, the remnants of Lucifer, the Asteroid Belt, is the site of a major uranium and core metal strike. Except for the names of specific mining areas, like the Halleujah Node, the names Heinlein includes in his discussion of the Asteroid Belt, including ones like Themis orbital pattern, are all legitimate astronomical and scientific names. See: **Bode's Law, Giuseppe Piazzi,** and **Kepler.**

Lummox (*SB*, 1): large and clumsy person. The extraterrestrial main character in *SB* is nicknamed Lummox for her great size and inadvertent destruction of property.

Machiavellian [Plot] (*RS*, 13): adjective form of the last name of Nicollo Machiavelli (b. 3 May 1649, d. 21 June 1527), author of the political treatise *The Prince*. Machiavelli has been popularized as the propagator if not the inventor of crafty and deceitful politics. In *RS*, Grandma Hazel, defending her grandsons in court on a charge of plotting to avoid Martian import taxes, argues that they are not capable of such a "Machiavellian plot."

Mad King Ludwig (*HSS*, 9): Ludwig II (b. 25 August 1845, d. 13 June 1886), king of Bavaria. Ludwig II was deposed in 1886 for mental illness and died the next day under mysterious circumstances. See: **Moors.**

Madame Curie (*BP*, 16): Marie Curie (b. 7 November 1867, d. 4 July 1934), chemist and physicist best known for her discovery of and work with radioactivity. In *BP*, it is the chosen English language name of one of the Venerian dragon scientists.

Madame Pompadour (*HSS*, 4): Madame de Pompadour, Jeanne-Antoinette Poisson (b. 29 December 1721, d. 15 April 1764), most famous as the socially and politically successful mistress of Louis XV of France. In *HSS*, Peewee's rag doll is named Madame Pompadour. Although it seems an odd name for a child's rag doll, Heinlein may have included "Madame Pompadour" as yet another example of a bright and successful woman.

Made Horns (*HSS*, 11): hand gesture in which the first and fourth fingers are held straight and the second and third fingers are curled into the palm of the hand. In Mediterranean countries, it is a gesture used to ward off evil or misfortune, and it is often used against the "evil eye." In *HSS*, the legionary makes horns at the Court of the Three Galaxies as he hears his recorded voice played back to him. See: **Legionary.**

"La Madelon" (*ST*, 6): French soldier's song from World War I. See: *"Le Regiment de Sambre et Meuse."*

"Mademoiselle from Armentières" (*ST*, 6): popular song sung during World War I that may date back a century before that. See: *"Le Regiment de Sambre et Meuse."*

Madison, James (*RP*, 4) *see* **James Madison [Marlowe].**

Madonna (*PM*, 2): general reference to a mother; specific reference to Mary, the mother of Jesus Christ and an important figure in medieval religious painting. In *PM*, Podkayne remarks on her mother's transformation from award-winning engineer to "Madonna" with the arrival of the triplets.

Magellan (*TfS*, 9): Ferdinand Magellan (b. ca. 1480, d. 27 April 1521),

Magnum

Portuguese born Spanish explorer best known as the first European to essentially circumnavigate the globe even though he was killed in the Philippines. In *TfS*, it is the name of one of the torch ships. See: **Lebensraum [Project]** and ***Lewis and Clark***.

Magnum Opus (*TfS*, 14): Latin for "great work." In *TfS*, Harry Gates is working on his magnum opus, a scientific study of the applicability of Bode's Law throughout solar systems. See: **Bode's Law**.

Magsaysay (*ST*, 14): Ramón Magsaysay (b. 31 August 1907, d. 17 March 1957), third Philippine president, known for his honesty and integrity. In *ST*, Johnnie, looking at the ships named for individual soldiers and thinking of his own Philippine heritage, says that there "ought to be one named Magsaysay." See: **Tagalog**.

Maître d'Hôtel (*BP*, 2): French for "master of the hotel," usually the person in charge of the dining room of the restaurant. In *BP*, it is the headwaiter at the Back Room, a restaurant to which Dr. Jefferson takes Don Harvey, who escorts them to their table. Don is somewhat shocked at what Dr. Jefferson refers to as a decadent fleshpot. The Back Room serves not only as a contrast to the ranch in New Mexico where Don has been in school but also to the more vibrant frontier culture of Venus. Dr. Jefferson also calls it Sodom and Gomorrah and suggests that its days — meaning not just the club but the Earth culture in which it flourishes — are numbered. See: **Sodom and Gomorrah, Tannhäuser, "These Our Actors ..."** and **Tromp of Doom**.

Malt (*HSS*, 2): powdered substance made from milk, malted barley, and wheat flour. It can be used to thicken and flavor milkshakes. See: **Soda Jerk**.

Malthus (*TiS*, 2): Thomas Malthus (b. ca. 13 February 1776, d. 23 December 1834), political economist whose most popular theory was that population growth would outstrip the planet's resources — with disastrous consequences. In *TiS*, Heinlein invokes Malthusian theory to explain why the emigration gates were such an important development. See: **Gulliver's Travels**.

"Maman" (*SC*, 15): French for "mother." In *SC*, Thurlow follows that with, *"Manan — Pourquoi fait-il nuit ainsi?"* "Mother — why is it always dark [night]?" See: ***"J'ai soif."***

The Man (*HSS*, 7): slang term for someone in authority, usually a law enforcement figure. In *HSS*, one of the humans working with the Wormfaces says that they don't have to worry about the Man "putting the arm" on them (i.e., arresting them) on Pluto.

Man in the Iron Mask (*TfS*, 16): name given to a Frenchman imprisoned from 1669 until his death in 1703. No one knows for sure who he was because of the "iron mask," actually a black cloth, that gave him his name. See: **Comte de Monte Cristo**.

Man Is Not a Rational Animal; He Is a Rationalizing Animal (*TiS*, 2): appears in other Heinlein writing. In *Rationalising: Webster's Quotations, Facts and Phrases* (2008), there are hundreds of quotations about people being rational, not rational, or rationalizers. None of these quotations provides a source for Heinlein's comment, although it does sound like something Jonathan Swift might have written. In *TiS*, Kip's sister uses this argument to persuade him not to create a scene with his parents before leaving.

Mandarin (*CG*, 18): standard language of China. In *CG*, Thorby realizes that the Sargonese language contains many Mandarin words.

Manhattan Project (*RSG*, 3): formally designated the Manhattan Engineer District, the Manhattan Project, as it is better known, was the effort spearheaded by the United States during World War II to develop the first atomic bomb under the direction of J. Robert Oppenheimer. In *RSG*, Cargraves talks about the Manhattan Project's foreshadowing of space flight and, later, uses it as an example of what young men can accomplish (4) as he tries to persuade one of the fathers to allow his son to participate in building the *Galileo*. See: **Einstein** and **Sir Isaac Newton**.

Maniac (*TiS*, 2): early computer, first successfully run in 1952. See: **Eniac** and **Univac**.

Mannerheim (*ST*, 12): Garl Gustaf Emil Mannerheim (b. 4 June 1867, d. 27 January 1951), Finnish military commander who became regent and then president of Finland. In *ST*, the name of a Federation spaceship on which Johnnie's high school friend Carmen Ibañez is in training.

Maori (*TiS*, 14; *PM*, 6): original and continuing Polynesian inhabitants of New Zealand. In *TiS*, the women of the community adopt the Maori grass skirt as everyday wear. In *PM*, Podkayne's Uncle Tom is of Maori ancestry. See: **Aasvogel** and **Uncle Tom**.

Marathon (*ST*, 13): site of a battle in Greece from which a runner ran over 26 miles to Athens to announce that the Greeks had defeated the Persians. According to legend, the messenger made his announcement and dropped dead. In *ST*, it is the name of one of the warships in the Federation fleet.

March of the Gladiators (*TfS*, 4): military theme also known as "Entry of the Gladiators" or "Thunder and Blazes" and most popularly used as an entrance march at the circus. In *TiS*, Pat Bartlett is humming the march when he thinks their parents have been convinced to let one of them go into space aboard the *Lewis and Clark*. See: *Lewis and Clark*.

Marching-and-Chowder Society (*RSG*, 1): uncertain origin; generic name for a group that gets together for a specific purpose. In *RSG*, Art refers to the Galileo Club as the Galileo Marching-and-Chowder Society.

Marco Polo (*TfS*, 9): Italian merchant (b. ca. 1254, d. 8 January 1324) best known for an extended journey through Asia and China with his father and uncle and for the account of that journey, which introduced Europeans to Asia and China. In *TfS*, it is the name of one of the torch ships. See: **Lebensraum [Project]** and *Lewis and Clark*.

Marcq St.-Hilaire (*RSG*, 12): French navigator Marcq St.-Hilaire. In 1875, St.-Hilaire developed what became known as the French *methodé du point raproché*, an obsolete method of navigation in *RSG* but one that Morrie will have to use flying near the moon as all of his navigation tables were tables for Earth. It is a way of using two estimates in sequence to find the probable position of one's vessel.

Margaret Mader (*CG*, 7): obvious reference to anthropologist Margaret Mead (b. 16 December 1901, d. 15 November 1978), a respected and controversial cultural anthropologist, especially for her reports on the healthy sexual attitudes in the South Pacific and arguments for broadened sexual life, an argument that contributed to the "sexual revolution" of the 1960s. In *CG*, Mader is an anthropologist aboard the *Sisu* whose studies of the Free Traders put her in the position to explain the society of the Free Traders to Thorby and to the reader. See: **Free Traders**.

Mark Twain's *Life on the Mississippi* (*RS*, 16): 1883 memoir by Mark Twain (Samuel L. Clemens: b. 30 November 1835, d. 21 April 1910) about his early career as a pilot-in-training on a Mississippi steamboat and his return many years later to travel the Mississippi by steamboat. In *RS*, Castor and Pollux are surprised to find a hard copy of Twain's book in Old Charlie's place in the Asteroid Belt.

Mark's *Standard Handbook for Mechanical Engineers* (*RSG*, 2): standard for over 70 years and edited by Eugene Avallone and Theodore Burmeister III, now in its 11th edition. In *RSG*, it is one of the books on the boys' clubhouse shelf. See: **Jules Verne**.

Marne (*ST*, 13): site of an early battle in World War I in which the French defeated the Germans, stopped their offensive, and set the stage for years of mostly trench warfare on the Western Front. In *ST*, it is the name of one of the warships of the Federation fleet.

Marquis de Sade (*SC*, 9): French aristocrat (b. 2 June 1740, b. 2 December 1814) who espoused a lifestyle unregulated by religion, law, or morality. His controversial writings, fiction and essays, as well as his actions, led to several prison sentences. The word "sadism" derives from de Sade's name.

Mauser

In *SC*, the Hog Alley Band members are known by pseudonyms, but the only historical one is the "Marquis de Sade," and there seems to be no reason for this ascription as all the other names, e.g., Senator Filibuster and Professor Farflung, are not names at all but activities or characteristics.

Marquis Howe (*RP*, 4): headmaster at the Lowell Academy on Mars in *RP* and possibly named for British General Howe, who battled the Americans at Bunker Hill, MA, at the outset of the Revolutionary War. In addition to a suitably "British" adversary for Jim, Howe's activities as headmaster broadly parallel his British model's actions early in the American Revolution. The name/title Marquis also suggests that Howe might be something of a martinet. See: **James Madison [Marlowe]**.

Marquis of Queensbury (*RS*, 2): formal rules of boxing as set forth in 1867 by John Sholto Douglas, the 9th Marquess of Queensberry (b. 20 July 1844, d. 31 January 1900). Since their publication, the Marquess of Queensberry rules have become a metaphor for fighting fairly. In *RS*, Grandma Hazel asserts that she can still physically discipline her son and asks if he wants "Marquis of Queensbury, dockside or kill-quick" rules.

Mars (*HSS*, 11): Roman god of war. In *HSS*, the legionary Iunio invokes Mars and Jove as he is being pulled by some invisible force out of the courtroom of the Court of the Three Galaxies. See: **Jove** and **Legionary**.

"Marseillaise" (*ST*, 6): composed in 1792 and became the rallying song of the French Revolution and ultimately the national song of France. See: *"Le Regiment de Sambre et Meuse."*

Martian Shandy (*TfS*, 4) *see* **Shandy**.

Marxist Theory (*ST*, 6): economic, political, and social theory named for Karl Marx (b. 5 May 1818, d. 14 March 1883) that advocates a labor theory of value and a move toward a classless society. In *ST*, Mr. Dubois "disproves" Marxist theory by demonstrating that work does not always add value to things and that value is relative and not absolute.

Masterrace (*RSG*, 16): Nazi concept that the Germanic and Nordic peoples were a pure race and culture as opposed to other cultures in which races mixed, causing the culture to degenerate. In *RSG*, Cargraves refers to their German prisoner as "Joe Masterrace," suggests that the "Master Race usually is stupid when it comes to a showdown" (17), and says, "I always have thought a man with a Master-Race complex was crazy as a hoot owl" (19). See: **Concentration Camps** and **Nazis**.

Mauser (*RSG*, 15): German arms manufacturer. Mauser rifles and pistols, for both military and hunting, have been made by the Mauser company since the 1870s, but the name Mauser in post-World War II years signified the rifles carried by the German soldiers. The civilian branch of the company exists today as Sig Sauer, one of the largest arms makers in the world, and its pistols are standard armament in contemporary novels of international intrigue. In *RSG*, the possession of a Mauser by one of the men who attacks the *Galileo* is a clue to his German identity.

Mavourneen (*PM*, 3): Irish (Gaelic) for "my darling." In *PM*, Podkayne's uncle calls her "mavourneen." Although Tom is of primarily Maori descent, his use of an Irish term is indicative of the mixed language of the people of Mars, who descended from convicts transported from Earth to Mars — just as nineteenth-century convicts, many of them Irish, were transported to Australia and nearby islands.

Maximilian (*SJ*, 1): possibly Maximilian I, Holy Roman Emperor (b. 22 March 1459, d. 12 January 1519). In *SJ*, the main character's name is Max, and although there are a number of Maximilians in history, including the ill-fated Maximilian I of Mexico, Heinlein may well have been thinking of the Holy Roman emperor known to have been a patron of the arts and sciences.

Mayflower (*FS*, 1): ship that brought the Pilgrims to the New World in 1620. In *FS*, the *Mayflower* is the ship that takes settlers from an overcrowded Earth to Ganymede, a moon of Jupiter's that has been chosen for terraforming. *Mayflower* is a logical choice for the name of the ship for more than just the obvious reason of transporting colonists. Ganymede is a harsh environment which, over a period of decades, the transplanted Earth people will try to make as much like Earth as possible, and the harshness of Ganymede certainly parallels the harshness of the New England climate with which the Pilgrims had to deal. Moreover, as Heinlein develops his juvenile series to parallel the settlement history of the North American continent, the *Mayflower* is a thematically appropriate name for the ship in this novel. See: **Daniel Boone, Johnny Appleseed, Plymouth Rock Colony,** and **Terraforming.**

Mayor Report (*ST*, 12): 1956 address, *Brainwashing: The Ultimate Weapon*, by U.S. Army major William E. Mayer in the Radiological Defense Laboratory of the San Francisco Naval Shipyard. In *ST*, Major Reid assigns one of the officer candidates a report on brainwashing and suggests that he look at the "Mayor Report."

"Meadowland" (*ST*, 13): one of several titles for a popular 1930s Russian song. In *ST*, it is the tune that calls Johnnie's classmate Bennie Montez to the ship to which he has been assigned.

Medusa (*SB*, 2): woman from Greek mythology with snakes on her head instead of hair. Anyone who looked directly at her was turned to stone; Perseus was able to behead her by looking at her reflection in his shield. In *SB*, Mr. Kiku has trouble facing a Rargyllian negotiator because Rargyllians have tentacles growing out of their heads that make Mr. Kiku so "ill" that he has to have a hypnotic treatment before he can meet with them.

Mein Kampf (*HSS*, 7): written in prison by Adolf Hitler in two volumes, 1925 and 1926, as both autobiography and political tract. See: **Hitler, O. Henry,** and **Saint Paul.**

Mendelssohn (*TiS*, 11): Jakob Ludwig Felix Mendelssohn Bartholdy (b. 3 February 1809, d. 4 November 1847), musician, conductor, and composer of the early Romantic period, probably best known as the composer of the "Wedding March." In *TiS*, Caroline plays Mendelssohn's "Wedding March" on her harmonica for weddings in the community.

"Mene, Mene, Tekel, Upharsin" Daniel v:25 (*BP*, 2, chapter title): words in the Old Testament that appeared on the wall at Belshazzar's feast and which Daniel interpreted to mean that God had damned the kingdom (Daniel 5:25). In *BP*, Heinlein begins chapter 2 with this quotation, thereby using it, first, as a prelude to the revolution in which Venus and Mars achieve their independence from an oppressive Earth and second as a parallel to the American revolution against England — part of his overall parallel of the juvenile series to American history.

Mercury Fulminate (*ST*, 6): explosive, $Hg(CNO)_2$, sensitive to heat, friction, and shock. In *ST*, Captain Frankel says that the recruits are as explosive as mercury fulminate and have to be watched at all times.

Mercutio (*RS*, 14): Romeo's best friend in William Shakespeare's 1591/1595 tragedy, *Romeo and Juliet,* who was killed in a sword duel by Juliet's cousin, Tybalt. When asked if he has been hurt, Mercutio says, "Aye, aye, a scratch, a scratch; marry 'tis enough" and "No, 'tis not so deep as a well, nor wide as a church / door; but 'tis enough, 'twill serve" (III, i, 89, 92–93) and then he dies. In *RS*, when asked in reference to the birthrate of flat cats what eight times five hundred and then eight times that is, Dr. Stone says, "Too many." Her husband replies, "My dear, that's the most masterly understatement since the death of Mercutio."

Merry Widow (*CG*, 2): 1905 comic operetta by Franz Lehar in which a widow's fortune is sought by several suitors for personal and political gain and won by the suitor willing to forego the fortune. In *CG*, it is the name of the first slave ship that Thorby can remember. The irony of a slave ship's being named the *Merry Widow* mirrors the ultimate ironies of the book that Thorby will be the one to begin to bring the slave trade to a halt and that the spaceship company founded by his ancestors has supplied ships and service ports to the slavers. See: **"Prometheus Bound."**

Mesa Verde (*TiS*, 10): cliff/cave dwellings and other dwelling places built by the Anasazi and dating from about A.D. 1200. In *TiS*, Rod Walker suggests that the growing community would be safer and better protected if they could find some caves to occupy instead of the open river bend which they currently occupy.

Mess Hall Lawyer (*BP*, 13) *see* **Bedroll Lawyer.**

Michelangelo (*TfS*, 1): Michelangelo di Lodovico Buonarroti Simoni (b. 5 March 1475, d. 18 February 1564), Italian painter and sculptor, perhaps second only in range of interests and abilities to Leonardo da Vinci, most famous for his sculpture *David* and his painting of the ceiling of the Sistine Chapel. In *TfS*, Pat Bartlett is Patrick Henry Michelangelo Bartlett, his given names coming from his father's interest in American history and his mother's interest in art. The names reflect Heinlein's belief in a well-rounded education. See: **Patrick Henry.**

Michelson-Morley Experiment (*TfS*, 8): late-nineteenth century experiment by Albert Michelson and Edward Morley that is now thought to be the first to provide evidence against the theory of a medium — aether — through which light traveled just as air and water were mediums through which sound could travel. In *TfS*, Heinlein refers to the Michelson-Morley experiment in a discussion of the relative passage of time aboard the *Lewis and Clark* compared to the passage of time back on Earth.

Midnight Sun (*RP*, 9): summer sun visible at midnight in the far northern latitudes. Norway is known as "The Land of the Midnight Sun." In *RP*, the powerful flashlight that Jim uses to produce light, and, inadvertently, oxygen, while inside a giant plant is a General Electric "Midnight Sun," so named for its powerful light.

Milk and Honey (*FS*, 13): from the "land of milk and honey" (Exodus 3:8). God says that he will come down and lead the Israelites out of Egypt and to "a land flowing with milk and honey." In *FS*, Bill, looking over the rocky and barren land his family has been assigned, says that it is not exactly "flowing with milk and honey." At that point, his father offers to send him back to college on Earth, but Bill refuses. See: **Golgotha** and **Promised Land.**

The Mill on the Floss (*RS*, 1): 1860 novel by George Eliot (Mary Ann Evans: b. 22 November 1819, d. 22 December 1880). Set in the second half of the nineteenth century, *The Mill on the Floss* is much less a historical novel than a novel of society, manners, and morality (or, at least, ethics). In *RS*, Roger Stone suggests that his sons should read great literature, and they reply that they do not want to read *The Mill on the Floss*, a large three-volume work less often taught at the high school level than Eliot's *Silas Marner*. Given the length and subject matter of *The Mill on the Floss*, one has to wonder if Heinlein was being serious about its being good reading for fifteen-year-old boys, although these twin boys could use some lessons in manners and ethics. Heinlein was also juxtaposing respected literary works with the low-quality space opera Roger Stone was writing. See: **Castor, Ivanhoe, Pollux, The Scourge of the Spaceways** and **White Knight**.

Mint Julep (*SC*, 8): strong drink made with mint leaves, bourbon, sugar (usually powered), and water. Mint juleps are traditionally associated with the southern states in the U.S. and are specifically associated with the Kentucky Derby horse race. In *SC*, Tex Jarman orders mint juleps for himself and his friends when they are on liberty even though they are not legally old enough to drink; he drinks most of them and suffers the consequences. See: **"Deep in the Heart of Texas"** and **"Ioway."**

Mirabile Visu (*HSS*, 5): Latin for "wonderful to Behold." In *HSS*, Kip says this when he finds his space suit. It is a reminder that, earlier in the novel as part of his education beyond what his high school offered, Kip learned Latin on his own. See: **M.I.T.**

Miracle Gro (*SJ*, 5): plant food that promises unusually productive results. In *SJ*, Max is given some Miracle Gro "hair restorer" to use as a disguise when his hair, removed for his fake identification, grows back.

"A Miss Is as Good as a Mile" (*RS*, 7): traditional saying asserting that a narrow escape is just as good as an escape with plenty of room to spare. In *RS*, Roger uses this phrase after their ship is nearly hit by an experimental satellite. See: **"They Went That-a-Way, Podnuh."**

"Mr. Chips" (*SJ*, 7): title character of the 1934 novel *Goodbye Mr. Chips*, by James Hilton (b. 9 September 1900, d. 20 December 1954), about a much-loved English schoolteacher. In *SJ*, Mr. Chips is the name of a spider puppy, so-called because of its six legs, that belongs to Eldreth (Ellie) Coburn, a young woman who has been dismissed from a number of private girls' schools.

M.I.T. (*CG*, 23; *HSS*, 1): Massachusetts Institute of Technology, one of the best engineering schools in the U.S. In *CG*, Thorby will finance an engineer who has ideas about dealing with the slavers. In *HSS*, Kip comments that M.I.T. does not give scholarships to students from his high school nor will he be able to get into Cal Tech from that high school. In this first chapter of *HSS*, Heinlein, in the person of Kip's father, is very critical of American secondary education and has Kip's father call the local high school's curriculum "occupational therapy for morons!" Throughout the novel, Kip makes comments in Latin and Spanish and makes references to literature, music, history, and science as Heinlein shows him to have gotten a thorough education almost in spite of his high school. See: **Dangling Participle** and **Skull-and-Bones.**

Mithrans (*TiS*, 12) *see* **Selenites.**

Moiety (*CG*, 8): two kinship groups that make up a society. In *CG*, the Free Traders have at least two moieties in the *Sisu*, both for social purposes for dividing up the duties aboard ship. See: **Free Traders.**

Molly Malone (*RS*, 17; *SJ*, 3): focus of the Irish song "Molly Malone," about a woman who sells cockles and mussels from a wheelbarrow in the streets of Dublin. The song dates back to the nineteenth century at least, and there is now a statue of Molly Malone in Grafton Street, Dublin. In *RS*, one of the flat cats in named Molly Malone. In *SJ*, it is the name of the truck in which Max gets a ride to Earthport.

Moneylender's Heart (*SJ*, 10): heart, or lack thereof, of someone who loans out money at high interest and can be ruthless about repayment. In *SJ*, Heinlein describes the temperature of Garson's Planet as "cold as a moneylender's heart."

Mongol (*TiS*, 1): ethnic group or groups of people now mainly located in Mongolia, China, and Russia. In *TiS*, Mongol policemen are herding over two million Asiatics, predominantly Chinese, through a gate to another planet in an attempt to relieve the population pressures in the "Australasian Republic." In the generally overcrowded world of the novel, the Asiatics are the most populous and the emigrants are very ill-equipped for whatever new world to which they are being sent. See: **Coolie** and **Heavenly Mountains.**

Monist (*TiS*, 2): belief that there is one god behind the separate manifestations in the world's religions. In *TiS*, Rod Walker's family is Monist. Later in the novel, some of the stranded students are described as Monist (14).

Monkey Suit (*HSS*, 9): slang term for a tuxedo, occasionally for a uniform or other formal dress. In *HSS*, Kip calls Peewee's new space suit a monkey suit; in this case, he may be saying as much because her suit fits as closely as an acrobat's tights.

Montgomery (*ST*, 13): probably Viscount Bernard Montgomery (b. 17 November 1887, d. 24 March 1976), British commander in North Africa during World War II whose command played an important role in driving the German and Italian forces out of North Africa. In *ST*, it is the name of one of the warships in the Federation fleet named for specific foot soldiers.

Moonstruck (*RSG*, 8): dazed or insane due to the effects of the moon.

In *RSG*, a name suggested for the rocket that Cargraves and the boys will try to fly to the moon. The name suggests both their fascination with this dangerous enterprise and the "insane" intent to do it. See: **Starstruck**.

Moors (*HSS*, 9): general term applied to both the historic and modern populations of North Africa. In *HSS*, Kip refers to the bedroom Peewee has designed for herself as a Disneyland-like Moorish harem as thought up by Mad King Ludwig, by which he probably means lots of hanging silks in bright colors. See: **Arabian Nights** and **Mad King Ludwig**.

Mopery and Dopery (*CG*, 10) *see* **Barratry**.

More Ways of Skinning a Cat (*PM*, 10): brief version of the popular saying "there's more than one way to skin a cat." In *PM*, Podkayne says that "there are more ways of skinning a cat than buttering it with parsnips." That version may be original with Heinlein, but other popular variations, also called folk proverbs, include the following: "There are more ways of killing a cat than choking it with cream," "There are more ways of killing a dog than hanging him," and "There are more ways of killing a cat than choking it with pudding."

Mormons [Pioneers] (*TiS*, 14): generally, the members of the Church of the Latter Day Saints, a religious movement founded by Joseph Smith in the early 1800s in New York State and most famous, historically, for moving west and founding a community in what is now Salt Lake City, Utah. In *TiS*, Rod Walker does not initially appreciate the Saturday night square dances because, Heinlein says, he did not know the history of the Mormon pioneers. The Mormon pioneers, like all rural and frontier societies, had to rely on themselves for entertainment, and so folk music and folk dances became a major part of the social interactions for the members of the community. That the students stranded on this planet begin regular Saturday night square dances is also part of Heinlein's continuing parallel of the juvenile series to American history. See: ***Joseph Smith***.

Morning Star (*PM*, 2): medieval weapon consisting of a handle and a spiked ball with a short chain connecting the two or a pole with a spiked head at the end. According to folklore, the morning star was a weapon developed for churchmen who were forbidden from carrying such weapons as swords and spears; but the use of the weapon was much more widespread than that. In *PM*, Podkayne says that she would not try to control her younger brother with anything less than a morning star.

Morning Star of Hope (*BP*, 6): bright object in the morning sky, often a planet and usually Venus. The Morning Star is also considered a sign of hope. In *BP*, *Morning Star of Hope* is the new anthem of the Republic of Venus.

"Morris Garage" (*TfS*, 1): British automobile maker best known for MG's T, A, and B series that introduced Americans to affordable, two-seat convertible sports cars in the two decades following World War II. In *TfS*, the Bartletts have an obsolete household robot from Morris Garage, the Mother's Helper model, as an indication of how tightly they have to manage their money, but they do have a household robot in Heinlein's future.

Moskva (*ST*, 12): Russian for Moscow, the capital of and largest city in Russia. In *ST*, it is the name of one of the warships in the Federation fleet.

Moulinet (*ST*, 3): French for "twirl"; more specifically, a fencing term for a circular cut. In *ST*, Zim makes a moulinet with his instructor's baton to show the enlistees the thing he is talking about.

Mount Etna (*BP*, 2): located in Sicily and one of the largest active volcanoes in Europe. In *BP*, Don Harvey has a dessert called a Mount Etna that is shaped like a volcano, has steam coming out of it, and is described as "fire and ice."

Mount Everest (*HSS*, 3): tallest mountain in the world and located in Tibet. See: **Andes.**

M-S-G (*RS*, 7): standard abbreviation for message. In *RS*, Hazel wonders how long traffic control has been holding a M-S-G that would have warned them about a satellite that just passed close by the *Rolling Stone*.

Mufti (*TiS*, 15; *ST*, 2): slang term for civilian clothes as opposed to military uniforms and may have come from a word for the clothing of Middle Eastern scholars. In *TiS*, Rod Walker is surprised to see his sister, an assault captain in the Amazons, in mufti. See: **Amazons.**

Mulligan [Stew] (*SJ*, 2): dish made of meat, vegetables, potatoes, and whatever else was available, usually associated with and shared among depression-era hobos. In *SJ*, Sam offers Max some "four-day old mulligan."

Multum in Parvo (*BP*, 16): Latin for "much in little." In *BP*, this title for chapter 16 refers to the apparently worthless ring that holds the key to the rebellion for Venus and Mars. See: **"Judge Not According to the Appearance."**

Muses (*PM*, 9): nine spirits in Greek mythology that inspire those who create in the arts and literature. In *PM*, Podkayne says that the Steinway piano in their suite at the Venus Hilton is sacred to the Muses and warns her brother not to touch it. See: **Steinway.**

"My Strength Is as the Strength of Ten Because My Heart Is Pure" (*SC*, 4; *FS*, 8; *HSS*, 7): famous quotation from Alfred, Lord Tennyson's (b. 6 August 1809, d. 6 October 1892) 1834 poem "Sir Galahad" (lines 3–4). In *SC*, Burke suggests that Matt's heart is pure, meaning that he is an innocent sort and will not be reralistic enough to succeed at the academy. In reality, it is the cynical Burke who will leave the academy and then get into trouble from which Matt and his friends have to rescue him. In *FS*, Bill mocks the phrase after losing a fight with a troublemaker. Heinlein may be suggesting that the ideals in some of Tennyson's work, such as Tennyson's Arthurian epic, *Idylls of the King*, do not hold true in the real world. In *HSS*, Kip says this in a self-mocking way when he is trapped and sees no way out to help Peewee or stop the Wormfaces.

NAA (*RSG*, 13): probably National Aeronautics Association, founded in 1905 to advance the "art, sport, and science of aviation in the United States" (Mission Statement). The NAA considers itself the historian and record keeper for U.S. aviation. In *RSG*, Art thinks that it might be the NAA that he can contact by radio from the moon.

Napery (*BP*, 14): table linens. In *BP*, Don Harvey is surprised to find a table in a dragon's house set with "fine napery" for his supper.

Napoleon (*RS*, 1; *SJ*, 12; *TfS*, 1; *ST*, 2): Napoleon Bonaparte (b. 15 August 1759, d. 5 May 1821). Crowned Emperor of France in 1804, Napoleon tried to conquer all of western Europe, including Russia and England. In Russia, his army suffered its first major setback, and in 1815, following abdication and then return to power, he was finally defeated by the Duke of Wellington at the Battle of Waterloo. Napoleon Bonaparte's name has become synonymous with both conquest and a desire for power. In *RS*, Roger Stone calls his sons, Castor and Pollux, "junior-model Napoleons." See: **Castor** and **Pollux**. In *SJ*, Bonaparte is the name of the principle city on Halcyon and is characterized as "not much of a city" in contrast to its name. In *TfS*, Napoleon is cited as an example of a great man who seemed destined from the beginning to be great. See: **Alexander the Great** and **Einstein**. In *ST*, Mr. Dubois refers to Napoleon in a discussion of whether or not violence solves anything. See: **Carthage.** Later, Johnnie recounts a joke about a cap trooper's reaction at seeing Napoleon's tomb (9), and finally, the O.C.S. commander uses an incident from the Napoleonic Wars to illustrate a way in which a cadet in training could suddenly become commander of his craft or unit (12). See: ***Waterloo*** and **Wellington.**

Napoleonic Wars (*ST*, 12): wars fought (1799–1815) between France and a number of European nations. See: **Napoleon.**

National Socialist Reich and **Nazi Reich** (*RSG*, 16): development in Heinlein's novel from the National Socialist Party of World War II Germany. A reich can be a state, a sovereign state, an empire, and much else. Hitler's Germany was the Third Reich. In *RSG*, Heinlein's Germans see the war as ongoing, and they believe that

Nautilus

they will return to Earth, conquer their enemies, and establish the National Socialist Reich.

Nautilus (*BP*, 5; *TfS*, 11): sea creature with a distinctive shell, but most notably the name of Captain Nemo's submarine in Jules Verne's 1872 novel, *Twenty Thousand Leagues Under the Sea*. In *BP*, it is the name of the rocket ship that the Venerian dragon scientist Sir Isaac Newton plans to take from the Circum-Terra space station to his home on Venus. In *TfS*, it is the name of one of the torch ships. See: **Jules Verne, Lebensraum [Project]**, and ***Lewis and Clark***.

Nazi V-2 Rockets (*RSG*, 9): ballistic rockets used against Britain and Belgium during the last stage of World War II. Although the V-2 was not developed soon enough to be militarily effective, it was psychologically effective and spurred late-war and postwar rocket experimentation and development in the United States and the USSR. In *RSG*, the computer that directs the *Galileo* is not different from the ones that drove the V-2 rockets; by suggesting this connection, Heinlein is indirectly preparing the reader for the Nazi outpost on the Moon. See: **German War Rockets**.

Nazis (*RSG*, 4): for National Socialism (German: *Nationalsozialismus*). Nazi has come to include the followers of Adolf Hitler and the ideology, policies, and practices of the German Third Reich government from 1933 through 1945. In *RSG*, Cargraves raises the specter of recent Nazism in chapter 4 to convince Art's mother, whose husband, Hans, was imprisoned by the Nazis, to allow her son, Art, to attempt the trip to the moon. Heinlein's deeper purpose here was to introduce the Nazis at this point as they would turn out to be the villains by the end of the story. German scientists made great progress with bomb-carrying rockets late in World War II, and given the Germans' well-known advances in rocketry and the 1947 publication date of *RSG*, it is logical in Heinlein's future that the Nazis preceded Cargraves and the boys to the moon and established a base there. See: **Concentration Camp, Kaiser Wilhelm Institute**, and **Nazi V-2 Rockets**.

Neanderthal (*SB*, 14; *TiS*, 109; *HSS*, 10): subspecies of, or separate species from, humans, the most recent of which lived more than 30,000 years ago. In *SB*, Heinlein has Mr. Kiku suggest that the Neanderthals battled the Cro-Magnons for the planet. See: **Caesar** and **Cro-Magnon Man**. In *TiS*, Jimmy says that when he recovers, his primitive, Neanderthal nature will be obvious, a suggestion that he will be able to deal with the survival conditions in which they find themselves. In *HSS*, it is one of the Earth people The Court of the Three Galaxies has captured to examine before deciding whether or not to exterminate humanity. See: **Legionary**.

Neap Tide (*BP*, 5): tide when the difference between high tide and low tide is at its least. Neap tide produces the smallest rise and fall of the water level and occurs during the quarter moons. In *BP*, a shuttle from the Circum-Terra space station to the moon is appropriately named the *Neap Tide*. See: **Spring Tide**.

"Neither a Borrower Nor a Lender Be" (*HSS*, 9): phrase from Shakespeare's 1606 *Hamlet* (I, iii, 75) that has become a common saying or proverb in English. In *Hamlet*, Polonius is lecturing his son, Laertes, who is about to leave for the university, and his speech is pedantic and full of platitudes. In *HSS*, Kip says this to Peewee when he tries to pay her for fixing his breakfast and she won't take the dollar. Peewee's reaction is to call Polonius "a stupid old bore." See: **Hamlet** and **Shakespeare**.

Nero (*TiS*, 7): Nero Claudius Caesar Augustus Germanicus (b. 15 December A.D. 37, d. A.D. 9 June 68), famously remembered for "fiddling while Rome burned" during the Great Fire of A.D. 64 (if true, he probably played the lyre, as the "fiddle" was not invented until much later). More recently, "fiddling while Rome burns" has come to mean "ignoring a developing problem." In *TiS*, Jimmy suggests that the signal fire he is building will make the Great Fire of Rome look like a bonfire. See: **Great Fire of Rome**.

Never-Get-Overs (*SJ*, 17): events, usually emotional, that one says he/she will "never get over." In *SJ*, Ellie excuses herself from work by saying that she has "come down with the never-get-overs" so that she can take a walk with Max. See: **Don Juan**.

New Canaan (*TiS*, 1): biblical name for the area now occupied by Israel, Lebanon, and other territories in that area; a land of merchants on the coast and agricultural lands in the interior. In *TiS*, it is the name of the planet to which a well-financed and well-provisioned emigrant group is headed. The use of "New" for settlements named after Earth cities parallels the settlement of North America, during which Europeans and then Euro-Americans used British and continental place names rather than adopt Native American place names.

New Joburg (*RS*, 16): city in the Asteroid Belt in *RS*, named for Johannesburg, South Africa. See: **New Canaan**.

New Melbourne (*CG*, 13): city on the planet Woolamurra in *CG*, named for Melbourne, Australia. See: **New Canaan** and **Woolamurra**.

Newton (*TfS*, 12) *see* **Sir Isaac Newton**.

Newton's Laws of Motion (*SC*, 5; *RS*, 4): (1) An object at rest will stay at rest unless acted upon by an unbalanced force. An object in motion continues in motion with the same speed and in the same direction unless acted

Nido

upon by an unbalanced force. (2) Acceleration is produced when a force acts on a mass. The greater the mass (of the object being accelerated) the greater the amount of force needed (to accelerate the object). (3) For every action there is an equal and opposite reaction. In *SC*, Heinlein suggests that all travel between planets is subject to the laws of motion and the law of gravity. In *RS*, Heinlein comments that automobile drivers on Earth careen around dangerously, in part because they no idea of these forces. See: **Sir Isaac Newton.**

El Nido (*CG*, 11): Spanish for "the nest." In *CG*, it is the name of one of the ships of the Free Traders. See: **Free Traders** and ***Hansea.***

Nijinski (*RSG*, 12): Vaslav Fomich Nijinsky (b. 12 March 1989, d. 8 April 1950), a Russian ballet dancer and choreographer of Polish descent considered one of the most gifted male dancers in the history of ballet. He could perform *en pointe*, a rare skill among male dancers at the time, and was known for his daring choreography and his leaps that seemed to defy gravity. In *RSG*, Cargraves' reference is included in a warning to Art about experimenting with low-gravity walking on the moon.

Nina (*TfS*, 13): one of Christopher Columbus' three ships on the 1492 voyage across the Atlantic Ocean to the New World (the Americas). In *TfS*, it is the name of one of the torch ships. See: **Lebensraum [Project]** and ***Lewis and Clark.***

Ninety and Nine (*TiS*, 12; *TfS*, 4): "If a man have an hundred sheep, and one of them be gone astray, doth he not leave the ninety and nine, and goeth into the mountains, and seeketh that which is gone astray?" (Matthew 18:12). In *TiS*, when Rod Walker and Roy Kilroy return, long overdue, from their search for caves into which to move the community, Grant Cowper comments that "there is more rejoicing for the strayed lamb than for the ninety and nine." In *TfS*, Tom realizes that the "half a loaf" argument will not work in this case as it will only fix their parents' attention on the dangers for the one twin going into space. See: **Half a Loaf.**

Nip-Ups (*SB*, 12): jump from lying on one's back to a standing position. In *SB*, Mr. Kiku imagines the Hroshii doing nip-ups at the sight of Lummox.

"No Army for Mine" (*ST*, 12): an antiwar song. See: **"Don't Wanta Study War No More."**

No Man Is an Island Complete in Himself (*PM*, Postlude): "No man is an island, entire of itself; every man is a piece of the continent, a piece of the main," from *Meditation XVII*, John Donne (b. 21 January 1572, d. 31 March 1631). In *PM*, these are among Podkayne's last words to her brother on her recorder, encouraging him to be less self-centered and more aware of his connection to others.

"No Tickee, No Washee" (*SB*, 5): mock Chinese for "if you do not have a laundry ticket, you cannot pick up the wash." In general American slang, it means if you do not have part A (identification, money, etc.), you cannot get B (admission, the product, etc.). In *SB*, Greenberg uses the phrase to mean that if a person does not have proper identification there is no way he or she could sneak onto the planet.

Noah (*TfS*, 10; *HSS*, 9): main character in the story of Noah and the Ark (Genesis 6–9), whom God instructs to make an Ark and take two of each animal aboard before the Great Flood to punish the sinners. In *TfS*, Tom contrasts Noah's ark, with its separation of genders, to the *Lewis and Clark*, on which the genders are free to socialize as they wish. In *HSS*, Kip mentions that a Vegan Noah would have to take twelve of each animal aboard his Ark to have all of the sexes.

Nobel (*SC*, 10): Alfred Nobel (b. 21 October 1833, d. 10 December 1896), Swedish arms manufacturer and inventor, most famous for inventing dynamite and for leaving his fortune to create the **Nobel Prize** (*RSG*, 1). In *SC*, Matt explains that the *Nobel* is used to inspect the atomic bomb rockets in orbit around Earth.

Noblesse Oblige (*CG*, 8): French for "nobility obligates," meaning that noble ancestry, wealth, or privilege requires one to behave in an honorable or responsible way. In *CG*, Margaret Mader explains this aspect of the highly stratified Free Trader society to Thorby.

The Noblest Fate That a Man Can Endure Is to Place His Own Mortal Body Between His Loved Home and the War's Desolation (*ST*, 6): probably Heinlein's version of Horace's Latin "Dulce et Decorum Est Pro Patria Morii" (Odes, III.2.13), "It is Sweet/Glorious and Honorable to Die for One's Country," and might also be Heinlein's answer to Wilfred Owen's (b. 18 March 1893, d. 4 November 1918) 1918 antiwar poem, "Dulce et Decorum Est." In *ST*, Mr. Dubois, Johnnie's high school teacher of history and moral philosophy, writes this in a letter praising him for choosing the Mobile Infantry and for sticking it out through the worst part of basic training.

Non Sequitur (*SB*, 5): Latin for "it does not follow," usually referring to a statement or response that does not logically follow from anything said previously. In *SB*, Mr. Kiku tells Greenberg that his logic in determining Lummox's intelligence is faulty.

Norbert Wiener (*CG*, 14): American mathematician and engineer (b. 26 November 1894, d. 18 March 1964) who founded the field of cybernetics, a field relevant to everything from systems control to social organization. During World War II, he helped develop weapons systems that would automatically aim and fire antiaircraft guns. In *CG*, it is the name of one of the ships of the Free Traders; in this case, it is the commodore's flagship. See: **Free Traders** and ***Hansea.***

Normandy Beach (*ST*, 13): site in France of the Allied invasion from England that began the liberation of Europe and the defeat of Hitler's Germany. In *ST*, it is the name of one of the warships in the Federation fleet.

Nos Morituri—(*HSS*, 8): Latin phrase, "Nos Morituri Te Salutamus" or "Morituri Te Salutant," which means "we who are about to die salute you," thought to be the traditional salute given by the gladiators to Caesar before the match began. In *HSS*, Kip says this to the Mother Thing as he goes outside into the frozen conditions on Pluto to set the beacon. Kip's use of Latin and other foreign languages, like his references to Shakespeare and other authors classical and popular, continues to remind the reader that Kip has significantly augmented the meager educational offerings at his local high school. See: **"Hail, Caesar, We Who Are About to Die —."**

Nosies (*SJ*, 4): slang for curious people, including the police. In *SJ*, Sam takes Max to a diner where there will be no "nosies leaning over our shoulders."

Novaës (*HSS*, 9): Guiomar Novaës (b. 28 February 1895, d. 7 March 1979), Brazilian pianist known for the individuality and poetic nuances of her playing. In *HSS*, Kip compares the ability of the Mother Thing's people to understand, which he finally calls empathy, to Novaës' understanding of the piano.

"Now I Lay Me Down to Sleep —" (*RS*, 5): traditional bedtime prayer: "Now I lay me down to sleep / I pray the Lord my soul to keep / If I should die before I wake / I pray the Lord my soul to take." In *RS*, Meade Stone begins to recite this prayer as the *Rolling Stone* is about to take off for the first time.

"Now Is the Time for All Good Men" (*RS*, 6): "Now is the time for all good men to come to the aid of their country," long thought to be a typing exercise. In *RS*, Pollux uses the first part of the sentence to suggest that it is time for him and Castor to come to the aid of their brother.

"Number Ten, Downing Street" (*TiS*, 12): London residence of the prime minister of England. In *TiS*, the small, hand-built, rock-walled building the community calls city hall was, when first built, ironically called "Number Ten Downing Street."

O. Henry (*HSS*, 7): pen name of William Sydney Porter (b. 11 September 1862, d. 5 June 1910), famous short-story writer best known for "The Gift of the Magi" and "The Ransom of Red Chief." In *HSS*, as Kip decides to occupy his time in captivity with chess problems and other intellectual pursuits to keep his sanity and to keep from feeling sorry for himself, he reminds himself that while in prison O. Henry wrote short stories, Hitler wrote *Mein Kampf*, and St. Paul wrote epistles. See: **Hilter** and **Saint Paul**.

Oak Ridge, TN (*RSG*, 2; *SC*, 11): established in the early 1940s as a military base for the Manhattan Project to develop the first atomic bomb. Shortly after the end of World War II, Oak Ridge was turned over to the Atomic Energy Commission, and the Department of Energy continues research there. In *RSG*, Heinlein makes working at Oak Ridge a logical part of Dr. Donald Cargraves' background. In *SC*, the *Oak Ridge* is the ship to which Tex is assigned for his first training cruise as a cadet before he wangles a transfer to the *Aes Triplex*.

O.B.E. (*SJ*, 8; *SB*, 2): Order of the British Empire, an award for civil or military service. In *SJ*, it is one of the many honorary titles held by Ellie Coburn's father, an imperial ambassador. In *SB*, Mr. Kiku has an O.B.E. It is an indication of his status. See: **Honoris Causa** and **Oxon**.

Obelisk [Mountains] (*RS*, 5): tall, four-sided monument ending in a four-sided pyramid at the top. The Washington Monument in Washington, DC, is an obelisk. In *RS*, the Obelisk Mountains are near the lunar spaceport.

Obrigado (*PM*, 10): Portuguese for "thank you." In *PM*, Podkayne talks about the effectiveness of the words "thank you," and then lists informal phonetic pronunciations (i.e., "mare-see" for the French "merci") for all of the languages in which she can say the phrase.

Occam's Razor (*TiS*, 11; *HSS*, 4): principle attributed to Franciscan friar William of Occam, a fourteenth-century logician, that states, "Entities should not be multiplied unnecessarily" and currently taken to mean that the simplest explanation or solution is the best one. In *TiS*, Roy Kilroy calls his knife Occam's Razor, an appropriate name for something that can cut away extraneous matter or cut to the heart of things. See: **Bluebeard, Colonel Bowie**, and **Lady Macbeth**. In *HSS*, Peewee suggests that the existence of UFOs is, by the application of Occam's razor, a logical possibility if not probability.

Ochee Chyornya (*ST*, 2): one of several spellings of the Russian words for "dark eyes," made popular in a Russian song of the same name. In *ST*, Johnnie calls Carmen Ibañez "*Ochee Chyornya*," an appropriate Russian label for a dark-eyed Spanish girl.

O.C.S. (*ST*, 11): Officers' Candidate School. In *ST*, one of Johnnie's fellow troopers suggests that he apply to O.C.S. because he has the ability to make it and will be the sort of officer men will willingly follow.

Oeroe (*RP*, 3): Greek water nymph, daughter of the river god Asopus, and the name of a river in Greece. In *RP*, it is the name of a canal on Mars.

Olympian Heights (*SB*, 9): top of Mount Olympus, the home of the gods in Greek mythology. Looking down from Olympian heights is looking down from a very high or godlike perspective. In *SB*, the Rargyllian negotiator suggests that the Hroshii look down on every other species from Olympian heights.

Once in a Blue Moon (*FS*, 8): extremely small chance of something happening; literally, two full moons in one month, something that happens an average of 41 times each century. In *FS*, Bill says that unless a ship went through the Asteroid Belt there wasn't a chance in a blue moon of being hit by a meteor. Of course, that is exactly what happens.

One Can Lead a Child to Knowledge but One *Cannot* Make Him Think (*ST*, 2): parody of the traditional saying "one can lead a horse to water but cannot make him drink." In *ST*, Mr. Dubois challenges and criticizes his students with this saying, meaning that all the memorized knowledge in the world will be of no use unless the students develop critical skills.

One Does Not Dip Water with a Knife (*CG*, 5) *see* **Dip Water With a Knife.**

Operation Samaritan (*SC*, 11) *see* **Good Samaritan.**

Oppernockity Tunes but Once (*PM*, 13): pun and the punch line to a "shaggy dog" joke based on "opportunity knocks once" or "opportunity seldom knocks twice" (proverbs). In *PM*, Podkayne feels that she might have missed an opportunity to escape her captors.

Oregon Boots (*RS*, 13): sturdy logging boots. In *RS*, Roger Stone says he will buy some Oregon boots for when he gets his sons out of jail. His intent, one suspects, is to kick their backsides.

Original Sin (*PM*, 1): according to Christian belief, the sin of Adam and Eve's disobedience that caused them to be exiled from the Garden of Eden and which we are all born with and carry until baptized. In *PM*, Podkayne suggests that she and her uncle have a streak of original sin, referring to their willingness to disregard the rules when they feel it necessary.

Orville and Wilbur (*HSS*, 9): Wilbur (b. 16 April 1867, d. 30 May 1912) and Orville (b. 19 August 1871, d. 30 January 1948) Wright, Americans generally considered the inventors and builders of the first successful airplane. In *HSS*, Heinlein uses the Wright brothers as an example of people who did something a lot of people thought could not be done.

Otis (*TiS*, 2): Elisha Otis (b. 3 August

1811, d. 8 April 1861), inventor of the elevator safety brake and founder of the Otis Elevator Company, the world's largest maker of elevators and escalators. In *TiS*, Heinlein makes the point that Rod Walker does not think about Ramsbotham, the transportation gate's inventor, when he uses it anymore than people of earlier generations thought about Otis when they took an elevator. Ultimately, Heinlein is talking about how people take inventions and technology for granted shortly after they become widespread.

Ouija Board (*RSG*, 19): fortune-telling or future-telling device that consists of a board with letters, numbers, and other symbols on it and a hand-held pointer that moves around to indicate answers from the spirit world to questions asked by whoever is touching the pointer. In *RSG*, Cargraves suggests that the German moon base commander use a Ouija board to find out the powers of a ship's master, a comment which indicates that the commander's fate is already known.

"Our Revels Now Are Ended" (*HSS*, 11) *see* **"These Our Actors …"**

Outback (*CG*, 13): most remote areas of Australia. In *CG*, it is the name of an area on the planet Woolamurra. See: **Cobber** and **Woolamurra.**

Outward Bound (*BP*, 3): ship featured in a Currier and Ives lithograph produced in the 1870s and currently located in the Bancroft Library, Berkeley, California. There is also a 1927 illustration, "Outward Bound," by Norman Rockwell. Heinlein might have been familiar with Rockwell's illustrations, as Heinlein began publishing in the "slick" magazines in the late 1940s, the same magazines, especially the *Saturday Evening Post*, for which Rockwell was doing cover art. See: **Saturday Evening Post.** In *BP*, it is the name of the rocket ship on which Don Harvey was born, the event giving him Federation citizenship rather than citizenship on one planet.

Overalls in the Chowder (*SB*, 13): "Who Put the Overalls in Mrs. Murphy's Chowder?" is a traditional Irish song about finding a pair of overalls at the bottom of a chowder pot during a party, but it is widely used to indicate that someone has ruined or spoiled something. In *SB*, Robbins says that he will tell "where the body is buried, how the apple cart was upset, and who put the overalls in the chowder," all phrases meaning that he will tell secrets that the secretary of Spatial Affairs would not want told.

Ovid (*HSS*, 10): Publius Ovidius Naso (b. 20 March 43 B.C., d. A.D. 17), Roman writer famous for his writings about love and seduction and for his mythological work, *The Metamorphoses*. In *HSS*, Kip says that the legionary captured by the Court of the Three Galaxies speaks a language that is a cross between Spanish and the Latin of Ovid and Caesar. See: **Caesar** and **Legionary.**

Oxford Accent (*RSG*, 13): upper-class British accent characteristic of someone who attended Oxford University. In *RSG*, Helmut von Hartwick, commander at the Nazi base on the moon, assumes an Oxford accent to conceal his true nationality as he attempts to locate the *Galileo* by radio so that his men can destroy it. See: **Lord Haw-Haw.**

Oxford University (*SC*, 5): highly respected British university. In *SC*, Matt comments that an older cadet might be assigned to study at Oxford's radiation laboratories or at the Sorbonne's law school. See: **Sorbonne.**

Oxon (*SB*, 2): short for Oxfordshire (originally Oxonia), a county in England, and used as an abbreviation for degrees from Oxford University. In *SB*, Mr. Kiku has an "M.A. (Oxon)." It is an indication of his status. See: **Honoris Causa** and **O.B.E.**

"Oyez" (*SB*, 4; *CG*, 21): Anglo-Norman directive to listen, literally "to hear," from the French *ouir*. Currently used in court with the meaning "hear ye." In *SB* and *CG*, it is the phrase used to begin court proceedings.

Oz (*PM*, 9): land in which L. Frank Baum (b. 15 May 1856, d. 6 May 1919) set his 1900 novel *The Wonderful Wizard of Oz* and its sequels. In *PM*, Podkayne says that her predominant ideas about Earth came from Oz stories and then she comments that the Oz stories are probably not a reliable portrait of what Earth is really like. She thinks Dorothy's conversations with the Wizard might be instructive but does not think she'll meet a tin woodman. She does, however, comment that there are "Tik-Tocks" (wind-up mechanical men) on Mars, although no one but children call them that. This intersection between Baum's novel and the real world of Mars echoes Heinlein's creation of the word "waldo," which has become a popular term for robotic arms.

OZMA (*PM*, 9): ruler of Oz whose story is told in the series after the first book, *The Wonderful Wizard of Oz*. In *PM*, Podkayne is the center of attention at the Dom Pedro Casino and feels like Ozma after she has ceased being Tip (a boy into whom she had been changed) and has become Ozma again. See: **Oz.**

Padre (*ST*, 1): Spanish for "father (sire)," "creator," or "priest," also traditional military slang for a priest, minister, rabbi, or other religious figure. In *ST*, Heinlein uses it in the military sense.

Pal Maleter (*ST*, 13): Hungarian hero (b. 4 September 1917, d. 16 June 1958) of the 1956 revolution who was seized illegally by the Soviets and executed. In *ST*, it is the name of one of the warships of the Federation fleet.

Palomar Catalog (*TfS*, 13): now the *Palomar MSU* [Michigan State University] *Nearby Star Survey*, a numerical catalog of stars and their properties. In *TfS*, some crew members of the *Lewis and Clark* give stars informal names because it is too complex to refer to each one by its Palomar catalog number.

Palomino (*TiS*: 1): horse with a golden coat and white mane and tail favored as show and parade horses, especially in California and the Southwest. In *TiS*, the leader of a well-equipped group of emigrants rides a "Palomino mare" and is "dressed as a California don"—possibly as a complement to his horse.

Pantywaists (*RS*, 15): literally, a child's garment in which short pants and a shirt are buttoned together at the waist; in slang terms, a sissy (probably because such garments were worn only by young children). In *RS*, Grandma Hazel suggests that the people of Mars are pantywaists, not the hardy frontier settlers she expected. See: **Scissorbills**.

Papoose (*FS*, 5): Native American word for "child," often referring to a child strapped into a cradleboard. In *FS*, a teenager named "Noisy" Edwards is strapped to his bunk in such a way that he cannot free himself after disobeying shipboard rules. See: **Tommyrot**.

Paramagnetics (*PM*, 9): study of a body or substance that, placed in a magnetic field, possesses magnetization in direct proportion to that field's strength. See: **Cambridge** and **Davis Mechanics**.

Paris-Match (*HSS*, 7): French weekly magazine that covers everything from national and international news to celebrity goings-on. See: ***The Anatomy of Melancholy***.

Parlor Pink (*ST*, 12): early- and mid-twentieth century derogatory term applied to one who will talk about being a revolutionary (in this case, communist) in the "parlor" (i.e., the safety of the living room) or one who sympathizes with the communist movement but is unwilling to actually do anything to support it. "Pink" and "Pinko" were applied to those with communist sympathies. In *ST*, one of Johnnie's classmates argues that revolution is now impossible as it requires aggressiveness and the aggressive ones have been separated out into the military where they use their aggressiveness for the government's purposes and leaving only "parlor pinks" to talk about revolution.

Parrot Fever (*TfS*, 5): bacterial infection carried by birds that can be transmitted to humans. See: **Housemaid's Knee**.

Passenger Pigeon (*ST*, 2): once the most common bird in North America, extinct since the late nineteenth and early twentieth centuries as a result of mass hunting of the birds as food for poor people and for pigs. See: **Carthage**.

Pathetic Fallacy (*HSS*, 5): tendency to treat inanimate objects as if they were human and had human emotions and responses. In *HSS*, Peewee says that she understands the pathetic fallacy (as well as fetishism, the belief that an object can have magical powers, and primitive animism, the belief that all objects have spirits in them) but still needs her doll so that she can sleep at night. She says it is a conditioned reflex, something that began to develop before she was aware of it.

Pathfinder (*SC*, 11; *BP*, 2): U.S., British and Canadian military units in World War II that parachuted in first to set up landing zones for the main body of paratroopers; also the title of a James Fennimore Cooper (b. 15 September 1789, d. 14 September 1851) 1840 novel in which Natty Bumpo (Hawkeye) continues his adventures during the French and Indian War. In *SC*, the *Pathfinder*, much like the military units and the Cooper character for which Heinlein may have named it, has been sent to chart a sector of the Asteroid Belt. The *Pathfinder* and has been out of contact for too long, and the *Aes Triplex* is being sent to search for her. See: ***Aes Triplex.*** In *BP*, *Pathfinder* is a ship that will make a one-way trip to settle another planet.

Patrick Henry (*TiS*, 1; *TfS*, 1): one of the radicals of the American Revolution (b. 29 May 1736, d. 6 June 1799), later governor of Virginia, famous for his "give me liberty, or give me death" speech made before the Virginia House of Burgesses in 1775. In *TiS*, Heinlein names Rod Walker's school Patrick Henry High School as part of his continuing parallel of the juvenile series to American history. In this case, Heinlein's reference to Patrick Henry is also an attempt to focus the reader on America's struggle to separate itself from England and, more important, establish its own form of government. The students abandoned and stranded on the planet Tangaroa are on their own and, assuming that they will never be rescued, struggle to develop a form of government that will work for them. See: **Ponce de Leon** and **Tangaroa.** In *TfS*, Pat Bartlett is Patrick Henry Michelangelo Bartlett, his given names coming from his father's interest in American history and his mother's interest in art. See: **Michelangelo.**

Pavlov (*ST*, 12): Ivan Pavlov (b. 14 September 1849, d. 27 February 1936), Russian psychologist and physician most famous for articulating the concept of classical conditioning and for the experiments with dogs that showed that they had a "conditioned reflex" to the presentation of food. Pavlov's name has become synonymous with the conditioned reflex, now called the Pavlovian response. Pavlov was awarded the Nobel Prize in physiology and medicine for his work on the physiology of digestion. In *ST*, Johnnie says that he and the rest of the soldiers fight not like Pavlov's dogs, i.e., by unthinking reaction, but for something that they believe is worth dying for.

Pawpaw (*SJ*, 17): tropical fruit with a mango/banana taste that grows in the southeastern United States. In *SJ*, Max and Ellie are fed a pawpaw-like fruit by the "centaurs" that have captured them.

"Pease Porridge Hot" (*TfS*, 10): "Pease porridge hot, / Pease porridge cold, / Pease porridge in the pot, / Nine days old" (traditional rhyme and, later, a children's folk game). In *TfS*, one of the crewmen tells Tom Bartlett that no one will have any intimacy greater than "Pease Porridge Hot," referring to the children's hand clapping game, with Prudence Mathews until she breaks free from the influence of her twin sister. See: **Galahad**.

Pecking Order (*TfS*, 1; *CG*, 8): method of establishing a hierarchy among birds according to which bird is able or allowed to peck with its beak at another bird. In *TfS*, Tom says that his twin brother, Pat, had "more grab" than he did and was higher in the pecking order. In *CG*, Thorby hits a Trader "cousin" back and is surprised when the cousin almost explodes; Margaret Mader, an anthropologist, says it has to do with "Peck rights."

Pegasus (*SC*, 18): winged horse of Greek mythology; also the insignia of the British 6th Airborne Division. In *SC*, it is the name of the ship that brings Matt and Tex back from Venus.

Percival Lowell (*SC*, 11; *RP*, 2): American astronomer (b. 13 March 1855, d. 12 November 1916) who studied the planet Mars extensively and supported the theory that there were "canals" on Mars as well as other features which suggested that the planet had once been inhabited. In *SC*, Captain Yancey mentions having served on the first *Percival Lowell*. In *RP*, Heinlein notes that the settlers do not use the Martian names for features such as "canals" but use the names given them by Percival Lowell. By doing so, Heinlein is drawing a parallel between the westward movement in the nineteenth-century United States and the outward movement of space exploration and settlement. In both cases, the new settlers use names familiar to them from home rather that adapt or adopt the names the natives used. See: **Canali**.

Persona Non Grata (*SB*, 14): Latin for "a person not welcome." In *SB*, Greenberg finds himself *persona non grata* in the Stuart house after Mrs. Stuart finds out that the Hroshii want Johnnie to go to their planet with them. See: **Hroshii** and **John Thomas [Stuart]**.

Peter and the Wolf (*HSS*, 9): 1936 musical composition by Sergei Prokofiev that tells the story of a young boy who captures a wolf and, as the story progresses, a different instrument plays the musical signature for each separate animal. In *HSS*, Kip feels like he might be caught in the middle of a performance of *Peter and the Wolf* or in a Wagnerian opera as he hears all of the musical voices of the Mother Thing's people. See: **Wagnerian Opera.**

Peter the Great (*TiS*, 1; *TfS* 12): ruler (b. 9 June 1672, d. 8 February 1725) who modernized, transformed, and made Russia a major power in Europe. But his wars abroad and victories over rebels at home cost many lives. In *TiS*, it is the name of one of the main emigration gates to new planets and suggests a transition from the Old World to the New World. See: **Emigrants' Gap** and **Witwatersrand.** In *TfS*, it is the name of a torch ship that shut down its engine for overhaul, could not start it again, and fell into the Sun. See: **Lebensraum [Project]** and *Lewis and Clark.*

Pharisees (*SJ*, 11): New Testament group described as focusing on laws, rules, and status. In *SJ*, Dr. Hendrix tells Max that what he did is not only wrong it is also undignified, and Hendrix then criticizes himself as a Pharisee for saying that. The conversation is part of Heinlein's long critique of the guild system in the novel. See: **Guilds.**

Phi Beta Kappa [Key] (*HSS*, 9): most prestigious of all academic honor societies in the United States, whose members wear a "key" or medallion, often on a watch chain or pinned to a collar or lapel. In *HSS*, Kip mistakenly thinks that the triangular pin worn by the Mother Things and a few others is something like a Phi Beta Kappa Key.

Phoenicians (*CG*, 12): Mediterranean trading culture that flourished between 1500 B.C. and 300 B.C. In *CG*, at one point, the Free Traders use a method of trading at least as old as that of the Phoenicians. In this method, one group puts out the goods it wants to trade and then the other group puts out its goods. Goods are added, subtracted, and rearranged until both sides feel that the trade is acceptable, and then each side takes the other's offerings away. This method works even when neither group speaks the other's language.

Physical Review (*TfS*, 3): journal of the American Physical Society "to advance and diffuse the knowledge of Physics." In *TfS*, a forthcoming article in *Physical Review* will discuss the evidence that telepathic communication is instantaneous, while all other forms have some lag time dependent on distance.

"The Picture of Dorian Gray" (*TfS*, 17): 1890 novel by Oscar Wilde (b. 16 October 1854, d. 30 November 1900) about a man who does not age, no matter how badly he behaves, while a picture of him in the attic does. In *TfS*, the aged Pat Bartlett mentions "The Picture of Dorian Gray" when talking with his brother, Tom, who still appears almost as young as they both were before Tom went off on the *Lewis and Clark*. See: **Lewis and Clark.**

"Pig-Headed" (*SB*, 6): willfully or perversely unyielding, obstinate; being unwilling to change having once made up one's mind. In *SB*, the Rargyllian negotiator considers the Hroshii to be "pig-headed."

Pike's Peak (*SC*, 5; *RS*, 4; *HSS*, 3): Colorado Rocky Mountain peak over 14,000 feet tall, with a base-to-summit elevation gain of almost 7500 feet. Numerous science fiction authors suggested the possibility of launching ships into orbit by catapulting them up tall mountain sides. In *SC*, Heinlein mentions the Pike's Peak catapult and later has Matt report to the Pike's Peak Catapult Station for a flight to Terra Station (10). In *RS*, Castor and Pollux are waiting for gaskets that have to be "jumped" to the moon via Pike's Peak. Later in the novel, the shuttle from Phobos down to the surface of Mars is not like the rocket operating between Pike's Peak and Earth's orbiting space station but more of a glider (11). In *HSS*, Kip mentions the Pike's Peak Hill Climb, a famous race to see which vehicle in each class (car, truck, motorcycle, etc.) can make it to the top the fastest.

Pinhead (*PM*, 13): very dull or stupid person; medically, a microcephalic who might have a tapering head and impaired mental faculties. In *PM*, "Pinhead" is the name Podkayne gives to the drug addicted Venerian keeping her prisoner.

Pinta (*TfS*, 9): one of Christopher Columbus' three ships on the 1492 voyage across the Atlantic Ocean to the New World (the Americas). In *TfS*, it is the name of one of the torch ships. See: **Lebensraum [Project]** and **Lewis and Clark.**

"Pint's a Pound the World 'Round" (*HSS*, 7): mnemonic device to remember that 16 ounces of water weighs approximately one pound. In *HSS*, Kip recites this phrase as he calculates how long it will take his cell to fill up with water so that he can escape out the top.

Pioneer Mothers (*TfS*, 3): name given to the strong and courageous women who helped settle the American West. In *TfS*, Pat uses the term ironically, labeling the female twins that refuse to go into space "Pioneer Mothers" in another instance of Heinlein's continuing parallel of the juvenile series to American history.

Pip (*RP*, 1; *SB*, 16): slight but nonspecific disorder or a skin disease common to tropical climates and characterized by surface lesions. In *RP*, Doctor Macrae tells Jim to sterilize the coffee cups so that no one comes down with the pip. In *SB*, Johnnie tells Betty that her new makeup application makes her look like "a zebra with the pip."

Pitcairn (*CG*, 18): group of islands in the southern Pacific Ocean made famous by the crew of the HMS *Bounty*, who settled there after seizing the ship

Plato

in a mutiny and leaving Captain Bligh and his supporters to survive on their own in one of the ship's boats. In *CG*, it is one of many properties, including a shooting lodge in Canada and a domehouse on Mars, owned by the Rudbeck family, an ownership to illustrate their wealth. See: **Captain Bligh** and **Yukon.**

Plato (*ST*, 12): Greek philosopher (b. 428 or 427 B.C., d. 348 or 347 B.C.) who, as a student of Socrates and teacher of Artistotle, helped found western philosophy. His most important work may be *The Republic*, in which he discusses theories of government and social and individual justice. In *ST*, one of Johnnie's teachers criticizes Plato for promoting an "antlike communism" in *The Republic*.

Plutocrat (*HSS*, 7): person who is able to exercise power by virtue of wealth. In *HSS*, Kip dismisses the idea that the Wormfaces could live on Pluto, punning on the word "plutocrat."

Plymouth Rock Colony (*FS*, 1; *TiS*, 15): colony established in 1620 by a religious group known as the Pilgrims. In *FS*, Bill's father, George, is trying to persuade him to stay on Earth by talking about how dangerous the trip to, and settlement of, Ganymede will be. Bill responds that almost half of the Plymouth Rock colony died in the first year, and as Bill points out, travel by rocket ship to Ganymede will take less time than it took the Pilgrims to cross the Atlantic by sailing ship. This comparison is part of Heinlein's ongoing depiction of the parallel between the exploration and settlement of outer space and the discovery and settlement of the North American continent. See: **Daniel Boone, Johnny Appleseed,** and *Mayflower*. In *TiS*, Deacon Matson tells Rod Walker that, even though he leaves and turns the planet over to professionals, the town they founded will not be lost but will go down in history along with Plymouth Rock, Botany Bay, and Dakin's Colony, the last a future colony from Heinlein's imagination (although the Dakin name might refer to William Dakin, zoologist and, during World War II, camouflage expert). See: **Botany Bay.**

Poetic License (*FS*, 7; *RS*, 2): freedom the audience allows an artist to take in deviating from known fact in order to produce a certain effect. In *FS*, as the boys are organizing Boy Scout troops aboard the *Mayflower*, someone points out that talking about "carrying the scouting trail out to the stars" was nonsense, as Ganymede wasn't a star, and Hank suggests such a statement can be allowed as poetic license. He then comments that carrying scouting to Ganymede is the first step in carrying it to the stars. In *RS*, chapter 2 is entitled "A Case for Dramatic License," and in that chapter, Grandma Hazel defends the outrageous plot she is creating by calling it "dramatic license." See: *The Scourge of the Spaceways.*

Pollard and Davidson (*RSG*, 2): Ernest C. Pollard and William L Davidson, authors of *Applied Nuclear Physics*, published in 1942. This book discusses nuclear energy and speculates on its future uses. In *RSG*, it is a book that could have been read by Heinlein's main characters, as they claim, and his use of actual authors instead of fictional ones is indicative of his attention to detail throughout the series. See: **Gamov.**

Pollux (*RS*, 1): twin brother of Castor in Roman mythology. They were the inseparable twin sons of Leda but by different fathers. Pollux's father was a god, Zeus, and the two brightest stars in Gemini are named for them. In *RS*, Pollux and Castor are sons in the Stone family, the main characters in the novel, and are known as the "unheavenly twins" for their propensity to get into trouble. See: **Castor.**

Polonius (*HSS*, 9) *see* **"Neither a Borrower Nor a Lender Be."**

Ponce de Leon (*TiS*, 4): Juan Ponce de León (b. 1474, d. 1521), Spanish explorer best known for searching for the fountain of youth in what is now the state of Florida. In *TiS*, it is the name of one of the high schools that has sent students on the survival test; the name is thematically appropriate for a high school that is sending its students to an unexplored planet. See: **Patrick Henry** and **Tangaroa.**

Porteño (*ST*, 10): Spanish for someone who lives in a port town or city, especially Buenos Aires. In *ST*, Kip hears that Buenos Aires has been destroyed by the Bugs and feels sorry for the one "Porteño" he knows. Kip will later learn that his mother was in Buenos Aires when it was bombed, perhaps a Heinlein suggestion that such events impact more than just those who happen to be there or from there.

Post Office (*HSS*, 1): kissing game played by young teenagers and preteens at parties as a way of getting to kiss someone without its meaning anything more than a game. In *HSS*, Kip says that he rarely got picked playing post office as a way of evaluating his chances of getting picked from any career to go to work in space or on the Moon.

Power of the Rods and the Ax (*ST*, 12): bundle of wooden rods bound together in a column with an ax blade sticking out, a traditional symbol of power dating back to the Roman Empire. In *ST*, Major Reid invokes the symbol of the rods and the ax to stand for political power or force.

Prairie Schooner (*TiS*: 1): another name for the covered wagons that transported people and goods into the American West, so called because of the arched canvas roof that could look, from a distance, like a sail. See: **Conestoga Wagon.**

Pratique (*SB*, 5): clearance given to an incoming ship by the health authority of the port after compliance with quarantine regulations or the presentation of a clean bill of health. In *SB*, the unexpected quarantine of a ship from Venus has serious political overtones.

Praxiteles (*PM*, 1): Greek sculptor (4th century B.C.) famous for statues of full-figured nude women. In *PM*, Podkayne, talking about her figure, suggests that Praxiteles would not have been interested in her slender shape.

"Prayer for Travelers" (*TfS*, 9): from *The Book of Common Prayer*, dating to the 1500s. In *TfS*, the crew of the *Lewis and Clark* sings the "Prayer for Travelers" after the *Vasco da Gama* is lost.

Predestination (*RS*, 14): belief that all things happen, are happening, and will happen as planned, usually by a deity, and that nothing humans can do will alter what happens. In *RS*, Pollux and his father, Roger, suggest predetermination and free will, respectively, to explain why things happened the way that they did. Castor says that both are very shaky theories.

The Prince of Wales (*SJ*, 3): traditional title of the heir apparent to the British Throne. In *SJ*, the starship *Asgard* was named the *Einstein* and *The Prince of Wales* in earlier configurations. See: **Asgard** and **Einstein**.

The Prisoner at the Bars (*SB*, 4, chapter title): slight modification of the phrase "the prisoner at the bar," which came from the actual bar that separated the lawyers from the common pleaders. In *SB*, Heinlein puns on the phrase, referring to the bars of steel in which Lummox is caged at her trial.

Pro Tem (*FS*, 7): Latin for "for the time" or, more loosely, "temporary." In *FS*, Bill is secretary *pro tem* as a Boy Scout troop is formed on the rocket ship.

"Prometheus Bound" (*CG*, 23): Greek titan who stole fire from the gods, gave it to man, and was condemned by Zeus to be chained to a rock forever and have his liver eaten every day by an eagle. The story has been the subject of many literary versions, including plays by Aeschylus and Shelley and a poem by Goethe. In *CG*, Thorby's identification code word to the military operative with whom he is working to end the slave trade includes "Prometheus Bound," a possible reference to the fact that he has to run his family's huge company and cannot work full time on the slave trade issue. See: ***Merry Widow***.

Promised Land (*FS*, 10): land to which God promises to lead the Israelites. In *FS*, Heinlein uses "Promised Land" as the ironic title of the chapter describing the settlers arrival on Ganymede and their frustration at the limited facilities and the bureaucracy that make their current situation difficult and will keep them from

P.T.A. Auxiliary (*HSS*, 1): student branch of the public school Parent Teacher Association. In *HSS*, Kip is in the auxiliary and has been told that his school is run along the most modern lines. His father's examination of textbooks and curriculum finds that not to be true as Heinlein critiques American education.

Purdah (*CG*, 8): state of isolation; in Muslim or Hindu societies, a system for keeping women separate. In *CG*, the society of the Free Traders has a complex system of rules based on genealogy that defines which males and females can marry. See: **Free Traders.**

"The Purloined Letter" (*HSS*, 8): 1844 short story by Edgar Allan Poe (b. 19 January 1809, d. 7 October 1849) in which a missing letter is left in plain sight in such a way that it will be overlooked by anyone hunting for it. In *HSS*, Kip remarks that the Wormfaces' hiding Peewee's small space suit inside Jock's larger one was a "purloined letter" gambit.

Put a Flea [Bug] in His [Your] Ear (*RP*, 9; *TiS*, 15): plant an idea in someone's mind. In *RP*, Frank's father says that he put a flea in the ear of the company resident agent who wants to arrest the boys. Given Frank's father's straightforward nature, he probably told the director what he would do if someone tried to arrest his son. In *TiS*, Rod is advised not to sign anything without fully investigating it. See: **Flea in Your Ear.**

"Put Not Your Faith in Princes" (*PM*, 11): "Put not your trust in princes, nor in the son of man, in whom there is not help" (Psalm 146:3). In this case, "the son of man" means other human beings. In *PM*, Podkayne's uncle suggests that the corporation on Venus lived by this dictum but understands it to mean that they should buy and sell without asking questions.

Putzie (*SJ*, 17): A Yiddish term, "Putz" has come to mean "foolish" or "worthless" person. In *SJ*, Ellie's boyfriend back on Hespera is named Putzie. After her failed romance with Max, and partly because he will go on to become an astrogator, she returns home at the end of the novel and marries him. Knowing Ellie's determination to have things her way, Max feels a bit sorry for Putzie.

P.W.s (*HSS*, 8; *ST*, 12): prisoners of war. In *HSS*, Kip differentiates between Peewee and the Mother Thing as hostages versus himself and the two gangsters as P.W.s. In *ST*, a discussion of prisoners of war leads to the conclusion that the number does not matter and that even if there is only one prisoner he or she must be rescued.

Quaker (*TiS*, 8): member of the Religious Society of Friends, more popularly known as the Quakers, a movement dating to the seventeenth century in England and long known

Quality

for social activism from protesting the slave trade to campaigning for minority rights to protesting war. In *TiS*, one couple is identified as Quakers.

"Quality of Mercy Is Not Strained, It Droppeth as the Gentle Rain from Heaven" (*TiS*, 2): from Shakespeare's 1596/1597 comedy, *The Merchant of Venice*. "The quality of mercy is not strained. / It droppeth as the gentle rain from heaven / Upon the place beneath. It is twice blest: / It blesseth him that gives, and him that takes" (IV, i, 179–182). In *TiS*, Helen Walker uses these lines as part of an argument with her superior officer that one of the women under her command should not be dealt with too harshly.

Queen Mary (*RS*, 6): most famously a British luxury liner, named for Mary (b. 20 May 1867, d. 24 March 1953), the consort of King George V (b. 3 June 1865, d. 20 January 1936), and now in permanent residence in Long Beach, CA. In *RS*, it is the name of a spaceship in transit near the *Rolling Stone*.

Queen of Sheeba (*FS*, 19): queen who traveled to Israel to ask questions of Solomon. She was reported to have been very rich and beautiful. In *FS*, Bill, sick with appendicitis, refuses to get up and see the alien artifacts that Hank has found, stating that he would not even "want to see the Queen of Sheeba."

"¿*Quién Es La Señorita?*" (*RP*, 4): Spanish for "who is that girl?" In *RP*, it is the title of a song that Willis repeats after hearing the record, an action that aggravates the friction between Jim Marlowe and Marquis Howe. See: **James Madison [Marlowe]** and **Marquis Howe**.

Quonset Hut (*RSG*, 13): developed for the military during World War II as cheap, lightweight, structures that could be erected by unskilled labor. The George A. Fuller construction company produced the huts near Quonset, Rhode Island. The huts had semicircular walls and flat ends; the standard huts were about 20 feet wide at the base, 48 feet long, and looked like a tube half sunk into the ground. After the war, the army sold Quonset huts to the public for use as everything from private homes to university student housing. In American popular speech, "Quonset hut" can refer to any inexpensive dwelling. Lightweight and collapsible, the Quonset hut is the perfect living space for Cargraves and the boys to erect on the moon in *RSG*.

Radio Paris (*RSG*, 13): French radio station best known for its broadcasts during World War II that promoted and propagandized the German and Italian war efforts. As with Berlin Sender, Heinlein sees this radio station in *RSG* reestablishing itself in the free world after the war. See: **NAA** and **Berlin Sender**.

Raising Cain (*FS*, 2) *see* **Cain**.

Rajah (*SB*, 1): Indian prince or Hindu noble. In *SB*, Johnnie is described as riding like "a rajah ready for a tiger hunt" on Lummox. The implied comparison of Lummox to an elephant gives some indication of Lummox's size.

Raleigh ["Sandman"] (*RS*, 8): major importer of multispeed (usually three speeds with hand brakes), lightweight "English" bicycles in the 1950s. In *RS*, the "Sandman" model is Heinlein's invention, but it is appropriately named in regard to its intended use on the deserts of Mars.

RCA New York (*RS*, 2): Radio Corporation of America, founded in the early twentieth century as an electronics company producing radios first, as the name suggests, and then branching into other electronic media. In *RS*, Roger Stone, and later Grandma Hazel, send their scripts to RCA New York. See: ***The Scourge of the Spaceways.***

Red Queen (*RP*, 14) *see* **Emulate the Red Queen.**

Reductio Ad Absurdum (*SB*, 13): Latin for "reduction to the absurd," an argumentative strategy that shows the conclusion to be false and therefore the premise or proposition also false, or disproof of a proposition or premise by showing that it leads to an absurd conclusion. In *SB*, Mr. Kiku uses that argumentative strategy with his boss, the secretary for Spatial Affairs.

Reeling, Writhing, and Fainting in Coils (*RS*, 8): some of the subjects the Mock Turtle says he was taught in school in Lewis Carroll's satire on education in *Alice in Wonderland* (chapter 9). In *RS*, these are the humorous suggestions for the subjects that young Lowell will study unless his mother opts for something else. See: **Alice** and **Lewis Carroll.**

"Le Regiment de Sambre et Meuse" (*ST*, 4): 1879 military march by Joseph Rauski based on words by Paul Cezano and music by Robert Planquette written after the Franco–Prussian War in honor of the bravery of the French conscripted soldiers. The march is played at West Point graduations and was made part of the Ohio State University marching band's repertoire by Eugene Weigel, who had learned it playing in the navy band during World War I. In *ST*, it is one of the songs the trainees sing, along with "The Caisson Song" and "The Halls of Montezuma," as they march back to camp from an overnight field maneuver. Johnnie comments that the music raises the men's spirits in addition to moving them along. Later in the novel, they sing "Marseillaise" "Madelon," "Sons of Toil and Danger, "Legion Étrangère," and "Mademoiselle from Armentières." Also, the bagpipers play "Alamein Dead." All are songs that have connections to specific military engagements (6). See individual titles.

Reich and New Reich (*RSG*, 19): German moon-base commander's terms for the government they will establish after conquering Earth. See: **National Socialist Reich** and **Nazis.**

Renshaw (*CG*, 3): Dr. Samuel G. Renshaw (b. 1892, d. 1981), Ohio State University researcher in learning and memory whose theories are still controversial even though his methods produced astounding results. Renshaw's work with navy personnel during World War II is considered to have saved lives and material. In *CG*, Baslim the Cripple trains Thorby to be a fast reader and have total recall using Renshaw's techniques.

Rensselaer (*HSS*, 3): Rensselaer Polytechnic Institute, commonly referred to as RPI, an engineering university located in Troy, New York. In *HSS*, it is one of the universities that reject Kip.

Repple-Depple (*ST*, 11): army slang for "replacement depot," the place where supplies and men are picked up to replace what has been lost on a mission.

The Republic (*ST*, 12) *see* **Plato.**

Richard E. Byrd (*TfS*, 6): American aviator and polar explorer (b. 25 October 1888, d. 11 March 1957), participant and leader of several Antarctic expeditions. In *TfS*, it is the name of one of the torch ships. See: **Lebensraum [Project]** and ***Lewis and Clark.***

Richardson (*RS*, 14): possibly Lewis F. Richardson (b. 11 October 1881, d. 30 September 1953), English physicist, psychologist, meteorologist, and pacifist who investigated mathematical methods of weather forecasting and attempted to apply the same methods to the study of the causes of war. In *RS*, Lowell goes to the settlement of Richardson to meet a Martian. There are actually Richardson craters on the moon and on Mars.

Richardson Medal (*TfS*, 17): medal given by the Optical Society of America for advances in the science and technology of light. In *TfS*, the members of the returning crew of the *Lewis and Clark* are given Richardson Medals. Interestingly, an actual Richardson Medal from the OSA was first given in 1966. Even though the OSA had been founded in 1916, Heinlein could have known about the society but would have made up the medal for his 1956 book. There is also a much newer Richardson Medal given occasionally by the International Glaciological Society. And there are others. Heinlein might also have named the medal for Lewis Richardson. See: **Richardson.**

Ring [Hotel] (*TfS*, 8): luxury hotel in the central district of Vienna, Austria. In *TfS*, Dr. Babcock claims that he wishes he had stayed in Vienna and asks Tom Bartlett if he has ever had coffee and pastries at that hotel.

Rio Grande (*HSS*, 10): river that forms some of the boundary between the United States and Mexico. In *HSS*, Kip says that he has not traveled much and has not even been "south of the Rio Grande," which would not have been too far from his home in Missouri.

Rip Van Winkle (*TfS*, 17): main character in the 1819 short story of the same name by Washington Irving (b. 3 April 1783, d. 28 November 1859) who thought he had spent a day in the Catskill Mountains bowling with little men and came home to find that twenty years have passed, his wife has died, his children are grown, and many of his friends are gone. In *TfS*, the crew of the *Lewis and Clark*, and the crews of the other torch ships, are called "Rip Van Winkles" because they seem not to have aged, while their Earth counterparts are very old or gone. See: **Lewis and Clark.**

Roanoke (*FS*, 11): early British colony in North Carolina that disappeared in a three-year period between supply ships. No evidence has ever been found that explains what happened to the colony. In *FS*, George points out that things are tough but that other colonies, like the Roanoke colony, disappeared without much of a trace left behind.

Robber Barons (*RS*, 4): nineteenth-century American capitalists who created huge fortunes for themselves through various unfair and cutthroat business practices. In modern slang, anyone who uses questionable business practices to become rich. In *RS*, Roger Stone refers to Castor and Pollux as robber barons when they first approach him about carrying cargo on the *Rolling Stone,* cargo they might sell for a profit on other planets.

Robinson Crusoe (*SJ*, 15): main character in the 1719 novel of the same name by Daniel Defoe (b. 1660, d. 24 April 1731) about a man who spends almost three decades on a desert island. In *SJ*, Ellie thinks that settling on a new planet out of touch with the rest of humanity will be like being Robinson Crusoe. See: **Swiss Family Robinson.**

Rodger Young [Range] (*RS*, 5; *ST*, 1): Rodger Young died in the Solomon Islands during World War II. His actions saved the rest of his platoon, and for that he was awarded the Medal of Honor. In *RS*, a range of mountains near the spaceport is named for him. In *ST*, the *Rodger Young* is the ship on which Johnnie Rico sees action. Heinlein added an endnote to *ST* explaining who Rodger Young was and what he had done to earn the Medal of Honor.

Rog (*ST*, 13) *see* **Rodger Young [Range].**

The Rolling Stones (*RS,* cover): title of Heinlein's sixth juvenile book. The title of the novel refers to the last name of the family members who are the main characters, but it is also a play on the proverb "a rolling stone gathers no moss," as the plot of the novel is structured by the Stone family's travels within the solar system. See: **Cherub, Roma, Terra.**

Rolls (*PM*, 9): short version of Rolls-Royce, considered by many to be the epitome of expensive luxury vehicles. In *PM*, Podkayne and her uncle and brother ride to their hotel in the chairman of the board's Rolls, and she interprets it as a sign of her uncle's importance.

Roman Judge (*RS*, 9): judge in the classical Roman courts whose word was final. In *RS*, Roger Stone calls his wife, a medical doctor, a Roman judge, indicating that her decision was the final one in medical matters.

Romany [Lass] (*CG*, 3; *PM*, 9): also called Romani, a people with origins in South Asia who have widely dispersed over the centuries, especially throughout Europe, and are more commonly known as Gypsies. In *CG*, *Romany Lass* is the name of a spaceship of the Free Traders, a group who, like the Gypsies, have no fixed homes but travel, in this case throughout the galaxy trading with people on various planets. See: **Free Traders** and **Hansea.** In *PM*, "Romany Rose" is the stage name of a singer at the Dom Pedro Casino. See: **Dom Pedro.**

Romeo and Juliet (*TfS*, 7; *PM*, 10): main characters in Shakespeare's 1591/1595 tragedy, *Romeo and Juliet*, each of whom committed suicide rather than be without the other. In *TfS*, Tom Bartlett says that if Romeo and Juliet were the only crew of a spaceship on a multiyear cruise that by the end of the trip "even Juliet would start showing black widow blood." The idea of Juliet killing Romeo is the exact opposite of what happens in Shakespeare's drama, and Heinlein's intent here is to explain why torch ships like the *Lewis and Clark* had two hundred or more in the crew. In *PM*, Podkayne asserts that her reaction to and relationship with Dexter will not be of the Romeo and Juliet kind, in which love obliterates common sense.

Route 66 (*RSG*, 5; *BP*, 2): famous highway that runs from Chicago to Los Angeles through Missouri, Kansas, Oklahoma, Texas, New Mexico, and Arizona. It was also the subject of a popular 1946 song by Bobby Troup, "Get Your Kicks on Route 66," and after the publication of *BP*, a 1960–1964 television series, *Route 66*. In *RSG*, it is a highway near where Donald Cargraves and the boys will build their rocket ship. In *BP*, it is the name of a shuttle rocket that serves the southwest United States. See: **Santa Fé Trail.**

Rubberneck (*SC*, 7; *TiS*, 1): slang describing people trying to watch something by craning or stretching their necks to get a better view. In *SC*, the instructor taking the cadets on their first walk in space suits tells them to stop "rubbernecking" and move around. In *TiS*, Rod stops at Emigrants' Gap to "rubberneck," i.e., watch people going through gateways to other worlds.

Rudyard Kipling (*ST*, 7) *see* **Kipling.**

Russell Diagram (*HSS*, 9): The Hertzprung-Russell diagram ranks each star according to brightness, temperature, and color. In *HSS*, the Vegan sunlight is very high on the Russell diagram and, therefore, almost intolerable for humans.

Russia 1917 (*ST*, 12): Russian revolutions that destroyed the tsar and his autocratic rule and led, eventually, to the establishment of the Soviet Union. In *ST*, Heinlein suggests that the government in the novel came about because former soldiers stepped in when the existing governments collapsed and organized a government in which only veterans could vote. Heinlein has received a lot of negative criticism for proposing this government, but careful readers will note that he justifies the government in *ST*, not philosophically, as the accusations have suggested, but by saying that the system continues because it works satisfactorily. See: **Yin and Yang.**

Russian Roulette (*RS*, 15; *SB*, 12; *TfS*, 4): "game" in which a person holds a six-shot revolver with a bullet in only one chamber (which is then spun so that no one knows where in the cylinder the bullet is) up to his head and pulls the trigger. More popularly, the term is applied to any situation in which someone chooses to take such a risk. In *RS*, living in the Asteroid Belt without a meteor shield is like playing Russian roulette: eventually a meteor will hit you. In *SB*, Mr. Kiku, the experienced under secretary for Spatial Affairs, defies his political appointee superior, saying that he will not play Russian roulette with Earth at stake. See: **Hroshii** and *Take Me Out to the Ball Game.* In *TfS*, Uncle Steve says that space exploration is like Russian roulette: "[Y]ou can win and win, but if you keep on, it will kill you, certain."

S-trajectories (*RSG*, 8): equations used to calculate any and all aspects of flight trajectories. Most of the equations can be used to calculate launch velocity, height of trajectory, time of flight, and landing site, but these equations can also be used to calculate trajectories for freefall and other space travel situations. In *RSG*, Morrie says that he's calculated those and Hohmann orbits until he is sick of them. See: **Hohmann Orbit.**

Saint Barbara (*SC*, 4): Christian saint and martyr, died ca. A.D. 200. Perhaps because of her association with lightning, she is the patron saint of artillerymen, military engineers, miners, and others who work with explosives or are in danger of death from thunderstorms and fires. Early in *SC*, a memorial service in which Saint Barbara is "asked to intercede for the souls of the men who were lost" is held for cadets who died in a rocket crash.

St. Bernard (*TiS*, 9): large breed of dog, averaging about 200 pounds,

Saint

commonly associated with rescue missions in the snowy Alps and often pictured with a flask of brandy around its neck. In *TiS*, the first house built by the stranded students would have been about right as a doghouse for a St. Bernard.

Saint Christopher (*CG*, 14): Roman Catholic figure, once considered a saint, best known for carrying a young Jesus Christ across a difficult river on his back, a feat that made him the patron saint of travelers. In *CG*, it is the name of one of the ships of the Free Traders and an appropriate one for a ship that travels the galaxy. See: **Free Traders** and ***Hansea***.

Saint Cyr (*ST*, 12): École Spéciale Militaire de Saint-Cyr, French for "Special Military School of Saint Cyr," the foremost military academy in France, founded in 1803 by Napoleon. In *ST*, it is an example of a military school that produces officers who have seen no previous military service, as opposed to the Federation, which requires that all officers come from the ranks of the trained troopers. See: **Sandhurst** and **West Point**.

Saint George (*FS*, 7): most popular as a dragon slayer and patron saint of the English monarchy. In *FS*, an English boy proposes the name for the scout troop, which sets off a conflict with an Irish boy. See: **Baden-Powell** and **Saint Patrick**.

Saint Louis (*CG*, 14): Missouri city on the Mississippi River named for King Louis IX of France that became a major river port as well as a jumping-off point for westward-bound wagon trains in the second half of the nineteenth century. In *CG*, it is the name of one of the ships of the Free Traders. See: **Free Traders** and ***Hansea***.

Saint Nicholas (*PM*, 9): historical Christian saint (b. ca. 270, d. ca. A.D. 347) of Greek extraction, known for his anonymous gift giving, on whom the modern Santa Claus is based. In *PM*, Podkayne remarks that the chairman of the board on Venus looks like Saint Nicholas.

Saint Patrick (*FS*, 7): patron saint of Ireland, best known for supposedly driving the snakes from the island. In *FS*, an Irish boy proposes the name for the scout troop in opposition to a boy who wants to name the troop for Saint George. See: **Baden-Powell** and **Saint George**.

Saint Paul (*HSS*, 7): Paul the Apostle (b. 4 B.C., d. ca A.D. 62–64), probably best known for his dramatic conversion to Christianity and for his epistles. See: **Hitler** and **O. Henry**.

Samaritan (*SC*, 11) *see* **Good Samaritan**.

"Samson in the Temple" (*PM*, Postlude): biblical story in which Samson's dying act is to bring down the Phillistine temple to which he has been chained. In *PM*, Podkayne's brother says that he should have returned to disarm the bomb that he had originally planned to use, like Samson, to destroy himself and his captors as a last resort. But because he did not do so, the bomb went off and killed Podkayne (in Heinlein's original version) or nearly killed her (a revision required by the first publisher of the novel).

San Martin (*ST*, 12): José de San Martín (b. 25 February 1778, d. 17 August 1850), along with Simón Bolívar, one of the leaders of South America's struggle for freedom from Spain. In *ST*, it is the name of the boot camp at which Johnnie's father trained.

Sandhurst (*ST*, 12): Royal Military Academy at Sandhurst, England's foremost military academy since 1802. Founded as the Royal Military College, the name was changed to Sandhurst in 1947. See: **Saint Cyr** and **West Point**.

Sandia Weapons Center (*BP*, 2): Sandia National Laboratories, established in 1949 to develop science-based technologies that support national security (www.sandia.gov). In *BP*, the transport that Don Harvey takes from Albuquerque to Chicago has to detour around Sandia Weapons Center.

Sandino (*ST*, 13): Augusto César Sandino (b. 18 May 1893, d. 23 February 1934), hero throughout Latin America for his rebellion against the U.S. military in Nicaragua (1927–1933). The current Sandinistas take their name from him. In *ST*, *Sandino*

is the name of one of the warships of the Federation fleet named for specific foot soldiers.

Sans Peur et Sans Reproche (*HSS*, 5): French phrase meaning "without fear and without reproach (blame)" or "beyond fear and beyond reproach" specifically applied to the French knight Chevalier de Bayard (b. 1473, d. 1524). In *HSS*, Kip applies this phrase to himself, somewhat humorously but also somewhat seriously, as Peewee's rescuer and protector. See: **King Arthur's Court.**

Santa Fé Trail (*BP*, 2): nineteenth-century route that connected several Missouri towns to Santa Fé, New Mexico. In *BP*, Don Harvey rides a winged rocket named *Santa Fé Trail* from his school in New Mexico to New Chicago, just south of Old Chicago, a radioactive field from some war that has concluded before the novel opened. See: **Abe Lincoln, Bedloe Crater, Route 66,** and **Statue of Liberty.**

Santa Maria (*SC*, 17; *TfS*, 9): Columbus' flagship on his first voyage. In *SC*, Tex compares the voyage of the astronauts in the *Astarte* to the voyage of Columbus in the *Santa Maria*. Oscar then comments: "They were men in those days"— a comment often made about how difficult things were for explorers in previous ages and how much more rugged they must have been. See: **Columbus.** In *TfS*, it is the name of one of the torch ships. See:

Lebensraum [Project] and ***Lewis and Clark***.

Sargon the Great (*ST*, 7) *see* **Sargon the Second**.

Sargon the Second (*TfS*, 7; *CG*, 1; *ST*, 7): Assyrian king (reign, 721–705 B.C.) who conquered a number of cities in Syria and Palestine, made captives of ten tribes of Israelis that became known as the Lost Tribes, and was known for his cruelty (2 Kings 17:6). In *TfS*, Tom Bartlett takes a history course from the captain of the *Lewis and Clark* and is impressed with his knowledge, commenting that, "he knew Sargon the Second and Socrates like brothers." Here, as in most of the juvenile series, Heinlein is extolling the importance of a good and broad education. In *CG*, Sargon is the capital of the Nine Worlds, an association of planets far from Earth and, more important, the home of the slave market where Thorby is sold to Baslim the Cripple. In *ST*, Johnnie refers to Sargon's conquest of the Sumerians.

The Saturday Evening Post (*SC*, 17): major American magazine publishing fiction, poetry, essays, articles, cartoons. The *Saturday Evening Post* was an elite short story market in the 1940s, and Heinlein published several short stories there, one of the first science fiction writers to begin publishing regularly in what were called the "slick" magazines. Heinlein's reference to a 1971 *Saturday Evening Post* in *SC* came two years after his first publication in that magazine and may be a small tribute to it.

"Sauve Qui Peut!" (*ST*, 10): French for "mad rush" or "stampede"; as a command, "Run for your life!" In *ST*, as the military raid on Klendathu turns into a shambles, this call is broadcast to tell whoever is still alive to make for the nearest transport and save himself.

La Savate (*TiS*, 14; *ST*, 5): style of fighting that combines traditional boxing and kickboxing maneuvers; *savate* is French for "shoe." In *TiS*, the students taking the survival test use *savate* and *shinobi* moves when they fight. In *ST*, it is one of the many fighting techniques Johnnie has to learn. See: **"Le Regiment de Sambre et Meuse"** and **Shinobi**.

Savoir-Faire (*PM*, 9): French for "knowing how to do [things]," especially a polished sureness in social behavior. In *PM*, Dexter tells Podkayne that she has savoir-faire.

"Scandal to the Jaybirds" (*SB*, 6): event or action so bad that it would be a scandal to creatures as foolish and silly as jaybirds. In *SB*, an Earth contact with the Hroshii would have been such an action. This is one of Heinlein's many attempts to show that humans might not be the most powerful race in the universe.

Schiaparelli (*BP*, 10): Giovanni Schiaparelli (b. 14 March 1835, d. 4 July

1910), Italian astronomer who observed, mapped, and wrote about Mars. It was Schiaparelli who called the lines that run across the surface of Mars "canali," by which he probably meant channels. However, Percival Lowell, among others, seized on the idea of canals on Mars as proof that there was, or at least there had been, some life on that planet. In *BP*, a communications station on Mars is named Schiaparelli Station. See: **Canali** and **Percival Lowell.**

Schnook (*RS*, 4): a stupid or easily duped person. In *RS*, Roger Stone says that his family all think that he is a schnook but asserts that he is not and that he is going to be in charge of this trip to other planets.

Scientific Method (*RSG*, 10): process for experimentation that constructs a hypothesis, conducts an experiment, analyzes the data, and draws a conclusion as to the validity of the hypothesis. In the discussion about proving that the far side of the moon is like the observed side in *RSG*, Cargraves suggests that the only way to know what the far side of the moon looks like is from experience, i.e., the scientific method. See: **Green Cheese.**

Scissorbills (*RS*, 15): small birds that fly along the top of the water and skim out small fish with their lower bills. In *RS*, Grandma Hazel suggests that the people on Mars are scissorbills, skimming money from the tourists. See: **Pantywaists.**

The Scourge of the Spaceways (*RS*, 1; *HSS*, 8): very profitable serial that Roger Stone is writing for the media but which he does not consider literature as it is primarily action-adventure plots with little or no believability or science. The term "space opera" has been applied to such fiction, suggesting that it has as little intellectual and artistic weight as the "soap operas" that have long been popular on radio and then television that were initially sponsored by soap manufacturers. Contrasting "space operas" to quality science fiction is something Heinlein does throughout the juvenile series. See: *Ivanhoe* and *The Mill on the Floss.* In *HSS*, Kip hears his space suit insulting him with this title and the equally insulting "Commander Comet" in an effort to goad him into getting up and continuing back toward shelter on Pluto. See: **Comic Strip.**

The Scum of the Waste Spaces (*RS*, 7): Roger Stone's mocking reference to *The Scourge of the Spaceways.*

Sears & Montgomery (*RS*, 5): Sears, Roebuck and Montgomery Ward, both founded in the late nineteenth century and rival department stores throughout the twentieth. In *RS*, Sears & Montgomery is one company that sells bicycles, among other things, on the moon.

Selenites (*SC*, 6; *TiS*, 12): former inhabitants of the moon who may have exterminated themselves by atomic

Semper

warfare (see *RSG*, 11). In *SC*, Matt does not understand why he has to study lunar archeology, as the Selenites have been dead for centuries, but his tutor says that it will keep his mind loosened up. Heinlein was a believer in a well-rounded education — as the cultural items in the juvenile series indicate. In *TiS*, during a discussion of the cave dwellings, someone asks where the original inhabitants went, and Roy Kilroy says that the same question might be asked about the Selenites and the Mithrans (people who once lived on the planet Mithras).

Semper Toujours (*PM*, 8): Latin/French combination that can be translated as "always, always." In *PM*, Clark questions Podkayne's desire to be a spaceship captain and closes with this phrase. "Semper" is most famous currently as part of "Semper Fidelis," the United States Marine Corps' motto, "Always Faithful." "Toujours" appears in many French phrases and idioms, such as "toujours amour," or "love always."

Serendipity (*TfS*, 16): finding of valuable or agreeable things for which one was not looking. In *TfS*, it is the name of the "irrelevant" ship that comes to bring the crew of the *Lewis and Clark* back home and, with other such ships, to take over the search for inhabitable planets. Irrelevant ships are the serendipitous result of the research on time and space possible because the telepaths were on Earth and onboard the torch ships, the former able to communicate instantaneously as the latter traveled more and more light years from Earth. Heinlein probably calls them "irrelevant" spaceships because they ignore or transcend Einstein's Theory of Relativity.

Shakespeare (*RS*, 2; *SJ*, 9): William Shakespeare (b. 26 April 1564, d. 23 April 1616), English playwright and poet. In *RS*, Grandma Hazel humorously worries that Shakespeare might sue her for stealing from his plays to write *The Scourge of the Spaceways*. See: **Hamlet** and ***The Scourge of the Spaceways.*** In *SJ*, Dr. Hendrix tests Max's memory by asking him to recite specific passages from *A Winter's Tale*, a Shakespeare play which Max had not read in years. Lines from and titles of Shakespeare's plays appear in several of the other novels, but Shakespeare's name does not.

Shakysides (*SC*, 9): one of four ships in a practice squadron used at the U.S. Naval Academy at Annapolis in the 1920s, according to what purports to be an excerpt from the 1926 yearbook from the academy. But both the tone of the piece and the places named suggest that this is a lampoon of the real thing. Still, Heinlein, at the naval academy from 1925 to 1929, may have gotten the name *Shakysides* from this source and used it as the cadets' name for the ship that takes them on a training cruise to the moon in *SC*. (www.e-yearbook.com/yearbooks/United_States_Naval_Academy_Lucky_Bag_Yearbook/1926/Page_302.html).

Shandy (*TfS*, 4): drink usually made with one part beer and one part ginger ale or lemonade; additions to the beer can vary. In *TfS*, Pat and Tom's Uncle Steve has a Martian shandy.

Shank's Ponies (*BP*, 9; *RS*, 5; *SJ*, 1): traveling on one's own feet, more commonly "shank's mare" in American slang. In all three references, travel by foot is necessary because there is no other means (*BP* and *RS*) or because travel by other methods is too expensive (*SJ*).

Share Croppers (*FS*, 11 chapter title and passim): people who live on someone else's land and receive housing, seeds, tools, and such which they pay for by "sharing" the crop with the landowner. In *FS*, the newly arrived colonists discover that there are too many of them to be set up in individual farms right away and many will have to be sharecroppers for some period of time, a situation which does not sit well with some of them.

Sheol (*ST*, 11): Hebrew word for the grave, the pit, or, more metaphorically, the afterlife. In *ST*, it is the name of one of the planets occupied by the Bugs.

Shillelagh (*HSS*, 5): wooden walking stick with a clubbed handle, can be used as a weapon. In *HSS*, Kip suggests that Peewee go for help while he guards the door with a shillelagh.

"Shines the Name, Shines the Name of Rodger Young" (*ST*, 13): line from "The Ballad of Rodger Young," Frank Loesser (b. 29 June 1910, d. 28 July 1969). In *ST*, it is the music that signals Johnnie that it is time for him to board his ship. Later in *ST*, the ship's captain plays another line from the song "To the Everlasting Glory of the Infantry," as Johnnie's platoon is getting ready to make a drop (14). See: **Rodger Young.**

Shingle Cut (*SB*, 5): straight hairstyle introduced in the 1920s that features short locks at the neck and increasingly longer locks as the cut progresses upward on the head so that the upper locks overlay the lower ones as upper shingles on a roof overlay lower ones. In *SB*, Mr. Kiku smiles at the thought of the Rargyllian translator, Dr. Ftaeml, with a shingle cut instead of the long tendrils that remind Mr. Kiku of the snake-headed Medusa.

Shinobi (*TiS*, 14): more commonly known as ninja, a style of fighting that uses unorthodox methodology and weapons (as opposed to the samurai and their strict rules of honor and conduct). See: ***La Savate.***

Shyster (*SJ*, 5): person, usually a lawyer, who uses unethical or unscrupulous methods or tactics. In *SJ*, Sam suggests that Max hire a shyster to get back his farm or the money that came from the sale of it.

Sibelius (*RP*, 3): Jean Sibelius, born Johan Julius Christian Sibelius (b. 8 December 1865, d. 20 September 1957), Finnish composer of the later

Romantic period and one of the most notable composers of the late 19th and early 20th centuries. His best-known work is the symphony *Finlandia*, and many of his pieces were inspired by the Finnish national epic, *The Kalevala*. His music played an important role in the formation of Finnish national identity. In *RP*, a transport driver on Mars is playing Sibelius, and Heinlein comments on the fact that the Mars colony is too new to have developed its own national or patriotic arts.

Siberia (*ST*, 4): cold and desolate area of the Soviet Union famous as a place to which political prisoners were sent. In *ST*, Johnnie wants his military companions to be from Camp Currie, where he trained, or its Siberian equivalent.

Sic Transit Gloria Mundi (*SJ*, 12): Latin for "and so the glory of this world shall fade" or "thus passes the glory of the world." In *SJ*, Sam uses this phrase to describe his having been busted in rank and then makes a pun, playing on the Mundi/Monday similarity, that Tuesdays are "usually worse."

Side Meat (*SJ*, 1): slab of meat taken from the side of a pig that can be salted for salt pork or smoked for bacon and is often a staple in poor, rural diets. In *SJ*, Max slices up side meat, which he cooks over a wood stove, and serves with eggs, biscuits, and coffee in a typical rural supper. See: **Barn Dances, Huskings, Squirrel Gun,** and **"Wagon Room."**

Silly Billy (BP, 12; *PM*, 13): silly or foolish person, a person who makes no sense; also, a billy goat with no sense. In *SB*, one of the Earth soldiers hunting Don Harvey refers to the "move-overs," sheep- or goat-like creatures among whom Don is successfully hiding, as "silly billies." In *PM*, Mrs. Grew calls Podkayne a "silly billy" for thinking that she can communicate with her Uncle Tom, whom Mrs. Grew has also captured.

Simón Bolívar (*SC*, 5; *SB*, 2; *ST*, 13): known as the "Liberator," (b. 24 July 1783, d. 17 December 1830) and credited as a leading figure in Spanish South America's fight for independence. Many South American countries consider him to be a national hero. In *SC*, the transport that takes the cadets from Terra Base to the P.R.S. *James Randolph* is named for him, by which Heinlein begins to depict his belief that a peaceful and united Earth as being necessary before real space travel can begin (as did other science fiction writers such as Arthur C. Clarke). In *SB*, it is the name of a starship that would be lost in unknown space and wander for years. In *ST*, it is the name of one of the Federation warships in the fleet.

Simon Legree (*RSG*, 5): cruel plantation owner in Harriet Beecher Stowe's (b. 14 June 1811, d. 1 July 1896) 1852 antislavery novel, *Uncle Tom's Cabin*, whose name has passed into common usage to denote someone considered to be a "slave driver," that is, someone who works others cruelly or unusually hard. In *RSG*, Ross calls Art "Simon Legree," using the name in a humorous or ironic way, when Art tries to get him up in the morning.

Sinister (*PM*, 9): referring to the left, as in left-handed or the left side of something; also, threatening or suggesting the possibility of evil. See: **Dexter.**

Sir Isaac Newton (*RSG*, 4; *SC*, 5; *BP*, 2; *TiS*, 2; *TfS*, 12): English mathematician (b. 4 January 1643, d. 31 March 1727) who laid the foundation for differential and integral calculus and published significant works on optics and gravitation. He was just over twenty when he invented calculus. In 2005 a survey of members of Britain's Royal Academy found Newton to be considered more influential on the history of science than Einstein. In *RSG*, Cargraves uses Newton as an example of what can be achieved by young men. See: **Einstein** and **Manhattan Project.** In *SC*, Heinlein refers to Newton's laws of motion and law of gravity as governing all interplanetary travel. In *BP*, "Sir Isaac Newton" is the name of a Venerian "dragon," a high-ranking person as well as a very important scientist (hence his chosen English-language name) who assists Don Harvey and who is also working with Don Harvey's parents and other rebels on Venus and Mars. In *TiS*, it is a name Rod Walker knows from books but does not think about. See:

Otis. In *TfS*, one of the scientists aboard the *Lewis and Clark* says that the proof of Bode's Law will be the "most important thing since Newton got conked with the apple." See: **Bode's Law.**

Sisu (*CG*, 4): Finnish concept or philosophy that what must be done, will be done, regardless of any other consideration; a special strength and determination to continue and overcome adversity. In *CG*, *Sisu* is the name on the Free Trader ship on which Thorby escapes from Sargon. The captain of the *Sisu* is under obligation to Baslim the Cripple to not only take Thorby with him but also deliver him to any vessel of the Hegemonic Guard; the task will involve the difficulty of getting him off the planet as well as the problem of finding the appropriate vessel to which to deliver him. See: **Free Traders** and **Hansea.**

Six Days Shalt Thou Work and Do All Thou Art Able, / The Seventh the Same and Pound on the Cable (*ST*, 12): parody of "Six days shalt thou labor, and do all your work" (Exodus 20:9). In *ST*, Johnnie quotes this traditional Mobile Infantry saying to emphasize how hard the training is.

Skeleton in the Closet (*SJ*, 10): idiomatic expression referring to a dark secret in someone's past. In *SJ*, Sam suggests that "everyone has a skeleton in the closet" when he is telling Max how he might finagle the records and become a legitimate guild member.

Skew-Flip Turn-Over (*HSS*, 4): maneuver in which a spaceship accelerates to a midpoint in its journey and then turns over and uses its engine to slow down to its destination. In *HSS*, the spaceship in which Kip and Peewee are prisoners does a skew-flip turn-over between Earth and the moon.

"Skin Head" (*TfS*, 7): slang term for a bald person, usually slightly derogatory. In *TfS*, the captain says that he will order the crew to stop calling the telepaths "freaks" and comments that he once saw a crewman try to knife another for continuing to call him "skin head." See: **"Fog-Eater," "Limey,"** and **"Yank."**

"Skinning the Cat" (*SC*, 14): move in gymnastics, usually done on the high bar or the parallel bars, in which the performer grasps the bar or bars with his or her hands, lifts their feet, then rotates the whole body between the arms, and stretches the body down from the bar. In *SC*, Matt has to "skin the cat" to get out of his seat after the rocket ship starts to tip over.

Skull-and-Bones (*HSS*, 3): secret society at Yale University, New Haven, CT. In *HSS*, Kip, describing his lack of funds and limited college prospects, comments that, in fiction, the All-American Hero arrives at college broke but ends up with money in the bank and an invitation to join Skull-and-Bones. He further comments that he is in no way an All-American Hero, but ironically, by the end of the novel, he has become a hero in his own way, has money in the bank, and has been offered a full scholarship to M.I.T.

"Sleep That Knits Up the Ravell'd Sleave of Care" (*HSS*, 5): from Shakespeare's 1606 tragedy, *Macbeth* (II, ii, 36). In *HSS*, one of the quotations Peewee uses to reinforce her suggestion that she and Kip can do nothing more productive at the time than sleep. This and the other two quotations about sleep indicate Peewee's erudition. See: **"Blessings on Him Who Invented Sleep, the Mantle that Covers All Human Thoughts"** and **"Tired Nature's Sweet Restorer, Balmy Sleep."**

Slings and Arrows of Outrageous Fortune (*TiS*, 1): from Shakespeare's 1603 tragedy, *Hamlet*, "To be or not to be; that is the question: / Whether 'tis nobler in mind to suffer / The slings and arrows of outrageous fortune, / Or to take arms against a sea of troubles, / And by opposing, end them?" (III, i, 58–62). In *TiS*, Deacon Matson uses this quotation to suggest that someone who becomes worn out thinking about the unfairness of life, as Hamlet wears himself out, will not be ready to deal with what is actually happening and is, therefore, not ready for the survival test.

Slipstick (*RSG*, 10; *SB* 11; *HSS*, 7): slang term for a slide rule, a device for making rapid calculations that looked like a wide ruler divided the long way into three sections, the middle of which could be slid (slipped) back and forth, hence slipstick. It is interesting that Heinlein, with his knowledge of computers, never saw the slide rule being replaced by the pocket calculator and has characters in the first, middle, and last books still using slide rules.

Smile When You Say That (*RS*, 1): common phrase that suggests a person has said something insulting and should smile or otherwise indicate that he is not serious. In *RS*, when Dealer Dan notes that Castor and Pollux are known as the "Unheavenly Twins," Pollux suggests that he should smile when he says that.

"Smiling, the Boy Fell Dead" (*RP*, 4): from Robert Browning's (b. 7 May 1812, d. 12 December 1889) "Incident of the French Camp." In the poem, a young soldier, wounded, brings Napoleon news of a victory and, smiling with pride at the news and at having accomplished the deed, falls dead at Napoleon's feet. In *RP*, Frank uses the quotation to suggest that Jim is "dead" after questioning Headmaster Howe's administration of Lowell Academy.

Smyth's *Atomic Energy for Military Purposes* (*RSG*, 2): complete title, *The Official Report on the Development of the Atomic Bomb Under the Auspices of the United States Government, 1940–1945*, author, Henry D. Smyth. In *RSG*, it is one of the books on the boys' clubhouse shelf. See: **Jules Verne.**

Socrates (*TfS*, 7; *HSS*, 11): Greek philosopher (b. ca. 470 B.C., d. 399 B.C.) considered one of the founders of western philosophy and known for the Socratic Method of Inquiry. Socrates chose to drink hemlock (poison) rather than be exiled from Athens. See: **Sargon the Second.** In *HSS*, Kip tries to remember what Socrates said to his judges (or Plato's version of it in the *Apology*), feeling that the human race has been prejudged just as Socrates had been: but he rejects using Socrates' words because it is the whole human race, not just one man, who are on trial before the Court of the Three Galaxies.

Soda Jerk (*HSS*, 2): one who works behind a "soda fountain" in a pharmacy and makes ice cream sodas and milk shakes and serves dishes of ice cream. As the second half of the twentieth century wore on, pharmacies ceased to be gathering places for young people, and the owners replaced the soda fountains with more shelving for merchandise. In *HSS*, Kip works as a soda jerk in a pharmacy.

Sodium Pentothal (*BP*, 3): drug known as "truth serum" or "the truth drug" that eases inhibitions and makes people talkative. In *BP*, Don Harvey in threatened with this drug twice: once by a political officer investigating him as he is trying to leave Earth, and later in the novel, by a political officer interrogating him on Venus who decides to wait for sodium pentothal rather that attempting to extract information through physical means (11).

Sodom and Gomorrah (*BP*, 2): two ancient cities in Palestine destroyed by God because of the indecent and perverse conduct of their inhabitants (Genesis 18, 19). In *BP*, Dr. Jefferson refers to New Chicago, and perhaps the entire Earth, as Sodom and Gomorrah, telling Don Harvey to study it, as he will not see its like again. See: ***Maître d'Hôtel***, **Tannhäuser**, "**These Our Actors ...,**" and **Tromp of Doom**.

Solomon (*FS*, 14; *SB*, 5; *TfS*, 4; *CG*, 7): biblical king of Israel (b. ca. 1011 B.C., d. ca. 932 B.C.) known for his wealth and his wisdom. In the most famous story about him, he told two women who claimed the same baby that he would saw it in half. One woman agreed, the other woman did not, so he gave the baby to the woman who did not want it sawed in half. In *FS*, a local disparages a gift of apple seeds and says that the giver acted as if he had handed him "the riches of Solomon." Bill Lermer suggests that the apple seeds are exactly that kind of wealth in this new land and runs the man off his land with a rake. See: **Johnny Appleseed**. In *SB*, Mr. Kiku remarks that Greenberg's decision in the Lummox case is of the kind that has not been seen since "Solomon ordered the baby sawed in half." In *TfS*, when Pat Bartlett suggests that his parents should be convinced to let one twin go into space because they would then be sure of having the other at home, his Uncle Steve suggests that he read about King Solomon. In *CG*, when Thorby tries on some new clothes aboard the *Sisu* and is delighted with his appearance, Heinlein suggests Thorby's pride by saying, "Yet Solomon in all his glory was not arrayed as Thorby," a reference to the following: "Consider the lilies how they grow: they toil not, they spin not; and yet I say unto you, that Solomon in all his glory was not arrayed as one of these" (Luke 12:27).

"**Sons of Toil and Danger**" (*ST*, 6): song from the 1925 operetta *The Vagabond King*, by Rudolph Frimi, Brian Hooker, Russell Janney, and W.H. Post, that rouses the rabble of Paris to defeat the Burgundians who are surrounding the city. See: "***Le Regiment de Sambre et Meuse.***"

Sorbonne (*SC*, 5; *ST*, 2): generally used to refer to the University of Paris, France. See: **Harvard** and **Oxford University**.

Southern Cross (*TiS*, 5): distinct formation of stars visible only from Earth's southern hemisphere. In *TiS*, "Jack" Daudet claims to have been able to recognize the Southern Cross for a long time.

Spaatz Field (*RSG*, 5): airport in Reading, Pennsylvania, named for

General Carl Andrew Spaatz (b. 28 June 1891, d. 14 July 1974), an early advocate of the military applications of air power and a leader in the creation of the U.S. Air Force as a separate branch of the military. Spaatz' pioneering efforts in military air power and his supervision of the use of atomic bombs on Hiroshima and Nagasaki make Spaatz Field a logical site for Cargraves and Morrie to get their rocket pilots' licenses in *RSG*.

"Spare the Rod and Spoil the Child" (*RS*, 15; *PM*, 1): from the Bible: "He who spareth the rod hateth his son; but he that loveth him correcteth him betimes" (Proverbs 13:24). In *RS*, Roger puns on the biblical injunction, saying, "Spare the child and spoil the fodder," when his wife says that she does not need their daughter to help with dinner. In *PM*, Podkayne says that this is her father's theory of child rearing.

"Sparks" (*BP*, 5): traditional slang term for a radio operator or for someone who repairs electronic devices. In *BP*, "Sparks" is the one to whom "Sir Isaac Newton's" damaged "voder" (voice translator) is taken for repairs.

"Speak for Yourself, John" (*SC*, 14): according to the folk history of the Pilgrims' Plymouth Colony (1620–1691), what Priscilla Mullins is supposed to have said to John Alden when he came to her with Myles Standish's proposal of marriage, more correctly, "Why don't you speak for yourself, John?" In American popular speech, the phrase is usually used, as Matt uses it in *SC*, to tell someone to speak only his or her own mind, not someone else's.

Speleologist (*CG*, 4): one who specializes in the scientific study and exploration of caves, commonly shortened to "spelunker." In *CG*, Heinlein calls Thorby a speleologist for his ability to navigate the underground ruins, in which he and Baslim the Cripple live, to avoid the police.

Spooky Smith [Sergeant] (*ST*, 9): perhaps Sergeant Arthur George Smith, the man to whom *Starship Troopers* is dedicated. In *ST*, it is the name of the training camp in the Canadian Rockies to which Johnnie is sent after basic training at Camp Currie.

Spring Tide (*BP*, 5): tide when the difference between high tide and low tide is at its greatest. Spring tide produces the largest rise and fall of the water level and occurs during the full or new moon. In *BP*, a shuttle between the Circum-Terra space station and the moon is appropriately named the *Spring Tide*. See: ***Neap Tide.***

Square Dance (*RS*, 1: *TiS*, 14): traditional folk dance in which four couples form a square and then go through various exchanges of partners and dance moves to the rhythm of the music and the instructions of the caller. In *RS*, Meade Stone is dancing in a square dance contest. In

Squirrel

TiS, the community holds Saturday night square dances. See: **Arkansas Traveler** and **Texas Star**.

Squirrel Gun (*SJ*, 2): small-caliber rifle, such as a .22, suitable for hunting squirrels. Hunting squirrels with a gun like a .22 works because the hunter can kill the squirrel with a headshot and not ruin the meat. In *SJ*, Max wishes he had brought his squirrel gun as he gets hungry, which suggests that squirrel had been a part of his regular diet and adds to Heinlein's exaggerated characterization of Max's rural background. See: **Barn Dances, Huskings, Side Meat,** and "**Wagon Room.**"

Stanford (*HSS*, 3): Stanford University, one of the best engineering schools in the U.S. In *HSS*, it is one of the schools to which Kip has applied.

Stapp (*HSS*, 2): probably John Paul Stapp (b. 11 July 1910, d. 13 November 1999), an air force flight surgeon who studied the effects of acceleration and deceleration on humans. See: **Haber** and **Strughold.**

Starstruck (*RSG*, 1): fascination with famous people; also astonished or captivated. In *RSG*, the name of the boys' experimental rocket and, later in the novel, a suggested name for the rocket to the moon (8), indicative of the boys' fascination with rocket travel and its possibilities. See: **Moonstruck.**

Statue of Liberty (*TiS*, 1): statue in New York Harbor that symbolizes America's traditional welcome to immigrants. In *TiS*, the original Statue of Liberty is gone as the result of a war long over when the book opens, but an exact replica stands at Emigrants' Gap, near New York City, to inspire those leaving Earth through the Gap. In this case, as part of his continuing parallel of the juvenile series to American history, Heinlein sees Earth as the Old World and the new planets for which the emigrants are leaving as the New World. See: **Abe Lincoln, Bedloe Crater,** and **Santa Fé Trail.**

Steinway (*PM*, 9): piano built by Steinway and Sons, German-American piano builders since the mid-nineteenth century and famed for the quality of their work. In *PM*, Podkayne finds a Steinway piano in their suite at the Hilton on Venus.

Stevenson (*RS*, 1): Robert Louis Stevenson (b. 13 November 1850, d. 3 December 1894), English author best known for his 1883 novel, *Treasure Island*. In *RS*, Roger Stone suggests that he can use a bit of the plot from Stevenson's *Treasure Island* (which, Stone says, Stevenson may have gotten from Homer) for the episode of *The Scourge of the Spaceways*, a serial stone writes for video production. See: **Homer,** *The Scourge of the Spaceways* and *Treasure Island.*

Stone Walls Do Not a Prison Make Nor Light Years a Separa-

tion (*TfS*, 6): variation on Richard Lovelace's "Stone walls do not a prison make, / Nor iron bars a cage," the first lines of his 1642 poem, "To Althea, from Prison." In *TfS*, Tom uses this phrase to describe the telepathic relationship of Uncle Alf and his neice, "Sugar Pie."

Stonehenge (*FS*, 19): prehistoric monument in southern England that was built of huge stones sometime between 3000 and 2000 B.C. Although burials took place there and certain astronomical measurements can be charted there, no one knows all of the uses to which Stonehenge was put or the full extent of its symbolism. In *FS*, a Stonehenge-sized boulder has broken away from the cliff, unveiling an opening into a cave in which there are, appropriately, ancient alien artifacts.

Stoop Labor (*FS*, 14): slang phrase for hard fieldwork done by hand with a lot of bending over. In *FS*, Bill goes to work on Johann Schultz's farm and characterizes the work there as "stoop labor."

"— stout-hearted men —," (*SC*, 204): popular song by Sigmund Romberg (b. 29 July 1887, d. 9 November 1951) and Oscar Hammerstein II (b. 12 July 1895, d. 23 August 1960) for the 1928 operetta *The New Moon*. The song praises "stout-hearted men" who will fight for and accomplish things as a team. Tex sings this brief lyric in *SC* when he is contemplating the *Astarte* and thinking about the bravery of the men who made that first ill-fated trip to Venus. See: **Astarte.**

Stranger in a Strange Land (*RS*, 13): "I have been a stranger in a strange land" (Exodus 2:22). In *RS*, Grandma Hazel uses this phrase to describe her situation as a newcomer to Mars as she prepares to defend her grandsons in court. This phrase would become the title of Heinlein's most successful and, though rivaled by *Starship Troopers*, most controversial novel. Even though it was not published until 1961, there is evidence that he was working on it in the early 1950s as he was writing the juvenile series.

Strughold (*HSS*, 2): Hubertus Strughold (b. 15 June 1898, d. 25 September 1986), German physician who emigrated to the United States after World War II and became known as "the father of space medicine" for his almost 200 papers on the subject. In *HSS*, Strughold's is one of the books, along with Haber and Stapp, that Mr. Charton, the pharmacist, loans Kip in his attempt to steer Kip toward a career in pharmacy that might also allow Kip to achieve his dream of going into space. See: **Haber** and **Stapp.**

Studebaker (*TiS*, 1): corporation that made wagons in the nineteenth century, switched to automobiles and trucks in the twentieth century, and ceased production in 1966. In

TiS, some of the emigrants have Studebaker Wagons and others have the better known Conestoga Wagons. See: **Conestoga Wagon.**

Sub Rosa (*BP*, 16): Latin phrase meaning "under the rose," commonly used to identify something being conducted in secrecy. The rose as a sign of confidentiality dates back at least to Greek mythology. In *BP*, it describes the testing in Earth laboratories of theoretical materials by the rebels from Mars and Venus.

"Sugar Bush" (*ST*, 10): popular song written by Josef Marais (b. 1905, d. 1978) that was very popular in the early 1950s. In *ST*, it is the recall Johnnie hears but not the one he was expecting. See: **Valley Forge** and **"Yankee Doodle."**

Sumerians (*ST*, 7): ancient civilization in what is now southern Iraq. See: **Sargon the Second.**

Suomish (*CG*, 6): or suomic, meaning Finnish or pertaining to the Finnish people. In *CG*, Thorby delivers a message in Suomish to the captain of the Free Trader vessel *Sisu*. See: **Sisu.**

Sure as Taxes (*SJ*, 2): "certain as death and taxes" (idiomatic expression); i.e., bound to occur, inevitable. In *SJ*, Max says, "Sure as taxes" when Sam doubts that Max's uncle was on the first trip to Beta Hydrae.

Suspenders and Belt Man (*SJ*, 14; *HSS*, 5): literally, a man who wears both suspenders and a belt to ensure that if one breaks he will still have the other to hold up his pants; figuratively, someone who has a backup plan or someone who covers all the contingencies. In *SJ*, Kelly says that he is double checking everything because he is "a suspenders and belt man." In *HSS*, Kip says that the Wormface would have secured the airlock as well as locking them in their room had he been "a suspenders-and-belt man."

Swamp Fox (*ST*, 13): Francis Marion (b. 1732, d. 26 February 1795), American Revolutionary War hero whose unorthodox tactics are considered the foundation of today's guerrilla warfare. In *ST*, it is the name of one of the warships in the Federation fleet named for specific foot soldiers.

Swing a Cat (*FS*, 7; *RS*, 5): variation on the phrase "there's not enough room in here to swing a cat." In *FS*, Bill comments that the *Mayflower* taking them to Ganymede was so crowded that there wasn't enough "room to swing a cat." Later in the novel, he uses the same phrase to describe his bedroom in the house his family has built on Ganymede (14). In *RS*, Roger Stone tells his sons that when they get the bicycles into the hold there won't be enough room "to swing a cat."

Swiss Family Robinson (*SJ*, 15): main characters in the 1812 novel of the same name by Johann David Wyss (b. 4 March 1743, d. 11 January 1818) about a family shipwrecked in the

East Indies. In *SJ*, Ellie thinks that settling on a new planet out of touch with the rest of humanity will be like being the Swiss Family Robinson. See: **Robinson Crusoe.**

Swiss Watch (*HSS*, 3): watch made by a watchmaker in Switzerland, long famous home of precision timepieces. In *HSS*, Kip compares the helmet of his space suit to a Swiss watch.

der Tag (*RSG*, 16): German for "the day." In *RSG*, Heinlein uses the term to refer to the timetable of the Nazi plans for conquering the Earth from their moon base station.

Tagalog (*ST*, 13): ethnic language in the Philippines. At the end of *ST*, Johnnie says something a classmate does not understand and explains that he was speaking in Tagalog, the language he and his folks sometimes used at home. In case the reader had not already figured it out before, Juan Rico, "Johnnie," is of Philippine descent. See: **Magsaysay.**

Tail-End Charlie (*ST*, 1): last person or thing in a line or a formation, or the crew member who operates the gun in the tail end of an aircraft, especially a bomber. In *ST*, Johnnie is the tail-end Charlie, the last one out of the spaceship, on the first mission described in the book.

Taj Mahal (*PM*, 9): mausoleum built in the 1600s by an Indian emperor in memory of his favorite wife and one of the most famous and recognizable structures in the world. In *PM*, it is the name of an ice cream flavor in an expensive sweet shop on Venus.

Take Me Out to the Ball Game (*SB*, 2): popular song about attending a baseball game and often sung during the seventh-inning stretch of a game. In *SB*, the secretary for Spatial Affairs whistles this tune, perhaps an indication that he, as a political appointee, is not as serious or knowledgeable about his job as is his under secretary. Heinlein may well have been critical of political appointees, who were coming under increased scrutiny and criticism at the time. In 1958, William J. Lederer and Eugene Burdick's *The Ugly American*, about American political appointees, among others (including tourists) and their mistakes abroad, would be published. See: **Hroshii** and **Russian Roulette.**

Take Off Your Skin and Dance Around in Your Bones (*ST*, 13): line from the 1929 jazz song "Tain't No Sin" (music, Walter Donaldson; lyrics, Edgar Leslie), offering advice for hot weather. In *ST*, Johnnie's captain says, in an exaggeration of course, that that's what he is to do if the major asks him to.

Tangaroa (*TiS*, 15): Polynesian sea god credited with separating the earth from the sky son of the goddess from whose body came the waters of the oceans. In *TiS*, the planet on which Rod Walker and the others have been stranded for some time has been named Tangaroa by the Terran Corporation.

Tannhäuser (*BP*, 2; *PM*, 9): main character in Wagner's opera of the same name. Tannhäuser struggles between his attraction to Venus and his love of Elizabeth, between the profane and the sacred. Elizabeth will not have him until he has the Pope's absolution, but by the time that comes, both of them, believing that the Pope will not absolve Tannhäuser, have died. In *BP*, Don Harvey sees a man portraying Tannhäuser but does not know who Tannhäuser was. Tannhauser's destruction may be Heinlein's comment on the Earth culture of the novel. See: **Mâitre d'Hotel, Sodom and Gomorrah, "These Our Actors ...,"** and **Tromp of Doom**. In *PM*, Podkayne and her family stay at the Hilton Tannhäuser, perhaps a portent of the political problems of the novel or the tragic end Heinlein had originally written for the book. See: **Wagnerian Opera**.

Tchaka (*ST*, 13): one of the ships of the Federation fleet. See: **Tshaka Memorial Park**.

Tell the Truth and Shame the Devil (*RS*, 13): "While you live, tell the truth and shame the devil" (proverb) variously interpreted as "tell the truth even when tempted to lie," "tell the truth even if there seems to be good reason not to do so," or "tell the truth even if you have good reason to conceal it." More literally, it means something like "tell the truth and shame the devil who is trying to make you lie." In *RS*, Grandma Hazel uses this proverb when defending Castor and Pollux in a Martian court.

Teller [University] (*TiS*, 8): Edward Teller (b. 15 January 1908, d. 9 September 2003), Hungarian-American physicist popularly known as the "father of the atomic bomb" and was also known as a difficult man with whom to deal on a personal level. In *TiS*, some of the students from Teller University refuse to work. They start a fight and are kicked out of the community while the ones who stay try to form themselves as the elite of the new governing body of the community. See: **"Fish, or Cut Bait."**

Tennessee Windage (*HSS*, 12): method of adjusting your aim to correct for poor sights or for anything else, like the wind, which might affect the flight of your bullet, more popularly Kentucky Windage. In *HSS*, Peewee's father suggests that, given the great distances Kip and Peewee have come and the space travel capabilities of the Vegans, it shouldn't surprise Kip that he and Peewee have been returned to Earth at almost the same time as they left, allowing for a little Tennessee windage.

Terra Firma (*FS*, 4; *TiS*, 1): Latin for "solid ground." In *FS*, Bill talks about terra firma (as solid ground) in opposition to the "free fall" (weightlessness) experienced when a rocket ship is in

Theory

free orbit, neither accelerating, decelerating, nor spinning to maintain an artificial gravity. In *TiS*, it is the feeling of solid ground under one's feet after going through one of the transportation gates.

Terraforming (*FS*, premise): creating an environment that will sustain human habitation on a planet, moon, or other satellite that, in its original state, would not support human life. In *FS*, although Heinlein does not rely on that word, the action of the novel is a description of humans' attempt to "terraform" Ganymede, one of Jupiter's moons. See: **Farmer in the Sky.**

Teutonic [Thoroughness] (*RSG*, 18): reference to the popular image or stereotype of Germans as masters of detail. In *RSG*, Cargraves is able to find out a great deal about the Germans and their plans from the detailed journals he captures.

Texas Star (*TiS*, 14): traditional square dance in which the pattern calls for the four men of the group to join left hands at right angles to one another, thereby forming a star, and then circle to the left with the women on their right arms; they then reverse arrangement and circle to the right. In *TiS*, the Texas Star is one of the square dances at the Saturday night parties. See: ***Arkansas Traveler*** and **Square Dance.**

"Thar She Blows!" (*SC*, 3): call from the lookout on a whaling ship that he has spotted a whale by the spout of water from its blowhole. More generally, it is a phrase used to recognize or signal the start of something. In *SC*, one of the cadets uses this phrase rather ineptly as the ride that tests the cadets' tolerance of gravity forces starts to drop.

Their Finest Hour (*HSS*, 7): phrase from British prime minister Winston Churchill's famous 18 June 1940 speech to the British House of Commons following the fall of France in World War II. He concluded: "Let us therefore brace ourselves to our duties, and so bear ourselves that if the British Empire and its Commonwealth last for a thousand years, men will still say, 'This was their finest hour.'" In *HSS*, Kip makes an ironic comment that, in the event the gangsters ended up as food for the Wormfaces, "as soup, they probably had their finest hour."

Theodora (*PM*, 10): Empress of the Byzantine Empire (b. ca. 497, d. 28 June 548) and by all accounts the real intellect and power behind the throne of Justinian II. In *PM*, Podkayne suggests that it would be acceptable to her to marry a man, let him run things, and then run him as Theodora did. See: **Catherine the Great.**

Theory of Colonial Expansion (*BP*, 1): probably a variation on Joseph Chamberlain (1836–1914) and his theory of imperialism; it could also be a reference to Neville Chamberlain (1869–1940), but the latter seems un-

There

likely, as Neville Chamberlain was for avoiding war at all costs. In *BP*, this is a book that has been banned on Earth but is popular on Venus and Mars. As *BP* was published in 1951 at the height of the McCarthy era, Heinlein's inclusion of a banned book may have been part of a protest against the kind of government regulations McCarthy and his followers wanted.

There Won't Be Enough Room in the Hold to Swing a Cat (*RS*, 5): *see* **Swing a Cat.**

"These Our Actors ..." (*BP*, 2; *HSS*, 11): from Prospero's speech in Shakespeare's 1610/1611 comedy, *The Tempest* (IV, i, 148–158), asserting that the entire play is disappearing and will leave nothing behind. The speech closes with these lines: "We are such stuff / As dreams are made on, and our little life / Is rounded with a sleep." In *BP*, Dr. Jefferson quotes bits of Prospero's speech as a way of saying that the Earth culture he knows will soon disappear. See: **Maître d'Hôtel** and **Sodom and Gomorrah.** In *HSS*, Kip quotes the same passage to illustrate human poetry to the Court of the Three Galaxies in his attempt to prove that the human race should not be exterminated; but he realizes that these lines, speaking as they do about the insubstantiality of things, are an ironic justification in his attempt to stave off humanity's extinction.

"They Got Me" (*TiS*, 8): clichéd remark from Western novels and movies indicating that the person who says it has been shot. In *TiS*, one of the troublemakers says this when he is hit with what he thinks is a poisoned dart from a dart gun.

"They Went That-a-Way, Podnuh" (*RS*, 7): clichéd remark from Western novels and movies indicating which way the outlaws went. In *RS*, Grandma Hazel uses the chiché after the Stone family's rocket ship is almost hit by an experimental satellite. See: **"A Miss Is as Good as a Mile."**

Thiamin Chloride (*SC*, 8): water-soluable B-complex vitamin, also spelled thiamine. Involved in electrolyte flow both in and out of nerve and muscle cells as well as other bodily functions, thiamin has been suggested for people suffering from chronic alcoholism or alcohol withdrawl. In *SC*, Oscar buys some thiamin chloride to help Tex recover from too many mint juleps. See also: **Mint Julep.**

Third Reich (*RSG*, 18): period of Hitler's government in Germany. See: **Hitler, National Socialist Reich,** and **Nazis.**

Thomas Paine (*SC*, 13; *TfS*, 1; *ST*, 6): American patriot (b. 29 January 1737, d. 8 June 1809) most famous for the pamphlet *Common Sense* and considered one of the Founding Fathers of the United States. In *SC*, the cadets are called upon to investigate some trouble on Venus because the ship that would normally do it, the *Thomas Paine*, is grounded. In *TfS*, Tom

Bartlett is Thomas Paine Leonardo da Vinci Bartlett, his given names coming from his father's interest in American history and his mother's interest in art. See: **Leonardo da Vinci**. In *ST*, Heinlein begins chapter 6 with a Thomas Paine quotation about highly valuing such things as freedom that are achieved with difficulty. See: **The Noblest Fate That a Man Can Endure Is to Place His Own Mortal Body Between His Loved Home and the War's Desolation.**

Thor (*RSG*, 8; *TiS*, 3): Scandinavian/Germanic Thunder God. In *RSG*, one of the boys suggests this for the name of the rocket ship, but more because it is powered by Thorium than for any similarities to the mythological figure. Ironically, later in *RSG*, one of the Nazi rocket ships is named *Thor* and is the rocket ship that carries Cargraves and the boys back to Earth after the *Galileo* has been destroyed by the Nazis (18 and 19). See: **Wotan**. In *TiS*, Thor is the name of the large and fierce dog one student is taking with him on the survival test.

Thos. Cook & Son (*HSS*, 1): British travel agency, Thomas Cook and Son, founded in the mid–1800s and still in business. In *HSS*, Thos. Cook & Son has partnered with American Express to offer tourist excursions to the Moon.

Three Men in a Boat (*HSS*, 1): 1889 humorous novel by Jerome K. Jerome. Although its initial critical reception was poor, the novel was extremely popular, made Jerome a lot of money, and has never been out of print since its initial publication. The novel is a humorous tale of three men boating on the Thames and the various adventures and misadventures they have on their trip. In *HSS*, Kip's father rereads the book often enough that Kip thinks he must know it by heart. The various humorous difficulties and misadventures of Jerome and his friends stand in stark contrast to the serious and dangerous journey that Kip makes in the course of the book, a journey dangerous not only to him and Peewee but to the entire human race. See: **Jerome K. Jerome**.

The Three Musketeers (*TiS*, 14): 1844 novel by Alexandre Dumas (père) (b. 24 July 1802, d. 5 December 1870) set in the France of Cardinal Richelieu and King Louis VIII in the early 1600s that features swordplay and codes of honor. In *TiS*, Rod Walker realizes that the romantic and swashbuckling adventures of the musketeers are just that and not applicable to his life.

Thule (*SJ*, 8; *TiS*, 2; *CG*, 16): most northern parts of Europe, sometimes called Ultima Thule, according to the ancients, variously referring to Iceland, Greenland, and the "unknown lands"; also, since just after the end of World War II, a U.S. Air Force Base in Greenland. In *SJ*, it is the name of an interplanetary rocket ship. In *TiS*, it is the name of a planet on which Helen Walker was stationed. In *CG*, Ultima

Tibetans

Thule is the planet on which Thorby transfers from the *Hydra* to the *Ariel*.

Tibetans (*RP*, 2): central Asian people who live at high altitudes. In *RP*, Heinlein mentions the Tibetans as one of two groups of settlers who can venture outside the pressurized buildings of the colony without a respirator to make up for the lack of oxygen on Mars. This emphasizes both the similarities and the differences between Mars and Earth. See: **Bolivian Indians**.

Tin Woodman (*HSS*, 10): metal man from L. Frank Baum's 1902 novel *The Wonderful Wizard of Oz* whose movements become jerky if his joints are not kept oiled. In *HSS*, Kip remarks that the robots who serve him and Peewee look nothing like the Tin Woodman and, in fact, do not look humanoid at all. See: **OZ**.

"Tired Nature's Sweet Restorer, Balmy Sleep" (*HSS*, 5): Line 1 of the poem "The Complaint: or Night Thoughts on Life, Death and Immortality," Edward Young (b. 3 June 1683, d. 5 April 1765). See: **"Blessings on Him Who Invented Sleep, the Mantle That Covers All Human Thought"** and **"Sleep That Knits Up the Ravell'd Sleave of Care."**

Titan (*PM*, 7): largest of Saturn's moons. In *PM*, it is a prison planet.

Titania (*PM*, 13): queen of the fairies in Shakespeare's 1594/1596 comedy, *A Midsummer Night's Dream*; also the largest moon of Uranus. In *PM*, it is the name Podkayne gives to the winged Venerian "fairy" who guards her when she is being held captive.

Tivoli (*SJ*, 3): most notably, an elaborate fountain in Italy. In *SJ*, the trucker who gives Max a lift mentions a truck stop named *Tivoli* that is highly automated.

"To Hear Is to Obey, Master" (*RS*, 6): paraphrase of "whoever comes to me, and listens to my words, and does [practices, obeys] them, I will show you what he is like" (Luke 6:47). In *RS*, Grandma Hazel responds this way when her son, Roger, asks her to help his wife, Edith, with the baby, who is not handling the blast-off well.

"To Understand All Is to Forgive All" (*BP*, 4; *ST*, 11): "To understand all is to forgive all," a French proverb and a quotation from Evelyn Waugh's (b. 28 October 1903, d. 10 April 1966) 1945 novel *Brideshead Revisited*. In *BP*, "Sir Isaac Newton" says this to Don Harvey after Don wishes a long and tedious life on a woman who shrieked at the sight of the Venerian "dragon." Heinlein usually has little patience with such ignorant people, and it is interesting that he creates a Venerian who is so tolerant. In *ST*, Johnnie rejects this idea when he thinks about a former enlistee who murdered a little girl and reserves his sympathy for the family of the victim. See: **Dillinger**.

Tomahawk (*SJ*, 1): hatchet-style weapon usually associated with Native

Americans, although iron-headed ones were made in Europe. In *SJ*, it is the name of one of the super-fast trains, all of which have throwing-weapon names. See: **Assegai.**

Tombaugh [Station] (*HSS*, 6): Clyde William Tombaugh (b. 4 February 1906, d. 17 January 1997), American astronomer best known for discovering the "planet" Pluto in 1930 (it is no longer classified as a planet). He also charted a number of asteroids and argued for the serious scientific research into unidentified flying objects. Some of his ashes are on the New Horizons spacecraft, launched in 2005 for a flyby of Pluto in 2014. Heinlein names a lunar station after Tombaugh in *HSS*, and the main characters are headed there when they are captured and then taken to Pluto.

Tommyrot (*FS*, 5): "foolishness," "silliness," or "nonsense." In *FS*, "Noisy" Edwards says that the shipboard rules are "tommyrot," goes off on his own, gets into trouble, and is punished. Edwards is a typical Heinlein example of how not to act. See: **Papoose.**

Too, Too Mortal Flesh (*PM*, 9): from Shakespeare's 1603 tragedy, *Hamlet*—"O, that this too too solid flesh would melt" (II, ii, 130)—in which Hamlet considers the overwhelming effect of his father's death and his mother's quick marriage to his uncle. In *PM*, Podkayne's Uncle Tom changes the quotation to argue that the flesh is less mortal and more resilient than people suppose.

Toomai-of-the-Elephants (*BP*, 14): character in Rudyard Kipling's short story "Toomai of the Elephants," published in the 1894 collection, *The Jungle Book*. Little Toomai, son of Big Toomai, the elephant driver, achieves the impossible; he sees the elephants dance, and on his return to camp, he is saluted by the hunters and the elephants, too. In *BP*, Don Harvey, riding on the Venerian dragon "Sir Isaac Newton," feels like Toomai of the Elephants and, unbeknownst to him as he rides, he will also become the focus of attention, the hinge upon which the ending of the novel turns, when he reaches Sir Isaac Newton's dwelling place. See: **Kipling.**

Tours (*ST*, 12): Battle of Tours, France, in October 732, in which Charles Martel defeated a much larger Muslim army and, according to some historians, saved Europe from large-scale invasion by North Africa. In *ST*, it is the name of one of the warships of the Federation fleet.

Treasure Island (*RS*, 1; *PM*, 13): 1883 novel by Robert Louis Stevenson about a voyage to find buried treasure. See: **Stevenson.** In *RS*, it is one of the sources Roger Stone draws on for material to help him write ***The Scourge of the Spaceways***. See: ***The Scourge of the Spaceways***. In *PM*, Podkayne refers to the book as an example of what she should have done when she

Tricorn

was captured. See: **Jolly Roger** and **Union Jack**.

Tricorn (*PM*, 3): three-cornered hat popular in the late-seventeenth and early-eighteenth centuries. In *PM*, it is the name of the spaceship on which Podkayne travels from Mars to Venus and one of a fleet of ships, including the *Trice* (very short period of time), the *Triad* (a chord of three tones in music), the *Triangulum* (the name of a spiral galaxy), and the *Tricolor* (a flag with three different-colored stripes such as the French and Irish flags), that travel among Earth, Mars, and Venus.

Tristan and Iseult (*HSS*, 5): main characters, along with King Mark, in a medieval romance that exists in many versions. Tristan travels to Ireland to bring Iseult back as wife to his uncle, King Mark, but the two fall in love on the voyage. Different versions have different endings, but all are tragic with Tristan and Iseult reunited, if at all, only in the grave, each often dying for love of the other. See: **King Arthur's Court**.

Trojan Horse (*BP*, 6; *ST*, 1): wooden horse with Greek soldiers inside which the Greeks tricked the Trojans into dragging inside the walls of Troy. The "Trojan Horse" trick was conceived by Odysseus, and when the Greek soldiers emerged from the horse and let the rest of the Greek army into the city, Troy and the Trojans were destroyed. In *BP*, the forces of the Venue Republic seize Circum-Terra, the space station, and use it as a Trojan horse from which to address the people on Earth. In *ST*, Johnny gets the shakes before a combat drop and wonders if the Greeks got the shakes when they climbed into the horse.

Tromp of Doom (*FS*, 12; *BP* 3): mangled reference to the last trumpet (trump) announcing the end of the world and the Last Judgment. In *FS*, Bill admits that he should not have confronted the local scouts but says that he will be talking instead of listening at "the Tromp of Doom." In *BP*, the comedian in the Back Room tells people the tromp will be the next sound they hear as he attempts to ease the tension caused by a blackout. In this case, given the other signs of impending war, he may be correct. See: **Maître d'Hôtel, Sodom and Gomorrah, Tannhäuser**, and **"These Our Actors ..."**

Truce of the Bear (*TiS*, 1): 1898 poem by Rudyard Kipling in which a man does not shoot a bear that appears to be approaching in peace and is then severely mauled and mutilated by the bear. It may be that Kipling meant this poem to be a warning about Britain's making a treaty with Russia. In *TiS*, Deacon Matson warns Rod Walker to "beware of the Truce of the Bear," suggesting that Rod will try to make alliances with people who are dangerous rather than deal with them as being dangerous (which, in fact, he does). See: **Kipling**.

Trygve Lie (*RS*, 6): Norwegian politician (b. 16 July 1896, d. 30 December 1968) and first elected secretary-general of the United Nations. In *RS*, it is the name of a rocket ship involved in a fatal collision.

Tshaka Memorial Park (*TiS*, 5): Shaka Zulu (b. ca. 1787, d. 22 September 1828), leader who conquered and united the Zulu tribes in southeast Africa in the early nineteenth century. In *TiS*, the Tshaka Memorial Park that Rod Walker mentions as the possible location for the survival test is probably named for Shaka Zulu. See: **Tchaka.**

Turkey in the Straw (*FS*, 2): American folk music and lyrics from the 19th century. In *FS*, Bill plays several tunes on his accordion to prove that he should be allowed to bring the instrument along as extra weight on the *Mayflower*. Heinlein also uses this well-known tune to introduce fictional titles: Nehru's *Opus 81*, Morgenstern's *Dawn of the 22nd Century*, and *The Green Hills of Earth*, the last a song created by a Heinlein character, Rhysling, in the 1947 short story "The Green Hills of Earth." See: **Kipling.**

Turtle (*HSS*, 11) *see* **Form a Turtle.**

Tweedledum (*TiS*, 2): character from Lewis Carroll's *Through the Looking-Glass* who prepares for a battle with his brother, Tweedledee, that never occurs. See: **Lewis Carroll** and **White Knight.**

"— 'Twere Well It Were Done Quickly'" (*HSS*, 10): "If it were done when 'tis done, then 'twere well / It were done quickly," from William Shakespeare's 1606 tragedy, *Macbeth* (I, vii, 1–2). Macbeth is speaking here of the proposed killing of King Duncan and realizes that the murder of the king will not be a single act, unconnected to anything else, but will have far-reaching consequences beyond just opening the way for him to become king. In *HSS*, Kip uses this phrase when he hears that the Wormfaces' planet has been rotated into a dimension without its sun and will slowly freeze; in this case, he seems to be saying that a terminal punishment should be carried out quickly.

"Two Peas in a Pod" (*SB*, 6): American idiomatic expression: "As alike as two peas in a pod." In *SB*, the Rarygillian negotiator suggests that there must be another race somewhere as like to humans as "two peas in a pod." See: **"As Cold as ..."**

Tyrannosaurus Rex (*ST*, 13): carnivorous dinosaur known for its size and believed to have been very ferocious. In *ST*, Johnnie thinks that he might be as obsolete as a *Tyrannosaurus rex* but also knows that he and his fellow soldiers can do things that the most well-equipped and highly technological ship cannot do.

Ugly Duckling (*SJ*, 21; *SB*, 9): reviled and ugly main character in the Hans Christian Andersen story of the same name who grows up to be a beautiful swan. In *SJ*, it is one of the star formations by which Max and his shipmates realize that they have returned to known space. In *SB*, it is the monstrous Lummox who turns out to be the long lost Hroshii princess. See: **Hans Christian Andersen.**

Ultima Thule (*CG*, 16) *see* **Thule.**

Ulysses Grant [Cowper] (*TiS*, 14): soldier and politician Ulysses S. Grant (b. 27 April 1822, d. 23 July 1885), 18th president of the United States and most famous for his service as general of the Union Army during the Civil War. In *TiS*, Grant Cowper's full name is Ulysses Grant Cowper; he is mayor of the settlement established by the students on the planet where they have been stranded and dies helping defend the town.

UN (*RSG*, 3; *HSS*, 10): United Nations, founded in 1945 after World War II to promote international communication and cooperation on all topics, especially those that would ensure peace and progress. In *RSG*, the UN oversees all matters pertaining to atomic energy and rocket development through the UN Trusteeship for Atomics and the rules of the UN Atomics Convention (the latter perhaps reminiscent of the Geneva Convention following World War II). See: **Doomsday Bomb.** In *HSS*, Kip likens the Court of the Three Galaxies to the League of Nations or the United Nations.

Unabridged (*HSS*, 9): complete, as in an unabridged novel or dictionary. In *HSS*, Kip discusses the Mother Thing's musical language and says his translations are very inexact but that an "Unabridged" would not be able to provide anything better.

Uncle Sam (*HSS*, 1): character representation of the United States of America officially based on Sam Wilson of Troy, New York (b. 13 September 1766, d. 31 July 1854), who supplied the army with meat in barrels marked "U.S." during the War of 1812. In *HSS*, Kip's father has a basket marked "UNCLE SAM" in which he places the cash he bundles up and sends to Washington, DC, to pay his taxes. His use of cash is protested by the IRS (Internal Revenue Service) and the FBI (Federal Bureau of Investigation), but he points out that cash is "legal tender for all debts" and that the government cannot require him to submit tax forms because it cannot require that a person know how to read and write. Kip's father is one of Heinlein's "independent" men, based on Heinlein's own Libertarian philosophies.

Uncle Tom (*BP*, 8; *PM*, throughout): from *Uncle Tom's Cabin* and used primarily, but not exclusively, by African-American people to refer to someone who betrays the minority or oppressed group by siding with or serving the majority or oppressive group. In *BP*, the term is used by a Chinese man to refer to a Chinese banker who made his fortune by staking prospectors to equipment and will not now lend money to indigent Venerian citizens who have been impoverished as a result of the rebellion. In *PM*, Uncle Tom is Podkayne's uncle, a convict transportee to Mars, or a descendant thereof, of Maori descent. In this case, Heinlein might be using the term ironically, as this Uncle Tom is pretending to be on one political side while actually representing another. See: **Aasvogel** and **Maori.**

Union Jack (*PM*, 13): slang term for the flag of Great Britain: England, Scotland, Wales, and Northern Ireland. In *PM*, Podkayne refers to it as the flag of the British Navy, using it as part of a metaphor, lowering the Jolly Roger and raising the Union Jack, for escaping from capture. See: **Jolly Roger** and *Treasure Island.*

United Nations (*HSS*, 10) see **League of Nations** and **UN.**

Univac (*TiS*, 2): Universal Automatic Computer, the first commercial computer produced in the United States. In *TiS*, Univac, Eniac, and Maniac computers are ancestors of the Rakitiac computer Ramsbotham uses to process the equations that lead to the Ramsbotham gate. See: **Eniac** and **Maniac.**

Valkyrie (*BP*, 1; *PM*, 1): female spirits or warriors in Norse mythology that carry out Odin's orders or requests. Valkyries wear armor and ride horses, sometimes give victory according to Odin's commands, and most popularly are the "choosers of the slain," who carry heroes slain in battle to Valhalla, the Hall of Heroes in Asgard, where they will feast and fight until Ragnarok, the final battle in which the gods and men fight with the giants and monsters until all are destroyed. In *BP*, it is the name of the ship that carries Don Harvey from Earth to Venus, where he will become a central figure in Venus' and Mars' rebellion against Earth. In *PM*, Podkayne says that her mother looks like a Valkyrie.

Valley Forge (*ST*, 10): Pennsylvania site of George Washington and the Continental Army's encampment during the winter of 1777–1778 in the Revolutionary War where they suffered from cold, malnutrition, and disease but from which they emerged the next summer to pursue and engage the British. In *ST*, the first transport ship to which Johnnie is assigned is named *Valley Forge*, and the military operation that follows is a disaster from which the military will have to regroup just as the Valley Forge experience was one from which the Continental Army had to regroup. See: **"Yankee Doodle"** and *Ypres.*

van Buren (*HSS*, 1): Martin van Buren (b. 5 December 1782, d. 24 July 1862), 8th president of the United States and holder of many other political offices, including vice president of the U.S. and governor of New York. In *HSS*, Kip's failure to be able to explain to his father why Van Buren did not win reelection is part of Heinlein's critique of American secondary education. See: **M.I.T.**

Vanderdecken (*BP*, 1; *TfS*, 15): one spelling of the name of the captain of the fabled ship that became known as *The Flying Dutchman*. Sailing around the Cape of Good Hope into a raging storm, Vanderdecken, according to legend, cursed the storm and God, saying that he would keep on sailing until Judgment Day if necessary rather than put into a sheltered bay. For his curse, Vanderdecken and his ship and crew were doomed to sail the seas until Judgment Day. In *BP*, the *Vanderdecken* is the ship on which Don Harvey was originally scheduled to return home to Mars. See *Valkyrie*. In *TfS*, Tom wonders if the new captain, who wants to continue the mission of the *Lewis and Clark* with a skeleton crew, thinks he is Columbus or *The Flying Dutchman*. See: **Columbus.**

Van Loon [Professor] (*PM*, 1): Hendrick Willem van Loon (b. 14 January 1882, d. 11 March 1944), a well-known history professor at Cornell University also famous for history books for young readers. His *The Story of Mankind* won the first Newbery Medal in 1922. In *PM*, Podkayne's father is Van Loon Professor of Terrestrial History.

Vasco da Gama (*TfS*, 6): Portuguese explorer (b. 1460, d. 24 December 1524) best known for sailing around the Cape of Good Hope, Africa, and on to India. In *TfS*, it is the name of one of the torch ships. See: **Lebensraum [Project]** and *Lewis and Clark.*

Venus de Milo (*HSS*, 10): one of the most famous works of ancient Greek sculpture believed to be a depiction of the goddess of love. The statue is partly famous for being both beautiful and armless. In *HSS*, Kip comments that his description of the Wormfaces read into evidence at the trial has been so truncated that it is hard to tell whether he is talking about the ugly aliens or the beautiful Venus.

Vercingetorix (*ST*, 13): Gaulish leader (b. ca. 82 B.C., d, 46 B.C.) who unified various tribes to fight against Julius Caesar, the account of which appears in Caesar's *De Bello Gallico*. In *ST*, it is the name of one of the warships of the Federation fleet named for specific foot soldiers. See: *De Bello Gallico.*

Victrix (*HSS*, 10): VI Legion, Victrix (Victorious), stationed at Eboracum in Britain during the Roman occupation. See: **Eboracum** and **Gaul.**

Viking Ships (*SC*, 19): wooden longships in which the Vikings sailed as far as North America about A.D. 1000. See: **Columbus.**

Virginia Bill of Rights (*TiS*, 10): drafted in 1776, the first statement of individual rights adopted by a state government and an important influence on the Declaration of Independence and the Constitution of the United States of America. In *TiS*, one of the stranded students suggests the adoption of the Virginia Bill of Rights as a first step toward forming a government; the proposal is part of Heinlein's continuing parallel of the juvenile series to American history.

Voortrek (*ST*, 10): South African "Great Trek" (1835–1840) of the Boers to escape British policies. In *ST*, it is the name of the ship on which Johnnie finds himself escaping after the Bugs hand the humans a severe setback in the "Klendathu debacle." See: ***Valley Forge.***

Vox Populi (*PM*, 13): Latin for "the voice of the people." In *PM*, Podkayne believes that there are things that are always wrong and that even if everyone agrees to do them, or approves them, they are still wrong. In this, she is mulling over her brother's philosophy that "anything that is moral for a group to do is moral for one person to do."

V-2 Rocket (*RSG*, 9) *see* **Nazi V-2 Rocket.**

"Wages of Sin Are Death" (*RS*, 5): "For the wages of sin is death; but the gift of God is eternal life through Jesus Christ our Lord" (Romans 6:23). In *RS*, Grandma Hazel quotes only the first part of this sentence as a comment on her son's (Roger) hangover. In fact, most contemporary people quote only the words Hazel quotes.

Wagnerian Opera (*HSS*, 9): any of the typically loud and heroic/tragic operas of Richard Wagner (b. 22 May 1813, d. 13 February 1883), which often feature figures from Norse mythology or medieval romance. See: ***Peter and the Wolf.***

"Wagon Room" (*SJ*, 1): staying away from someone or giving someone plenty of room. "Wagon room" would be the prairie equivalent of the nautical phrase "wide berth." In *SJ*, that Max has always given Biff Montgomery "wagon room" is part of Heinlein's characterization of Max as coming from an extremely rural background. See: **Barn Dances, Huskings, Side Meat,** and **Squirrel Gun.**

Walker, Boyd and Asimov (*HSS*, 2): 1952 book, *Biochemistry and Human Metabolism,* by Burnham S. Walker, William C. Boyd, and Isaac Asimov. In *HSS*, Mr. Charton, the pharmacist, loans Kip this book to help him with biochemistry.

Walpurgis (*SC*, 13): Walpurgis Night, a pre–Christian rite of spring still celebrated on 30 April or 1 May in some northern European countries. On Walpurgis Night, bonfires are lit and some practices or pranks by "unruly spirits" take place, much the same as they do on Halloween. In *SC*, Captain Yancey's comment that he would rather fly a broom on Walpurgis than try to land on Venus suggests that the Venerian atmosphere is very turbulent.

The Walrus and the Carpenter (*HSS*, 5): characters from the 1872 classic by Lewis Carroll (Charles Lutwidge Dodgson: b. 27 January 1832, d. 14 January 1898), *Through the Looking-Glass*, who convince the Oysters to take a walk along the beach with them and then eat up every one of them. In *HSS*, Kip smashes doors in the Wormfaces' spaceship "as fast as the Walrus and the Carpenter opened oysters." See: **Lewis Carroll.**

Waltzing Matilda (*ST*, 6): 1887 Australian ballad by Banjo Patterson; also Australian slang for traveling on foot with one's goods (Matilda) on one's back. In *ST*, Captain Frankel suggests to Sergeant Zim that they are both getting soft and should get together in the gym and go "waltzing Matilda."

Wanderjahr (*RS*, 4): German for "a year of wandering." More generally, this is the year of travel before settling down to one's trade or vocation; it was once a common practice in Europe. In *RS*, Roger Stone says that this trip is going to be his *wanderjahr*.

Wanderlust (*PM*, 3): strong desire to travel. In *PM*, it is the name of the spaceship that Podkayne had expected to take from Mars to Earth.

War Whoop (*PM*, 4): yell Native Americans made when attacking white settlements or wagon trains. In *PM*, it is the name of a newspaper or journal on Mars indicative of the frontier status of the human settlements there — another parallel to the settlement of the American West.

Washington [George] (*RS*, 5): 1st president of the United States (b. 22 February 1732, d. 14 December 1799). In *RS*, Roger Stone invokes Washington's owning slaves to counter Pollux's invoking Lincoln and Churchill in an argument about transporting whisky-making equipment and ingredients to Mars.

Waterloo (*ST*, 13; *PM*, 13): site of the 1815 battle in which the English forces under the Duke of Wellington defeated Napoleon's army and ended his rule as emperor of France. In *ST*, it is the name of one of the warships in the Federation fleet. See: **Napoleon** and **Wellington.** In *PM*, Podkayne believes that Abraham Lincoln was at Waterloo. See: **Abe Lincoln.**

Webcor Wire Recorder (*HSS*, 3): precursor to the tape recorder built by the Webster-Chicago Corporation. In *HSS*, Kip builds part of his space suit's communications system from parts of an old Webcor wire recorder.

Welched (*RSG*, 4; *SB*, 17): also welshed, an insulting reference to Wales and the Welsh people that, as a verb, means to fail to pay a debt or to fail to fulfill or run out on an obligation. In *RSG*, Cargraves says that if he accepts Mr. Jenkins' offer to hire engineers to help him build the rocket ship he'd be welching on the proposition he made to the boys. In *SB*, former secretary of Spatial Affairs McClure "welches" on his agreement to be ambassador to the home planet of the Hroshii.

Wellington (*RS*, 19; *ST*, 2): Arthur Wellesley, 1st Duke of Wellington (b. May 1769, d. 14 September 1852), most famous for defeating Napoleon at the Battle of Waterloo. In *ST*, Dubois uses Wellington as an example that violence does settle things. See: **Napoleon** and ***Waterloo.***

"West of the Pecos" (*TiS*, 11): reference to the rugged region of the western part of Texas where the legal system had little jurisdiction; more generally, any distant and rugged terrain where one makes his or her own rules. In *TiS*, when they are searching for caves to which to move the community, Roy Kilroy uses the phrase to suggest to Rod Walker that they are in a region where they must make their own rules about continuing on or trying to get back on schedule.

West Point (*HSS*, 9; *ST*, 12): United States Military Academy at West Point, New York, an elite school for future army officers. In *HSS*, Kip compares himself to the mule at West Point, the college's mascot, and suggests that, like the mule, he understands very little of his surroundings on the Mother Thing's planet. See: **Saint Cyr** and **Sandhurst.**

"What Can't Be Cured Must Be Endured" (*BP*, 10): traditional proverb found in many literary sources but not ascribed to a specific source. In *BP*, Don Harvey thinks it might have been said by Confucius and uses it to characterize his present situation, working for Old Charlie at the Two Worlds Dining Room.

What's in a Name? (*PM*, 2): From Shakespeare's 1591/1595 tragedy, *Romeo and Juliet:* "What's in a name? That which we call a rose / By any other name would smell as sweet" (II, ii, 1–2). In *PM*, Podkayne quotes Shakespeare in regard to what to name her new sibling triplets. Heinlein may have been punning on the difference between the smell of a rose and a baby's diaper. See: **Augean Stables** and **Romeo and Juliet.**

When in Rome One Should Shoot Roman Candles (*SB*, 6): phrase that pops into Greenberg's head when he speculates that the Rargyllian has his tail wrapped around him so that he might dress as an Earth person. See: **Ask Me No Questions and I'll Sell You No Pigs in a Poke** and **Chesterfieldian.**

"While I Was Musing the Fire Burned" Psalm xxxix:3 (*BP*, 10): excerpt from the Psalm: "My heart was hot within me; while I was musing the fire burned: then I spoke with my tongue" (Psalm 39:3). In *BP*, this is the title to chapter 10, a chapter in which the Federation troops land on Venus, control New London, and take Don Harvey into

Whirligig

custody. With that chapter title Heinlein could be referring to Don's working at the Two Worlds Dining Room and not realistically planning for the future while things heat up all around him, but the entire Psalm suggests that there are deeper feelings and forces at work that Don does not yet recognize.

Whirligig [Albert] (*HSS*, 9): object, often solid or stationary, that has one or more parts that move or "whirl" around and around driven by the wind, by friction, by hand, or occasionally by a motor. Humorous weathervanes are an example. See: **Einstein**.

"Whistle Stop" (*TfS*, 13): small station at which trains stop only when signaled; more generally, a small town or community. In *TfS*, Tom refers to a planet that the *Lewis and Clark* investigated as "Whistle Stop," indicating that it was probably not a planet that humans could emigrate to.

White Knight (*RS*, 3; *TiS*, 2): rescues Alice from the Red Knight in *Through the Looking-Glass*. In *RS*, when Castor asks Grandma Hazel why she still carries a gun when most people have given up the practice, she asks him if he remembers "the reason the White Knight gave Alice for keeping a mouse trap on his horse." Castor does not know that the reason is because the White Knight wants to be prepared for everything — as does Grandma Hazel. In *TiS*, Rod's sister looks over the large pile of gear he is planning to take along on his survival test and asks if he is planning to be Tweedledum or the White Knight (the former prepared for a battle that never happened, and the latter tried to be prepared for everything). She will argue that he should take as little gear on the test as possible. See: **Alice, Lewis Carroll,** and **Tweedledum**.

"Whopper" (*SJ*, 14): lie, usually a big lie. In *SJ*, the first officer tells a "whopper" to the passengers about the condition of the ship to keep them from panicking; Max, who comes from a place where the "'whopper' was a respected literary art," is astonished at how well the first officer pulls it off.

Why Did the Bear Go Round the Mountain? (*RS*, 19): children's rhyme or song, "The Bear Went Over the Mountain," in which the bear goes "to see what he could see." In *RS*, Grandma Hazel wants to go farther out into the solar system, rather than go back to the moon, because she wants to go where she has not already been. Ironically, when the bear goes over the mountain in the children's rhyme, all he sees is the other side of the mountain. But Hienlein is probably using the rhyme to suggest that Americans (and perhaps people in general) have always had the urge to see what is beyond the next hill.

"Wicked Flee When No Man Pursueth" (*BP*, 3; *ST*, 8): "The wicked flee when no man pursueth; but the righteous are bold as a lion" (Proverbs 28:1). In *BP*, the Federation officer questioning Don Harvey quotes this proverb in regard to Dr. Jefferson's attempts to elude pursuit, suggesting that Dr. Jefferson has some connection with the rebel elements on Mars and Venus — as, indeed, is the case. In *ST*, Johnnie uses this comment to explain why someone might turn himself in, take his punishment, and then go on with his life, a free man.

Wild West (*RSG*, 6): generally America west of the Mississippi in the second half of the nineteenth century, but more specifically the stereotyped West of popular fiction that includes frontier explorers, wagon trains, Indians and cavalry, gunslingers and town-tamers, and the like. In *RSG*, Cargraves uses the term in its negative, i.e., lawless and chaotic, aspects when he cautions the boys about dealing with trespassers on the property. Ironically, such a shootout happens between the boys and the Germans on the moon (15).

"Will to Fail" (*TfS*, 5): psychological condition in which the person wants to fail but does not consciously know that he or she wants to fail. In *TfS*, the young woman both Tom and Pat date tells Tom that he likes having his brother push him around because he has a "will to fail." See: **Death Wish.**

William Tell (*PM*, 11): legendary fourteenth-century Swiss marksman who was forced to shoot an apple off his son's head to attain his freedom (he had been imprisoned for failing to properly salute a local official) and then later helped lead the rebellion that led to the formation of the Swiss Confederation. In *PM*, Podkayne says that all she knows about Switzerland is the story of William Tell and the apple. But what she knows is relevant, as her Uncle Tom compares Mars' political situation to that of Switzerland. It will also be important later, as Tom refuses to compromise his political stand even though his neice and nephew are being held hostage.

Willy Ley (*RSG*, 2; *RS*, 5): German-American writer (b. 2 December 1908, d. 24 June 1969) who wrote about rockets and space flight for a popular audience. See: **Ley's *Rockets*** and **Leyport.**

Winged Victory (*SC*, 8): one of the masterpieces of Hellenistic sculpture from ca. 190 B.C. *The Winged Victory of Samothrace* probably commemorated a major military victory. In *SC*, the scooter that takes the cadets from the *James Randolph* to Terra Station, the orbiting space station, has to be aware of an incoming ship named *Winged Victory*.

Winston Churchill (*RS*, 5; *ST*, 11): prime minister of England (b. 30 November 1874, d. 24 January 1865) during World War II. In *RS*, Pollux invokes Churchill's drinking of whiskey in an attempt to justify transporting whiskey-making equipment and ingredients to Mars. In *ST*, Churchill Road is the main road from the military base to the city of Espiritu Santo and is lined with shops intent on separating a military man on leave from his money. See: **Espiritu Santo**.

"With Your Shield or on It" (*HSS*, 5): "Come back with your shield — or on it" (Plutarch, *Moralia*, 241), the phrase with which Spartan mothers supposedly sent their sons off to battle. In *HSS*, Kip hands Peewee his jackknife with this phrase, but it also reflects his attitude toward protecting Peewee. See: **King Arthur's Court**.

Witwatersrand [Gate] (*TiS*, 1; *TfS*, 11): range of hills in South Africa, part of the Continental Divide separating the waters that flow into the Atlantic, on the west, from the waters that flow into the Indian Ocean, on the east. In *TiS*, it is the name of one of the emigration gates to the new planets and suggests moving from one side to another. See: **Emigrants' Gap** and **Peter the Great**. In *TfS*, Sugar Pie, the Earth telepathic partner of Uncle Alf onboard the *Lewis and Clark*, attends normal school in Witwatersrand. See: **Einstein** and **Lebensraum [Project]**.

Woolamurra (*CG*, 12): Wallamurra, a section of the city of Cairns, Australia. In *CG*, Woolamurra is the name of a frontier planet whose major city is New Melbourne. It is a planet on which, as one of the locals says, "Any cobber with strong arms and enough brain ... can go outback and make a fortune." The references — Woolamurra, New Melbourne, cobber, and outback — make this planet reminiscent of Australia and make it the perfect place if Thorby wants to escape and be his own man. See: **Cobber** and **Outback**.

Wotan (*RSG*, 16): leader of the Germanic mythological pantheon (Odin in the Scandinavian pantheon). In *RSG*, it is the name of one of the German rocket ships that can travel from the Earth to the moon. See: **Thor**.

Wright Field (*RSG*, 9; *HSS*, 3): built in Dayton, Ohio, by the Army Air Corps and opened in 1927 to explore and develop aircraft for military uses. The field was named in honor of the Wright brothers, and during World War II the number of buildings there increased from 40 in 1941 to over 300 by 1944. In 1947, Wright Field was combined with nearby Patterson Field to become Wright-Patterson Air Force Base, and research continues there to this day. In *RSG*, it is one of the places Dr. Cargraves has worked. In *HSS*, a reporter who has seen astronauts get into their space suits at Wright Field helps Kip get into the one he has won. In both cases, Heinlein extrapolates the current air force base into a base associated with space travel and exploration.

Xenology (*SB*, 3; *PM*, 4): scientific study of all aspects of extraterrestrial life. In *SB*, Greenberg asks John Thomas Stuart if he has studied xenology when he is discussing the three characteristics of species at the human level: speech centers, manipulation, and, as a product of those two, record keeping. In *PM*, Podkayne comments that xenoarcheologists always keep gas masks handy when opening a Martian tomb and that the air in a spaceship smells even worse than the air from a tomb.

Xenophon (*ST*, 13): Greek mercenary, soldier of fortune, admirer of Socrates, and historian (b. ca. 430 B.C., d. 350 B.C.). In *ST*, it is the name of one of the warships of the Federation named for specific foot soldiers.

Xerxes (*ST*, 12): fifth-century king of Persia who led an unsuccessful attempt to conquer Greece. In *ST*, Johnnie mentions Xerxes' campaign as one of the many things that the officer candidates had to learn and understand.

Yale (*BP*, 1): one of the most prestigious universities in the United States. In *BP*, Don's roommate gives up going to Yale for pilot training, believing that a war with Earth on one side and Venus and Mars on the other is coming soon.

Yale & Towne (*TfS*, 7): company that has been making locking mechanisms since the mid-nineteenth century. In *TfS*, Tom Bartlett has a Yale & Towne lock on his wardrobe.

"Yank" (*BP*, 1): slang term for Americans, especially American soldiers stationed in Britain and the rest of Europe during and after World War II. In *BP*, Heinlein uses it as an example of the kind of slang term that can be harmless or, if said in a certain tone of voice or in a certain context, an insult. Heinlein includes it here to illustrate the way "fog-eater" can be a slang term as well as an insulting term for someone who lives on Venus. See: **"Fog-Eater," "Limey,"** and **"Skin Head."**

"Yankee Doodle" (*ST*, 10): song popularized by the American forces during the Revolutionary War, although it may originally have been sung by the British to make fun of the Americans' rag-tag uniforms. In *ST*, it is the recall song that was supposed to guide Johnnie and the others in his unit back to their transport, appropriately, the *Valley Forge*. See: **Valley Forge.**

Yin and Yang (*ST*, 12): Chinese philosophical concept that everything contains its opposite. The yin-yang circle is divided into a large white part containing a small black part and a large black part containing a small white part to illustrate the concept. The parts can represent light and dark, male and female, good and evil. In *ST*, one of Johnnie's teachers suggests that the present government

York

is an example of yin yang in that those who are willing to sacrifice the most (those who enlist) are those who are accorded the most power (the vote).

York (*HSS*, 3): supplier of residential and commercial heating and cooling systems located in York, Pennsylvania. In *HSS*, Kip's space suit has an air conditioning system made by York. The suit itself was made by Goodyear, today a manufacturer of tires and other rubber products, and also contains additional equipment from General Electric, today a maker of small and large appliances.

You Can't Fight City Hall (*HSS*, 7): literally, the government is stronger than the individual, and so it is pointless to try to fight it; figuratively, the individual should accept the power structure, whatever it is, and go along with it. In *HSS*, the fat gangster justifies his actions with this phrase. See: **Handwriting on the Wall.**

The Young Rocketeers (*SC*, 4): fictional title based on early-twentieth-century series book titles. Early series books, many published by Edward Stratemeyer's company, had titles that emphasized technology: *The Railroad Boys*, *The Airplane Boys*, and *The Young Engineers*, for example. The fact that Matt has read a book entitled *The Young Rocketeers* in *SC* shows not only Heinlein's familiarity with such literature but also reflects an early version

of proposed titles for his own juvenile series: *The Young Atomic Engineers.*

Ypres (*ST*, 10): Belgian city that was the site of some of the fiercest battles of World War I and the site where the Germans first used mustard gas on a large scale in the war. In *ST*, the ship that collides with the *Valley Forge* destroying both ships and crews is the *Ypres*. Later in *ST*, there are new ships with those names (13). See: **Valley Forge.**

Yukon (*CG*, 18): northern and western part of Canada with a rugged terrain and an arctic climate. In *CG*, the Rudbeck family owns a "shooting lodge" in Yukon, along with a domehouse on Mars and Pitcairn Island, evidence of their vast wealth. See: **Pitcairn.**

Zero (*TfS*, 16): name of one of the new "irrelevant" spaceships. See: **Serendipity.**

Zeus (*RP*, 1; *BP*, 2): head of the Greek pantheon of gods. In *RP*, the name of the month before November on Mars, a planet named for another Greek god and needing extra months because its year is longer than that of Earth. In *BP*, Dr. Jefferson offers to take Don out for "such food as Zeus promised the gods — but failed to deliver."

Zoot Suit (*RSG*, 5): popular clothing style in the late 1930s and 1940s featuring excessively padded shoulders and wide-legged pants that were severely tapered (or "pegged") at the ankles. In *RSG*, Cargraves' best business suit causes Art to ask why he is wearing a "zoot suit," suggesting that Cargraves' attire is outrageous or out of place in a desert setting where a rocket ship is being readied for a trip to the moon. The popularity of the zoot suit among African Americans and Hispanic Americans and the so-called Zoot Suit Riots between servicemen and Mexican-American youth make this an odd reference for Heinlein to use.

Zulu (*TiS*, 1): major South African clan or tribe. In *TiS*, Caroline is described as a "big Zulu girl."

Appendix I: Plots of Heinlein's Juvenile Novels

The twelve books that make up Heinlein's "juveniles proper" chart the movement of Earth people out into space. The first novel, *Rocket Ship Galileo*, begins the process simply enough with a trip to the moon. The next five books, *Space Cadet* through *The Rolling Stones*, move humanity from Mars to beyond the Asteroid Belt. The last six, from *Starman Jones* to *Have Space Suit—Will Travel*, go beyond our solar system and even beyond our galaxy. While it is true that the action of *The Star Beast* takes place on Earth, it is the result of one of the first exploratory voyages beyond our solar system, and although *Have Space Suit—Will Travel* begins and ends on Earth, Kip and Peewee travel out to the Lesser Magellanic Cloud and back by the interstellar equivalent of a great circle route, not only bringing them back where they started but also ending the series where it started.

Starship Troopers was rejected by Scribner's, the publisher of the first twelve books, for its perceived militaristic attitudes; and although it does have a young hero coming of age as its main character and plot, the book is markedly different from the preceding twelve. Although much of the setting is in the classroom, recounted mostly in flashbacks by the main character, the emphasis on military service as the only qualification for citizenship, voting, and government office as well as the continuing philosophical justification of war caused the publisher and many critics a great deal of uneasiness. (And some people just thought it was a poorly written novel.)

Many Heinlein fans and some Heinlein critics do not know that he wrote short stories with female main characters and published some of them

Appendix I

in magazines for young female readers. Indeed, some of these were not science fiction or fantasy at all. But with *Podkayne of Mars*, Heinlein created his first juvenile novel with a female main character; and it is important that the main character is female, not male. Some of her ideas and actions are typical of the cultural period in which the novel was written, and some challenge women's traditional roles. The controversial ending (see summary below) is some testament to that fact.

The following summaries in no way do justice to the various ideas and themes Heinlein explores in these books but are intended, rather, to provide enough of the plot of each novel that the place and function of each of the entries can be fully understood.

Rocket Ship Galileo (1947): In the first Heinlein juvenile novel published by Scribner's, atomic scientist Dr. Donald Cargraves enlists the help of his nephew, Art, and Art's two rocket club friends, Morrie and Ross, in building a rocket ship that will be able to get them all to the moon. Heinlein spends quite a bit of time in this first juvenile explaining the scientific and technological aspects of the project. But there are also forces at work trying to prevent the building of the rocket ship, and when Cargraves and the boys successfully arrive on the moon, they find that the Nazis have beaten them to it and are planning to attack Earth.

Space Cadet (1948): Matt Dodson and friends, new cadets at the Interplanetary Patrol Academy, spend the first part of the novel being educated at an academy based on West Point and Annapolis where various "unfit" candidates are weeded out and a cadet's education is described in detail. The second part of the novel involves the search for a missing patrol ship in the Asteroid Belt and the rescue of an independent ship that has crashed on Venus while under the command of someone who had washed out of the academy.

Red Planet (1949): Jim Marlowe and Frank Sutton are sent away to school, where they discover a plot to deprive the colonists of their right to move to a warmer region of Mars for the winter. The antagonists in the novel are business and political interests on Earth, and the plot of the novel recalls the American Revolution against the absentee British government. In addition, Jim has befriended a Martian Roundhead and made it his pet, an action that becomes central to both the political plot and the relationship between the native Martians and the colonists from Earth.

Appendix I

Farmer in the Sky (1950): Bill Lermer accompanies his father, his father's new wife, Molly, and Molly's daughter, Peggy, to Ganymede, a moon of Jupiter, where settlers are trying to terraform the place (i.e., make the air breathable and the land arable) so that the colonists will have an Earth-like environment. Heinlein's American history parallel here is both the initial settlement of America, during which groups like the Puritans suffered substantial hardships and losses, and the westward movement of the nineteenth century, during which settlers were given land if they agreed to settle on and improve it.

Between Planets (1951): Don Harvey, at school on Earth, receives a message to return home to Mars. While he is in transit, hostilities break out between Earth on one side and Mars and Venus on the other. Don is forced by circumstances to go to Venus, and when Earth attacks, he joins the rebels as Heinlein creates another parallel to the American Revolution. Along the way, Don has made friends with a Venerian scientist who calls himself "Sir Isaac Newton," an action that has important consequences by the end of the book, as Don unknowingly carries a secret important to the revolution.

The Rolling Stones (1952): Having bought and refurbished a rocket ship, the Stone family leaves their home on the moon to travel to Mars. Finding Mars a bit too settled for their liking, they go on to the Asteroid Belt. As in *Rocket Ship Galileo*, there is some discussion of the details of space travel and shipboard living. In the end, instead of heading back to the Moon, they continue on, to be followed by thousands like them, "outward bound to the ends of the universe" (19) as Heinlein creates another parallel to the American westward movement of the nineteenth century.

Starman Jones (1953): Max Jones sneaks onto a spaceship with the help of an older and sharper character, Sam Anderson, who arranges for false papers identifying them as members of the Clerks and Stewards Guild. Max, however, has an eidetic memory and has memorized his late uncle's astrogation books. When the ship becomes lost, the captain dies, and one of the other astrogators destroys the books on board, it is up to Max to become captain and navigate the ship back to known space — where, if he succeeds, he will be a hero but will have to "face the music" about his false papers.

Appendix I

The Star Beast (1954): Young John Thomas Stuart IX is custodian of Lummox, an animal of almost dinosaur shape and size that an ancestor brought back from an intergalactic voyage. When a powerful race comes looking for its lost princess, it slowly becomes obvious that Lummox is that princess, and the aliens threaten to destroy Earth if she is not handed over. Much of the novel focuses on the efforts of Mr. Kiku, "Under Secretary for Spatial Affairs," to bring the situation to a peaceful close, and Heinlein uses the situation to comment on bureaucratic politics.

Tunnel in the Sky (1955): Rod Walker and the other members of his high school course in advanced survival are transported to a distant planet for their final exam. But due to sun spots, they are forced to stay there for years instead of days, along with students from other high schools and universities. The first part of the novel focuses on theories and practices of survival; the second part on the evolution of a government and a social structure among the students, who are intelligent and who can create anything they wish to on this planet that only they inhabit.

Time for the Stars (1956): Tom and Pat Bartlett are, like many identical twins, telepathic, and when exploratory ships are sent out at near-light speeds to find habitable planets for Earth's expanding population, only telepathy is an effective way of communicating. But as the twin on Earth ages at the normal rate, the twin on the ship, traveling near the speed of light, ages much more slowly. In addition to the theoretical implications of speed-of-light travel and the perils found on new planets, the difficulties of twin relationships are a major part of the plot.

Citizen of the Galaxy (1957): Thorby, a young slave, is bought by Baslim the Cripple in a slave market on a far distant planet. When Baslim is arrested, Thorby begins a long journey to find out who he is and where he is from. Thorby lives first with a matrilineal and matriarchal group of Free Traders, based loosely on the Gypsies, and then on a military ship patrolling for pirates. When his identity is revealed, he must return to Earth to reclaim control of his parents' company, a company that, under the direction of his Uncle Jack, may be supporting the slave trade.

Have Space Suit—Will Travel (1958): In the last of the juveniles proper, Kip Russell wins a space suit in a slogan contest and restores it to its original functional condition. He is then kidnapped by the Wormfaces, the first aliens in the juveniles that want to conquer Earth. Kip must help a human girl, Peewee, and another alien, the Mother Thing, thwart the Wormfaces. He must then defend Earth and her people in an intergalactic court that sees Earth as a potential threat and is, for its own security, considering destroying the planet and all who occupy it.

Starship Troopers (1959): Rejected by Scribner's for the juvenile series, *Starship Troopers* was published in abridged form in *The Magazine of Fantasy & Science Fiction* and complete in hardcover by Putnam's. The following year, it won the Hugo Award. The novel, though it features several battles, is about the high school education, basic training, and officers' candidate school training of the main character, Johnnie Rico, a plot that allows Heinlein much opportunity to discuss social, military, and political issues as the Bugs threaten to conquer human-occupied space.

Podkayne of Mars (1963): Although this novel might have appeared in the juvenile series, Heinlein had broken with Scribner's after they rejected *Starship Troopers*. Podkayne and her genius brother, Clark, are traveling with their uncle, Tom, from Mars to Earth by way of Venus. Tom is on a political mission that has some clandestine aspects, and Podkayne and Clark are kidnapped in an attempt to force Tom to act in a particular way. At the end of Heinlein's original version of the novel, Podkayne dies. The publisher made him rewrite that ending. Both are now available.

Appendix II: Some Speculations About Terms and Names Not Found

Included in this appendix are the names and terms that I believe meant something to Heinlein but for which I could not find a specific reference. I have listed them in the order in which they appear in the series.

Rocket Ship Galileo

"A school is a log with a pupil on one end and a teacher on the other" (10): According to *American Authors 1600–1900*, "It was president Garfield who first ... defined a university as 'Mary Hopkins on one end of a log and a student on the other.'" *American Authors 1600–1900*, Eds. Stanley J. Kunitz and Howard Haycraft, New York: Wilson, 1964: 384. The phrase as Heinlein uses it seems older, but I have found no other sources. Also in *Farmer in the Sky* (7, below).

Space Cadet

Hayworth Hall (1): hall to which Matt reports at the patrol academy. I suspect it might have been a name, possibly a building name, at Annapolis, but research and telephone calls to the naval academy yielded nothing.

Oubliette (2): dungeon accessed through a hole or door in the top. In *SC*, Burke throws his cigarette into the "oubliette," perhaps a slang reference to an ashtray with a hole in the top.

P.R.S. *James Randolph* (6): patrol ship that orbits the Earth and is a classroom of the Patrol Academy. This might be the name of an instructor at Annapolis, but James Randolph is a common name. My graduate assistant, Kimberly Thompson, found a World War II aircraft carrier, USS *Randolph*, but it was named for Peyton Randolph, the president of the First Continental Congress http://en.wikipedia.org/wiki/USS_Randolph_(CV-15).

The Cross-Eyed Pilot (14): song that Tex plays on his harmonica after the Little People have taken the cadets to an underground city. It may well be a phrase that results from the misunderstanding of another phrase. For example, the joke about children singing "gladly, the cross-eyed bear" is a result of their misunderstanding the hymn line "gladly the cross I'll bear." Similarly, "José, can you see" comes from a misunderstanding of the line in "The Star-Spangled Banner" "Oh, say, can you see." There may have been an original phrase behind Heinlein's "The Cross-Eyed Pilot," or he may have been making a joke on the fact that pilots need exceptionally good vision.

Goodman's Integrations (*SC*, 12): There is an Abraham Goodman Laboratory for Astronomical Observations at the University of North Carolina-Chapel Hill, but alas, there is no connection.

Red Planet

"It was a great fight, Maw, but I won" (14): Doctor Macrae quotes this sentence after he has successfully negotiated with the Martians. The sentence is a quotation within a quotation, suggesting Macrae is quoting something, but I could not find the source.

Farmer in the Sky

Billy-Be-Switched (10): proverbial comparison and intensifier probably invented by Heinlein. Bill says that it was "as cold as Billy-be-switched," meaning that it was extremely cold.

... a university consists of a log with a teacher on one end and a pupil on the other (7): Also in *Rocket Ship Galileo* (10, above).

Kneiper [Ridge/Cut] (16/20): ridge with a cut through it between the Lermer property and the town. Kimberly Thompson suggested Gerard

Appendix II

Kuiper (1905–1973), whose astronomical work in the 1940s might have caught Heinlein's attention and the man for whom the Kuiper Belt of asteroids is named, as a possible source for "Kneiper" (http://en.wikipedia.org/wiki/Gerard_Kuiper). Interestingly, Heinlein uses "Kuiper" for the name of the purser of the *Asgard* in *Starman Jones* (6).

Between Planets

Busby [J.S.] (13): Don's commanding officer when he joins the rebels on Venus. There are numerous Busbys on various military lists, but none of them appear to have been a guerilla warfare leader.
Reynolds Gun (10): weapon carried by the military from Earth. There are too many people with the last name Reynolds to make any guess at the person for whom the Reynolds gun is named.

The Rolling Stones

Halleujah Node (12): rich ore discovery in the Asteroid Belt. Halleujah, or Hallelujah, is what one shouts in a secular context when he or she has found or discovered something. In the history of gold and silver mining in the American West, there must have been one or more mines called the Hallelujah Mine (as there is currently in Peterson, Nevada), though I have found reference to none thus far.

Starman Jones

Imperial House (3): hotel at Earthport, probably just a generic name, given the number of "Imperial" houses and hotels in the world.
Insult Him Until He Apologizes (15): no definite source found. Sam tells Max that he has done the right thing in dealing with a superior officer who treats Max unfairly until Max forces him to abide by the legal regulations. See: **Step on Their Toes Until *They* Apologize** (*SB*, 15, below)
Why the Preacher Danced (6): phrase justifying a choice. In *SJ*, Sam says

Appendix II

something is "what the doctor ordered and why the preacher danced." "What the doctor ordered" is a well-known traditional phrase, but I could find no source for "why the preacher danced."

The Star Beast

Rangtangtoo (5): Kiku's term for Greenberg after Greenberg allows Betty to get the better of him in the initial court case involving Lummox. Rangtangtoo sounds like a combination of elements of names (o**rang**utan and kanga**roo**, for example) that might be the invented label for some exotic "animal" in a carnival side show exhibit; it also sounds like something from a Mark Twain story.

Step on Their Toes Until *They* Apologize (15): no definite source found. Mr. Kiku explains this to his superior as his strategy in negotiating with the Hroshii, an alien race that considers Earth people to be animals and is threatening to destroy the planet. See: **Insult Him Until He Apologizes** (*SJ*, 15, above).

Tunnel in the Sky

Cat's Way of Saying Good-Bye (2): probably a creation of Heinlein's playing on the apparent standoffishness of cats versus the apparent fawning of dogs. Rod's sister says that she prefers the cat's way of saying good-bye.

Ortega (2): inventor of the torch ship, the primary means of interstellar transportation in *Time for the Stars*. Kimberly Thompson found that part of Route 74 in California, opened in 1934, was named for the Spanish explorer Jose Ortega. It would make sense that Heinlein would name the inventor of the torch ship after an explorer of the American West. (http://en.wikipedia.org/wiki/Ortega_Highway).

Summerfield (3): gun that Rod could have taken on his survival test. This could be suggestive of Springfield, a well-known maker of firearms.

Templeton Gate (1): Transportation Gate nearest the departure gate for

Appendix II

the survival test Rod and his classmates will take. Kimberly Thompson discovered that the U.S. Army Corps of Engineers built the Templeton Gap Floodway in 1949 to divert floodwaters from downtown Colorado Springs. Although Rod Walker lives near the Grand Canyon, it is not clear that the Templeton Gate is in Colorado. (http://www.springsgov.com/Page.aspx?NavID=2743).

Time for the Stars

Lundy (12): explorer mentioned in the same sentence with Balboa and Columbus, probably someone in Heinlein's future as, throughout the series, he often pairs known names and terms with invented ones.

Macdougal's Operation (8): spinal surgery to enable Pat to walk again. I have not found a medical history that lists this as an operation performed in the 1940s or 1950s.

Ortega (1): inventor of the torch ship, the primary means of interstellar travel until the "irrelevant" ships are invented. See: **Ortega**, above, under *Tunnel in the Sky*.

Citizen of the Galaxy

Fraki (7): Free Traders' word for someone who lives on a planet, an insult.

Havermeyer Labs in Toronto (23): no source, although there is or has been a Havemeyer [*sic*] lab at Columbia University.

N-Space (10): fourth dimension, null-space — "null" meaning "no" or "nothing" — through which a ship passes when it goes irrelevant to get from one point to the next.

Starship Troopers

Do You Know How to Lead a Pig? (2): proverbial question quoted by Johnnie's father. Although no source was found for this proverb, it "sounds" traditional. Johnnie's father is suggesting that his teacher is leading them to enlist by telling them not to do it.

Klendathu (10): home planet of the Bugs. Given that one of the planets held by the Bugs is named Sheol (see main entries), it seems logical that Klendathu might have a cultural source (although it actually sounds like something out of an H.P. Lovecraft story).

Works Cited

Erisman, Fred. "Robert Heinlein, the Scribner Juveniles, and Cultural Literacy." *Extrapolation* 32, no.1 (1991): 45–53.

Heinlein, Robert A. *Grumbles from the Grave*. Edited by Virginia Heinlein. New York: Ballantine, 1989.

Kristeva, Julia. *Desire and Language*. 1969. Oxford: Blackwell, 1989.

Lewis, C.S. "On Stories." In *On Stories and Other Essays on Literature*. 1966. Edited by Walter Hooper. San Diego, CA: Harcourt, 1982. 3–20.

Sullivan, C.W. III. "Heinlein Criticism and the Scribner's Juveniles." *Journal of the Fantastic in the Arts* 17, no. 2 (2006): 168–180.

_____. "Heinlein's Juveniles: Growing Up in Outer Space." In *Science Fiction for Young Readers*. Edited by C.W. Sullivan III. Westport, CT: Greenwood, 1993. 21–35.

_____. "Heinlein's Juveniles: Space Opera vs. 'The Right Stuff.'" *Foundation* 10, no. 2 (Spring 2008): 61–70.

_____. "Heinlein's Juveniles: Still Contemporary After All These Years." *Children's Literature Association Quarterly* 10.2 (1985): 64–66.

_____. "Real-izing the Unreal: Folklore in Young Adult Science Fiction and Fantasy." In *Literature for Children: Contemporary Criticism*. Edited by Peter Hunt. London: Routledge, 1992. 141–155.

_____. "Robert A. Heinlein: Reinventing Series SF in the 1950s." *Extrapolation* 47, no. 1 (2006): 66–76.

Works Cited: Heinlein's Juvenile Novels Plus Two in Chronological Order

Rocket Ship Galileo. 1947. New York: Ballantine, 1977.

Space Cadet. 1948. New York: Ballantine, 1948.

Red Planet. 1949. New York: Ballantine, 1977.

Farmer in the Sky. 1950. New York: Ballantine, 1975.

Between Planets. 1951. New York: Ballantine, 1978.

The Rolling Stones. New York: Ace, 1952.

Starman Jones. 1953. New York: Ballantine, 1975.

The Star Beast. New York: Ace, 1954.

Tunnel in the Sky. New York: Ace, 1955.

Time for the Stars. 1956. New York: Ballantine, 1978.

Citizen of the Galaxy. New York: Ace, 1957.

Have Space Suit—Will Travel. New York: Ace, 1958.

Starship Troopers. 1959. New York: Ace, 1987.

Podkayne of Mars. 1963. New York: Avon, 1964.

Works Consulted

A Heinlein Concordance. The Heinlein Society. www.heinleinsociety.org/concordance/index.htm.

Frank, Marietta. "Women in Heinlein's Juveniles." In *Young Adult Science Fiction.* Edited by C.W. Sullivan III. Westport, CT: Greenwood, 1999. 119–130.

Franklin, H. Bruce. *Robert A. Heinlein: America as Science Fiction.* New York: Oxford University Press, 1980.

Heinlein, Robert A. "Science Fiction: Its Nature, Faults and Virtues." In *The Science Fiction Novel.* Edited by Basil Davenport. Chicago: Advent, 1959. 17–63.

Knight, Damon. *In Search of Wonder.* Chicago: Advent, 1956.

Lundwall, Sam. *Science Fiction: What It's All About.* 1969. New York: Ace, 1971.

Molson, Francis J. "The Winston Science Fiction Series and the Development of Children's Science Fiction." *Extrapolation,* 25, no. 1 (1984): 34–50.

Moskowitz, Sam. *Seekers of Tomorrow: Masters of Modern Science Fiction.* New York: Ballantine, 1967.

Panshin, Alexei. *Heinlein in Dimension.* Chicago: Advent, 1968.

Sands, Karen, and Marietta Frank. *Back in the Spaceship Again: Juvenile Science Fiction Since 1945.* Westport, CT: Greenwood, 1999.

Williamson, Jack. "Youth Against Space: Heinlein's Juveniles Revisited." In *Robert A. Heinlein.* Edited by Joseph D. Olander and Martin Harry Greenberg. New York: Taplinger, 1978. 15–31.

Wollheim, Donald. *The Universe Makers: Science Fiction Today.* New York: Harper, 1971.

www.ingramcontent.com/pod-product-compliance
Ingram Content Group UK Ltd.
Pitfield, Milton Keynes, MK11 3LW, UK
UKHW042013140426
5217IPUK00015B/1150